# HOAXES, MYTHS, AND MANIAS

# HOAXES, MYTHS, AND MANIAS

## Why We Need Critical Thinking

## ROBERT E. BARTHOLOMEW
## BENJAMIN RADFORD

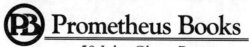

## Prometheus Books

59 John Glenn Drive
Amherst, New York 14228-2197

Published 2003 by Prometheus Books

Inquiries should be addressed to
Prometheus Books, 59 John Glenn Drive, Amherst, New York 14228–2197
VOICE: 716–691–0133, ext. 207; FAX: 716–564–2711
WWW.PROMETHEUSBOOKS.COM

07 06 05 04 03    5 4 3 2 1

Library of Congress Cataloging-in-Publication Data

Bartholomew, Robert E.
    Hoaxes, myths, and manias : why we need critical thinking / Robert E. Bartholomew and Benjamin Radford.
        p. cm.
    Includes bibliographical references and index.
    ISBN 1–59102–048–4 (pbk. : alk. paper)
    1. Critical thinking—Study and teaching (Secondary) I. Radford, Benjamin, 1970–
II. Title.

BF441 .B297 2002
160—dc21

                                                                          2002036721

Printed in the United States of America on acid-free paper

*For Gary Kruml and John Peterson, extraordinary teachers, and for Warren Zevon, whose ride came too soon.*

# CONTENTS

# PART 3:  THE CROSS-CULTURAL PICTURE

# PART 4: THE HISTORICAL PICTURE

# ACKNOWLEDGMENTS

Portions of chapter 2 first appeared in R. E. Bartholomew, "The Martian Panic Sixty Years On: What Have We Learned?" *Skeptical Inquirer* 22, no. 6 (1998): 40–43. Part of chapter 3 appeared in R. E. Bartholomew, "Before Roswell: The Meaning behind the Crashed UFO Myth," *Skeptical Inquirer* 22, no. 3 (1998): 29–30, 59. Some material in chapter 7 first appeared in R. E. Bartholomew, "Culture-Bound Syndromes as Fakery," *Skeptical Inquirer* 19, no. 6 (1995): 36–41. Parts of chapter 10 appeared in R. E. Bartholomew, "Rethinking the Dance Mania," *Skeptical Inquirer* 24, no. 4 (2000): 42–47. Part of chapter 15 appeared in R. E. Bartholomew, "Collective Delusions: A Skeptic's Guide," *Skeptical Inquirer* 31, no. 3 (1997): 29–33. All material from *Skeptical Inquirer* is reproduced by permission of Barry Karr, Committee for the Scientific Investigation of the Claims of the Paranormal, P.O. Box 703, Amherst, NY 14226–0703.

Part of chapter 8 was originally published in R. E. Bartholomew and J. O'Dea, "Religious Devoutness Construed as Pathology: The Myth of "Religious Mania," *International Journal for the Psychology of Religion* 8, no. 1 (1998): 1–16. Parts of chapters 6, 9, and 14 first appeared in R. E. Bartholomew, "Monkey Man Delusion Sweeps across India: Western Delusions Are No Less Bizarre," *The Skeptic* 9, no. 6 (2002): 13. R. E. Bartholomew, "Commentary: Deviance, Psychiatry and Relativism—An Important Borderland," *The Skeptic* 8, no. 3 (2000): 36–40; and R. E. Bartholomew, "Penis Panics: The Psychology of Penis-Shrinking Mass Hysterias," *The Skeptic* 7, no. 4 (1999): 39–43. They are reproduced by permission of The Skeptic Society, Box 338, Altadena, California.

A portion of chapter 12 appeared in R. E. Bartholomew, "From Airships to Flying Saucers: Oregon's Place in the Evolution of UFO Lore," *Oregon Historical Quarterly* 101, no. 2 (2000): 192–213. It is reproduced by permission of the Oregon Historical Society, 1200 S.W., Park Avenue, Portland, Oregon.

# PART I

# THE
# BROAD
# PICTURE

# I

# WHY DEVELOP
# A CRITICAL EYE?

*I have no riches
but my thoughts.
Yet these are
wealth enough for me.*

—Sara Teasdale[1]

L ike eating, breathing, and complaining about taxes, thinking is an activity that is typically taken for granted. In most schools throughout the world, students are taught three basic skills that will prepare them to function in society: reading, writing, and arithmetic. Although all of these areas require thinking, they do not necessarily involve *critical* thinking—what psychologist Dennis Coon defines as "an ability to evaluate, compare, analyze, critique, and synthesize information."[2] In some countries, authorities might not want pupils to develop critical thinking skills, as it may lead to challenges to long-standing political, religious, and social dogmas. Yet, in the United States and other countries where freedom and democracy are cornerstones of government and citizens take pride in making intelligent, informed decisions about every aspect of life, critical thinking is typically a small part of the school curriculum.

Each waking hour of each day, month after month, year after year, we have the opportunity to practice our thinking—for it is a skill that involves such things as expressing opinions, discussing events, analyzing situations, and solving problems. Yet, for all of this opportunity to practice, few of us think with any concrete analysis or scrutiny of *how* we are thinking. Many educators neglect the importance of thinking about thinking. Many people assume that just because they have the capacity to think, they can think well. They may believe that thinking takes no effort. Certainly, we can all think to some degree; we couldn't function if we didn't. But there is a difference between thinking about things and thinking about them critically and analytically. An apt analogy is writing. For those who don't see much difference between ordinary ways of thought and critical thinking, there would be little difference between the simple sentences strung together by a grade schooler and the writings of William Shakespeare or Ernest Hemingway. Most people can write readable sentences, but the ability to write well takes time, effort, practice, and training. It is a skill; perhaps with some element of innate ability, but a skill nonetheless. Critical thinking is also a skill, and it can be learned.

This book is a series of case studies in critical thinking so readers can examine topics along with us to see where the inquiry leads. A benefit to this approach is that the topic is limited, and usually quite specific, allowing for a deeper analysis of the issue. At times readers may even fault our analyses of the topics presented. They may see other explanations, other avenues of inquiry. We welcome this, as it is the methodology of science. A hallmark of science is that assertions are subject to attack and revision. If readers question assumptions—the public's, their own, or ours—we have succeeded in instilling a good foundation for critical thinking. We hope to challenge students to dig deeper into issues, to encourage people to develop a critical eye and ear, to help recognize faulty arguments in the world around them.

Critical thinking is a way of thinking and a tool of analysis that can be compared to the scientific method. Just as there are many ways to find out about the world, there are many ways to think about the world. But some ways are better than others; scientifically testing drinking water for lead or other toxins is better than letting others drink it and waiting for any negative results. In nature, for example, when our ancestors wanted to know why the sun rose and set, there was no sure way to find out, no scientific method to resort to. As a result, several explanations were put forth; one of them was reflected in mythology, that the sun was pulled across the sky by a flying chariot. We know now, of course, that sunrise and sunset are the products of the Earth's movement around the sun, all the while rotating on its axis.

On a simpler level, if you want to know why dew forms on grass, there are several ways you could go about it. You could make wild guesses, supposing that maybe it is residue from low-flying UFOs. You might guess that the grass itself exudes the dew. Or you might inquire at the library or ask an expert. You could conduct your own study, carefully recording when and under what conditions dew appears. If you think that the weather has an effect, see how the local humidity readings correlate with the dew. You might guess the correct answer on the first wild guess, or you might consult a local "expert"—who turns out to be wrong. You may even do the experiment yourself and come to the wrong conclusions. But critical thinking will help keep you on the right track. Science makes mistakes, but it is also self-correcting. When conclusions are drawn, other scientists criticize and examine the study and methodology for flaws. If a theory about how the world works holds up to repeated tests and criticisms, it can usually be relied on as accurate.

## CRITICAL THINKING BASICS

There are many components involved in the process of learning to think critically. Entire books have been written on the subject, but some of the most important guidelines can be distilled into a short list. Psychologists Carole Wade and Carol Tavris outline eight essential guidelines involved in learning to think critically. We list them here, with our explanations.[3]

1. *Ask questions; be willing to wonder.* Creativity is sparked by an

openness to question the world around us. Critical thinkers are not only willing to examine ideas and beliefs they disagree with, but ones they hold true as well. New claims and assertions should be examined and questioned, along with old ones that seem unlikely or for which the evidence is weak.

2. *Define the problem.* In order to solve a problem, a critical thinker must ask what the question is in the first place. Many times, proposed solutions fail because they are not addressing the correct problem. One example is famine relief; the obvious solution to the problem, sending more food, may not help at all if the famine is instead caused by inability to transport food to the needy. In that case, more trucks or road repair may be more effective than sending additional food. Defining the problem includes defining the parameters of the topic and the terms used as well.

3. *Examine the evidence.* Critical thinkers demand good evidence before accepting an assertion or belief as true. Your opinions and beliefs about the world are important to who you are as a person; do not sell them cheaply. Instead, the critical thinker asks what evidence supports a particular claim—and what evidence refutes it. As much relevant evidence as possible should be examined.

4. *Analyze assumptions and biases.* Critical thinkers need to be aware of their biases and prejudices in order to keep those influences to a minimum. Does a person benefit by convincing you of a certain claim? What might influence his or her opinions? This applies to advertisers, officials, and experts, but also to ourselves as well. Voltaire is credited with saying, "Every man is the creature of the age in which he lives; very few are able to raise themselves above the ideas of the time." Bear in mind that your thinking may be skewed by conscious or unconscious bias, and analyze how this could affect a conclusion.

5. *Avoid emotional reasoning.* Feelings and intuition are not sufficient to base an argument on. Give little credit to a person who can only support his or her opinions by simply saying, "Well, that's how I feel, so it must be true." We are all entitled to our views, but anyone may have any opinion about anything; they need not be based in fact, truth, or reality at all. Emotion and feelings have their place, but not as guides to the truth. Science and our understanding of the world progress on facts, not feelings.

6. *Don't oversimplify.* We live in a complex world, and it is common

for people to make generalizations or stereotypes about people or issues. But issues are rarely, if ever, clearly right or wrong, all good or all bad. Critical thinkers avoid easy generalizations and understand that there may be several viewpoints that make valid claims. Often investigators find that "the devil is in the details," meaning that a claim that seems true or impressive may turn out to be false once the specifics of the claim are examined.

7. *Consider other interpretations.* Tavris and Wade state that critical thinkers should strive to be creative in formulating reasonable hypotheses that offer potential explanations of behavior and events. "The ultimate goal is to find an explanation that accounts for the most evidence with the fewest assumptions. But critical thinkers are careful not to shut out all competing explanations too soon. They generate as many interpretations of the evidence as possible before settling on the most likely one." For example, many people believe that strange lights in the sky are alien spacecraft. Yet there are many possible explanations for lights in the sky, from an optical illusion to aircraft to the planet Venus to an unusual type of lightning. These other explanations don't mean that alien spacecraft don't exist, simply that we should eliminate the more likely explanations before accepting that one.

8. *Tolerate uncertainty.* It is important to maintain an open mind and be receptive to new ideas and possibilities. Sometimes people become dogmatic, whereby they assert their personal views as absolute truth. Science cannot answer every question, and some answers may be posed in the form of probabilities or chances of likelihood. Critical thinkers are not afraid to admit that they are not sure of something.

## CRITICAL THINKING AND EVERYDAY LIFE

Principles of critical thinking aren't only of use to rocket scientists and the academic elite. They are for everyone, and we can all learn to improve our thinking skills. In advertising, for example, critical thinking will likely make you a better consumer. You are better able to separate false claims from the true ones, and improbable claims from the likely ones, with a solid base of critical thinking skills.

If an ad for a product says, "Nothing works better," what does that really mean? That it is the best product of its kind? Not necessarily; assuming the ad is truthful, all the product is claiming is that nothing works *better* than it—still leaving the likely possibility that most of the competing products work about the same. If five leading brands of paint or pain reliever or motor oil all perform at the same level, all five could make the claim that "Nothing works better" and be completely truthful. Notice that the claim isn't really about the product itself, but about competing products.

Critical thinking can also help the environment, not only by finding solutions to ecological problems, but also by reducing the amount of superstitious thinking. Some herbal medicines, for example, are made from endangered animals. Tiger bones, rhinoceros horns, and bear gall bladders are only a few of the many substances believed in some cultures to have special healing powers—despite the lack of any evidence that they work. With fewer than 5,000 tigers reportedly surviving in the wild, we can't afford to let ignorance and myth further reduce their numbers. Jackie Chan, the martial arts film star, has publicly crusaded against such medicines.

The same is true for quack medicines that promise to heal everything from hair loss to AIDS to cancer. Though many patients may rationally question whether an unproven alternative medicine remedy will work for them, they are desperate and will pay any price to try. There have been many cases of ill patients dying because they left traditional therapies that were working for them in the hope of a miracle cure that never materialized. One reason that AIDS is ravaging Africa so badly is the common superstition that if an HIV-infected man has sex with a virgin, he will be cured. This is totally untrue, yet widely believed and acted upon—spreading the infection even further. Critical thinking helps you to look beyond emotional explanations and to recognize when we are manipulated.

## LOGIC, OPINIONS, AND EMOTIONS

Possession of emotions is one of the things that defines us as people. While other animals may be said to have moods, instincts, or even thoughts, the human animal is the only one with true emotions as we know them. We experience avarice and anger, joy and jealousy, hatred and love. Without emotions we would be little more than automatons, moving mechanically through life without feeling or really living. Yet emotions fail us spectacularly when they are used to make decisions and think critically. Emotions frequently hinder us in our search for the truth and our efforts to think clearly. Thinking based on emotion is likely to lead us astray for the following reasons:

- People are vulnerable to emotional appeals, and those require no basis in reality. There's a reason that advertisers use emotion to sell products and activists use it to scare people: Emotion moves people. If a person can't convince you of the worth of their cause through logic or rationality, emotion is always the easy route. We may dearly want to believe that our dead grandmother is talking to us though a spirit medium. But many "psychics" have been found guilty of robbing grieving relatives in part by telling them that they can communicate with their dead loved ones.

- Emotions ignore complexity. Emotions are frequently extreme and can blind people to important shades of gray in situations and problem-solving discussions. Like bumper sticker slogans, emotions are frequently reduced to likes or dislikes, and are rarely open to other information. But the world isn't black and white or easily understood; it is a complex web of choices, decisions, and causes that emotions are simply poorly equipped to deal with.

- People are notoriously poor at predicting their future feelings. Making decisions based upon those feelings ("If I buy this product or move there, I'll be happy") is a sure road to disappointment. As it turns out, people's predictions are flawed by at least one major emotional miscalculation: They tend to dramatically overestimate how long a feeling will last. In *New Scientist* magazine, writer Kathryn Brown discussed research into the problem: "People greatly overestimated how long a new love or a broken relationship would twist their emotions into knots, compared with reports from people in love or recently jilted. . . . On average, researchers say, we imagine a heavy blow or a piece of good fortune will devastate or thrill us for far longer than it actually does. 'People recover very quickly from emotional events, good and bad,' says [researcher Timothy] Wilson. 'We just don't expect to.'"[4] The same phenomenon applies to material gains and purchases. Just as children will be overjoyed at a new toy one minute and leave it forgotten an hour later, adults do much the same thing. Garages all over the world are littered with exercise equipment and gadgets whose excitement has worn off long before the credit card bills are paid off. The consumer who succumbs to manipulative, emotional appeals to spend money on pseudoscience or worthless devices is asking to be taken advantage of. Thinking critically can help its practitioners by reminding them of the larger picture.

- Feelings and emotions can inhibit rational problem-solving. Because emotions are usually considered sacred and beyond questioning (and therefore outside the realm of debate), nothing puts a stop to a discussion faster than saying, "Well, that's just the way I feel." Feelings have no truth value, no inherent validity. Feelings, unlike factual statements, are neither true nor false, valid nor invalid; they simply are. Feelings can and should be taken into account in discussions and analyses, but it's important to recognize their limits. Each person is entitled to his or her feelings and opinions, but hopefully most people can offer at least some reason or evidence to support them other than just "that's just how I feel." Marilyn vos Savant, the *Parade* magazine columnist and person with the world's highest IQ, tackled the logic-versus-emotion question this way in her column of December 7, 1997:

  Question: "You always seem to answer your questions based on logic. Do you ever allow intuition or emotion to factor into your answers? Do you believe that intuition, emotion, and other ways of making decisions are as valid as logic?"— Michael Mount, Tampa, FL

  Answer: "Good logic always takes emotion into account as an important factor, so our feelings are never neglected. But intuition—the sensation of knowing without the use of reasoning— is as lightweight as a first impression, and I wouldn't use it to make a decision unless I had no other information at all."

It is a popular fallacy that logic and emotion are mutually exclusive ways of dealing with the world, that the two can't work together. Nor is logic something practiced solely with Venn diagrams in stuffy college philosophy classes. Logic can easily apply to everyday life. For example, say a person has an irrational fear of crowds but wants to attend a music concert. The fact that emotion is involved doesn't break logic down; the logic simply takes the emotion into account. Logically, the person shouldn't be afraid of crowds. But since she is, and wants to attend, other avenues must be considered: she could arrive early to get a balcony seat so no one sits in front of her, or she could buy up the seats surrounding her and leave them empty. Emotional or irrational situations still have logic within them. Jealousy, for example, may in some cases be an irrational emotion, but the actions of a jealous person are likely to be predictable and logical. Logic is successful due in part to the fact that it can be insulated from emotion; logic thus accommodates illogic. In the end, logic and rationality are not cold, impersonal tools coveted by Vulcans, mathematicians, and scientists. We each use them in our own way and at our own times. The challenge is to be able to set aside (or overcome) emotions and irrational ways of thinking. A clear head, unclouded by emotion, is the best defense we have against those who would exploit and manipulate us.

Closely tied to emotions, opinions are sometimes used as a substitute for facts. But, as with emotions, lay opinions will only take you so far. As Vincent Ruggerio wrote in his book *Beyond Feelings,*

> Is everyone entitled to his or her opinion? In a free country this is not only permitted but guaranteed. In Great Britain, for example, there is still a Flat Earth Society. As the name implies, the members of this organization believe that the earth is not spherical but flat. In this country, too, each of us is free to take as bizarre a position as we please about any matter we choose. When the telephone operator announces, "That'll be 95 cents for the first three minutes," you may respond, "No, it won't—it'll be 28 cents." When the service station attendant notifies you, "Your oil is down a quart," you may reply, "Wrong—it's up three."
>
> Evidence that opinions can be mistaken is all around us. The weekend drinker often has the opinion that as long as he doesn't drink during the week, he is not an alcoholic. The person who continues driving with the oil light flashing on the dashboard may have the opinion

that the problem being signaled can wait until next month's service appointment. The student who quits school at age sixteen may have the opinion that an early entry into the job market ultimately improves his job security. Yet however deeply and sincerely such opinions are held, they are wrong.[5]

It's important to note, however, that experts can be wrong too. While they are more likely to be better informed and better educated than the man or woman on the street, that does not always guarantee that they can speak knowledgeably about any given topic. This is especially true when an expert is giving an opinion outside his or her field. If a heart surgeon is giving her evaluation of a new surgery technique, for example, she is probably qualified to give an informed opinion. If, however, that same surgeon is quoted offering advice on investing, astronomy, or car repair, one might want to be wary.

Another example is the testing of psychics. In many cases, people claiming to have special mental powers have been tested and examined by scientists—physicists, psychologists, and so on—in laboratory settings. And many times the scientists were very impressed with the results of their experiments, believing that those who apparently bent metal with their minds or moved objects without touching them did indeed have the powers they claimed. Yet it wasn't until professional magicians were invited to join the scientists that the "psychics" were found to be cheating. It wasn't that the scientists were stupid, or easily fooled. But they were not experts in detecting the sleight of hand used by both the magicians and the "psychics."

# CASE STUDIES IN CRITICAL THINKING

There are several ways one can go about investigating a topic. This book uses case studies, where one topic is examined in depth, and the limits of the subject are clearly drawn. Usually a single question or topic is addressed. In section II, we focus on domestic topics such as the 1938 *War of the Worlds* radio panic and the 1947 Roswell, New Mexico, UFO "crash." Even those who aren't old enough to have lived during the time likely know something about these notorious cases—not to mention modern films and television shows about them. We re-examine these cases critically in chapters 2 and 3, trying to separate fact from fiction. In chapter 4, the simple answers that many of us "know" turn out not to be so clear-cut after all, such as what happened in the case of the phantom gasser of Mattoon, Illinois. A mysterious figure was seen lurking around Mattoon, spraying victims with a paralyzing chemical. Special investigators and the FBI were called in. Yet no concrete evidence was found that the "mad gasser" really existed. Was it a media-led case of mass hysteria or a real threat? In chapter 5, we discuss a Massachusetts businessman who managed to fool many New Englanders into believing that he had invented the world's most sophisticated flying machine.

In section III, we expand our focus to cross-cultural issues. Chapter 6, "What Is Normal?" discusses extreme examples of diverse cultural beliefs and traditions, and the tendency for psychiatrists and physicians to place illness labels on unfamiliar conduct codes. In our ever-shrinking global village, cultures are interacting more than ever before. Especially in the past decade, with the explosion of the Internet, we have increased opportunities to interact with others of different faiths, cultures, and customs. It is closed-minded to assume that another culture is "bad" or "wrong" because its members hold beliefs and opinions that may be different than ours. Some people refuse to eat pork or beef; others may drink their cattle's blood; still others may believe in supernatural powers or believe that their genitals can disappear. We should celebrate our differences, not fear one another because of them. After all, isn't that what meeting other cultures is all about? If we all shared the same culture, the world would be a dull place indeed. Chapter 7 looks at parts of Southeast Asia where seemingly polite and demure women, when startled, may respond with vulgar obscenities and lewd gestures. This response, totally out of character, is said to be involuntary and may last for minutes. To some, these examples may seem like madness or psychosis. But some psychologists and sociologists argue that it is a mass delusion, and a natural outgrowth of that culture's beliefs and customs. Chapter 8, "Exploring Tolerance: Religious Devoutness or Bizarre Ritual?" examines the interpretations of scientists who not only viewed various religious rituals and beliefs as false and misguided, but as exemplifying mental disorder.

In some African and Asian cultures, people believe that their genitals are shrinking and receding into their bodies. At times men may even accuse others of stealing their genitals, apparently believing their own to be pilfered or shrunken. In chapter 9, these genital-shrinking scares are explored. Are these people mentally disturbed, or is this an extreme example of the impact of culture on beliefs?

In section IV we continue to ask, "What is normal?" but shift our focus to examining the importance of one's social and historical context. Chapter 10 explores the curious case of the dancing mania, in which religious people in medieval times would reportedly break into spontaneous dancing frenzies. During these dances, which could last for days, some participants would tear their clothes off and prance naked; others would make animal noises; others might laugh, cry, or scream uncontrollably; while still others made obscene gestures and rolled around in dirt. Some attributed the craze to madness; others said it was the result of a spider bite. A critical and historical inquiry, however, points to other explanations. Chapter 11 looks at the history behind the "Jumping Frenchmen of Maine." Is their exaggerated response to the startle reflex an innate nervous condition or a local habit developed in the lumberjack camps? The influence of the mass media on creating popular myths is the subject of chapter 12, which examines the origin of the flying saucer myth which was spawned from the publication of a single, erroneous newspaper article in 1947. In chapter 13 British folklorist David Clarke examines evidence for the existence of mysterious black helicopters that have been spotted across England in recent decades and how they reflect popular fears. In chapter 14 we explore the fascinating case of India's so-called monkey man. Chapter 15 addresses mass delusions and ends with a caveat: No one, regardless of his or her culture, nationality, or education level, is completely immune from the effects of social delusions. We must learn to recognize them and minimize their impact.

The cases examined in this book touch on many areas of critical thinking. Some highlight the danger of superficial investigation; others demonstrate the importance of not jumping to conclusions based on first impressions. The nature of memory and collective beliefs are also addressed. In the end, what people believe *does* matter, because they act on their beliefs—and those actions change the world around us. Following each chapter in this book, we will offer a set of review or study questions that are intended to guide and challenge readers on key points to determine whether they understand the material and how it relates to basic principles of critical thinking.

# REVIEW QUESTIONS

1. Define critical thinking. How does critical thinking differ from noncritical thinking?
2. List the eight essential guidelines involved in learning to think critically as outlined by psychologists Carole Wade and Carol Tavris.
3. Is it possible to be completely neutral and unbiased on any given topic? If not, how can we reduce the influence of prejudice and preconceived notions?
4. Believers in pseudoscience (beliefs or practices that are mistakenly thought to be based on scientific principles) often claim that they are open-minded and receptive to new possibilities while scientists are close-minded, rigid, and intolerant of unproven claims. Refute this argument and assume that the scientist involved is using the eight guidelines of critical thinking.
5. A person's environment influences his belief systems. How do the eight guidelines serve to reduce these influences which may hinder someone from making more objective decisions?

# NOTES

1. Cited in R. T. Tripp, *The International Thesaurus of Quotations* (New York: Harper & Row, 1970), p. 638.

2. D. Coon, *Introduction to Psychology: Exploration and Application* (Pacific Grove, Calif.: Brooks/Cole Publishing, 2000), p. 21.

3. Carole Wade and Carol Tavris, "Thinking Critically and Creatively," *Skeptical Inquirer* 14, no. 4 (1990): 372–77.

4. Kathryn Brown, "Feeling Just Fine," *New Scientist* (October 4, 1999): 36.

5. Vincent R. Ruggerio, *Beyond Feelings: A Guide to Critical Thinking* (New York: Mayfield Press, 1998), p. 35.

# PART 2

# THE AMERICAN PICTURE

# 2

# WAS THERE REALLY A MARTIAN PANIC IN 1938?

It's well known that the *War of the Worlds* radio play triggered a mass panic across the United States involving millions of people—or did it? You decide.

Shortly after 8 o'clock on Sunday evening October 30, 1938, many Americans became anxious or panic-stricken after listening to a realistic, live, one-hour radio play depicting a fictitious Martian landing at the Wilmuth farm in the tiny hamlet of Grovers Mill, New Jersey. Those living within the immediate vicinity of the bogus invasion appeared to have been most frightened, although the broadcast could be heard in all regions of the continental United States and no particular location was immune. The play included references to real places, buildings, highways, streets, prestigious speakers, and had convincing sound effects and special bulletins. The drama was produced by a twenty-three-year-old theatrical prodigy named George Orson Welles (1915–1985), who was accompanied by a small group of actors and musicians in a New York City studio of the Columbia Broadcasting System's Mercury Theatre. The actual broadcast script was written by Howard Koch, who loosely based it on an 1898 book by acclaimed science fiction writer Herbert George (H. G.) Wells (1866–1946), *The War of the Worlds*.[1] In the original Wells novel, the Martians had landed in nineteenth-century Woking, England. The broadcast remains arguably the most widely known delusion in United States and, perhaps, world history, and many radio stations around the world continue to broadcast the original play each Halloween eve.

It is timely to reflect on the lessons we can glean from the incident by using the wisdom that hindsight can provide.

1. *Human perception and memory reconstruction are remarkably flawed.*

Today many people seem to forget that the Martian "invasion" illustrates far more than a short-term panic. It is a testament to the remarkable power of expectation on perception. A person's frame of reference has a strong influence on how external stimuli are interpreted and internalized as reality.[2] Perception is highly unreliable and subject to error.[3] This effect has long been known to be pronounced under situations of stress, ambiguity, and uncertainty.[4] This message cannot be overemphasized and continues to go widely unheeded. Visual misperceptions contribute to many reports of such diverse phenomena as religious signs and wonders, UFOs, and Bigfoot.

In his famous study of the Martian panic, Princeton University psychologist Hadley Cantril discusses the extreme variability of eyewitness descriptions of the "invasion." These examples have usually been overlooked in subsequent popular and scholarly discussions of the panic. One person became convinced that he could smell the poison gas and feel the heat rays as described on the radio, while another became emotionally distraught and felt a choking sensation from the imaginary "gas."[5] During the broadcast several residents reported to police observations "of Martians on their giant machines poised on the Jersey Palisades."[6] After checking various descriptions of the panic, Joseph Bulgatz reported that a Boston woman said she could actually see the fire as described on the radio;[7] other persons told of hearing machine gun fire or the "swish" sound of the Martians. A man even climbed atop a Manhattan building with binoculars and described seeing "the flames of battle."

The event also reminds us that the human mind does not function like a video camera capturing each piece of data that comes into its field of vision. People interpret information as it is processed. These memories are not statically locked away in the brain forever, but are reconstructed over time.[8] Cantril cited the case of Miss Jane Dean, a devoutly religious woman, who, when recalling the broadcast, said the most realistic portion was "the sheet of flame that swept over the entire country. That is just the way I pictured the end."[9] In reality, there was no mention of a sheet of flame anywhere in the broadcast.

## 2. *The mass media is a powerful force in society.*

Not only does the Martian panic demonstrate the enormous influence of the mass media in contemporary society, but in recent years an ironic twist has developed. There is a growing consensus among sociologists that the extent of the panic as described by Cantril was greatly exaggerated.[10] The irony here is that for the better part of the past sixty years many people may have been misled by the media to believe that the panic was far more extensive and intense than it apparently was. However, regardless of the extent of the panic, there is little doubt that many Americans were genuinely frightened and some did try to flee the Martian gas raids and heat rays, especially in the New Jersey–New York area.

Based on various opinion polls and estimates, Cantril calculated that of about 1.7 million people who heard the drama, nearly 1.2 million "were excited" to varying degrees.[11] Yet there is only scant anecdotal evidence to suggest that many listeners actually took some action after hearing the broadcast, such as packing belongings, grabbing guns, or fleeing in motor vehicles. In fact, much of Cantril's study was based on interviews with just 135 people. Bainbridge is critical of Cantril for citing just a few colorful stories from a small number of people who panicked. According to sociologist Walter Bainbridge, on any given night, out of a pool of over a million people, at least a thousand would have been driving excessively fast or engaging in rambunctious behavior. Reports of people exhibiting panic behavior between 8 and 9 P.M. on October 30 did not necessarily have anything to do with the broadcast. From this perspective, the event was primarily a news media creation. Another sociologist, David Miller, supports this view, noting that while the day after the panic many newspapers carried accounts of suicides and heart attacks by frightened citizens, they proved to have been unfounded but have passed into

American folklore.[12] Miller also takes Cantril to task for failing to show
substantial evidence of mass flight from the perceived attack,[13] citing just
a few examples and not warranting an estimate of over 1 million panic-
stricken Americans. While Cantril cites American Telephone Company
figures indicating that local media and law enforcement agencies were
inundated with up to 40 percent more telephone calls than normal in parts
of New Jersey during the broadcast, he did not determine the specific
nature of these calls:

> Some callers requested information, such as which units of national
> guard were being called up or whether casualty lists were available.
> Some people called to find out where they could go to donate blood.
> Some callers were simply angry that such a realistic show was allowed
> on the air, while others called CBS to congratulate Mercury Theater for
> the exciting Halloween program. . . . we cannot know how many of
> these telephone calls were between households. It seems . . . (likely)
> many callers just wanted to chat with their families and friends about
> the exciting show they had just listened to on the radio.[14]

Criminologist Erich Goode agrees with Miller's assessment, but also notes
that to have convinced a substantial number of listeners "that a radio
drama about an invasion from Mars was an actual news broadcast has to
be regarded as a remarkable achievement."[15] Either way you view it,
whether tens of thousands of people became panic-stricken, or over a million, there is no denying that the mass media has significantly influenced
public perception of the event. There is also no disputing that similar
broadcasts have resulted in full-fledged panics, as we will discuss next.

### 3. *It can't happen again.*

Only someone with an ignorance of history would assume that similar panics could not recur. More recent mass panics and delusions have
involved the pivotal role of the mass media (especially newspaper and television). For instance, the media was instrumental in triggering a widespread delusion about the existence of imaginary pit marks on wind-
shields in Washington State during 1954 that were erroneously attributed
to atomic fallout.[16] Mass delusions can also have a humorous side. During
March 1993, excitement was created in Texas after the *Morning Times of*

*Laredo* published a hoax account of a giant 300-pound earthworm undulating across Interstate 35. Many citizens in the vicinity of Laredo believed the story despite claims that the worm was an incredible seventy-nine feet long! What is not humorous is the relative ease with which a spate of media hoaxes were perpetrated across the country in the early 1990s, prompting the Federal Communications Commission to impose fines of up to $250,000 for TV stations knowingly broadcasting false information. But could a repeat of the 1938 Martian panic occur? The answer is yes.

A widespread panic was triggered following a broadcast of the Welles play by a Santiago, Chile, radio station on November 12, 1944. Upon hearing the news of the "invasion," many fled into the streets or barricaded themselves in their homes. In one province troops and artillery were briefly mobilized by the governor in a bid to repel the invading Martians. The broadcast was highly realistic and included references to such organizations as the Red Cross and used an actor to impersonate the interior minister.[17]

On the night of February 12, 1949, another radio play based on *The War of the Worlds* resulted in a pandemonium in Quito, Ecuador, with tens of thousands of panic-stricken residents running into the streets to escape Martian gas raids. The event made headlines around the world, including the front page of the *New York Times*.[18] The drama described strange Martian creatures heading toward the city after landing and destroying the neighboring community of Latacunga, twenty miles south of Quito. Broadcast in Spanish on Radio Quito, the realistic program included impersonations of well-known local politicians and journalists, vivid eyewitness descriptions, and the name of the local town of Cotocallo. In Quito, a riot broke out and an enraged mob poured gasoline onto the building housing the radio station which broadcast the drama, then set it alight, killing five people. While the *Times* article states that fifteen people were killed in the rioting which ensued, filmmaker Eric Geringas recently interviewed a local man who witnessed the events, and was emphatic that only five died. It appears the *Times* correspondent may have added a "1" in front of the five by mistake. There was no follow-up article by the paper.[19]

The tragic sequence of events began when a regular music program was suddenly interrupted with a news bulletin followed by reports of the invading Martians wreaking havoc and destruction while closing in on the city. A voice resembling that of a government minister appealed for calm so the city's defenses could be organized and citizens evacuated in time. Next the "mayor" arrived and made a dramatic announcement: "People of Quito, let us defend our city. Our women and children must go out into the surrounding heights to leave the men free for action and combat." Positioned atop the tallest building in the city, La Previsora tower, an announcer said he could discern a monster engulfed in plumes of fire and smoke advancing on Quito from the north. It was at that point, according to a *New York Times* reporter, that citizens "began fleeing from their homes and running through the streets. Many were clad only in night clothing."[20]

Other radio adaptations of *The War of the Worlds* have had less dramatic consequences, but still resulted in some frightened listeners in the vicinity of Providence, Rhode Island, on the night of October 31, 1974, and in northern Portugal in 1988.[21]

# WHAT OF THE FUTURE?

Since 1938, the world's rapidly expanding population has grown increasingly reliant on the mass media and people generally expect it to contain immediate, accurate information on nearly every facet of their lives. By most projections, the twenty-first century will see an even greater dependence on information and mass media. While it may be true that you cannot fool all of the people all of the time, as the *War of the Worlds* panics and other mass scares attest to, you need only fool a relatively small portion of people for a short period to create large-scale disruptions to society. That is the lesson we can glean from the reaction to the 1938 broadcast. It can and will happen again. Only the mediums and forms will change as new technologies are developed and old delusional themes fade away while new ones come into vogue.

Each era has a set of taken-for-granted social realities that define it and manifest in unique delusions. During the Middle Ages scores of popular delusions, panics, and scares surrounded the belief that humans could transform into various animals, especially wolves.[22] In the seventeenth and eighteenth centuries, most recorded delusions were precipitated by a widespread fear of witches and manifested in episodes of mass demon possession and moral panics involving a hunt for those believed to be witches.[23] These episodes often resulted in torture, imprisonment, or death for various minority ethnic groups including Jews, heretics, deviants, the aged, women, and the poor.[24] Twentieth-century mass delusions overwhelmingly involve two themes. The first is a fear of environmental contaminants mirroring growing concern about global pollution and heightened awareness of public health. This situation has triggered scores of mass hysterical illness in schools, factories, and occasionally communities, and numerous delusions without psychological illness.[25] The second series of delusions has spread widely in Western countries that have become dependent on child daycare facilities. Their prominence since the mid-1980s coincides with a series of moral panics involving exaggerated claims about the existence of organized cultists kidnapping or molesting children. These myths function as cautionary tales about the inability of the weakened nuclear family to protect children.[26]

At the dawn of the twenty-first century and a new millennium, we can only ponder what new mass scares and panics await us. It is beyond the realm of science to accurately predict what these will entail. But it will be vital for scientists to respond to the challenge of this new era of ideas and technologies that will bring about an as yet unforeseen set of circumstances that characterize and define each age. For mass panics and scares can tell us much about ourselves and the times in which we live. Part of this challenge is to remember the lessons of the past.

\*    \*    \*

Applying basic critical thinking principles to the Martian "panic" leads to the realization that the extent of the public's reaction to the broadcast—one of the most famous chapters in the annals of social psychology—has been greatly exaggerated. It appears that only a tiny fraction of those who tuned in or heard about the broadcast from others actually panicked and tried to flee. Until relatively recently, researchers discussing this episode have failed to clearly define and distinguish between the terms "panic" and "scare" as they relate to the collected evidence. There is very little evidence that more than a tiny group of people panicked. In many introductory college textbooks on sociology or social psychology, the event continues to be erroneously categorized as an example of "mass hysteria."

Hadley Cantril should have conducted more interviews with a statistically significant sample size. He also needed to separate his emotions from the *zeitgeist* or spirit of the times. His assumption that many listeners panicked is based more on the tide of popular opinion when he began his study shortly after the incident—more on emotion than evidence. Early on, Cantril should have considered a variety of interpretations of the data in his book, but instead he ended up rubber-stamping his initial assumptions and did not even mention the possibility that the episode was a form of mass media creation. In fact, the authors of most college textbooks on mass psychology have, until recently, continued to cite Cantril's study as valid without ever examining the evidence on which he based his claims. Like Cantril, they were guilty of giving in to their assumptions and biases and failing to consider alternative explanations.

# REVIEW QUESTIONS

1. Cite specific examples of how the Martian invasion scare supports the position that human perception and memory are flawed.
2. Mass delusions such as the Martian scare did not occur in a social vacuum. Even before the broadcast aired, what preexisting conditions served to foster the episode?
3. Do you agree with the assessment that the extent of the Martian panic was exaggerated by the news media?
4. What could those affected have done to find out if there really was a Martian or German invasion?
5. What could Hadley Cantril have done to make the results of his survey more convincing?
6. If a similar scare occurred today, what form might it take? Do you think the alien invaders would look like they were described in 1938? Why or why not?
7. How do you explain the report of the man who described seeing the "flames of battle" from a Manhattan building? Do you think he was mistaken, lying, or misinterpreting?
8. Which word best describes what happened in parts of the United States on October 30, 1938—a panic or a scare? What about Quito, Equador, in 1949?

9. Why should we remember the Martian scare of 1938?
10. What do mass panics and scares tell us about ourselves and the times in which we live?

## NOTES

1. H. G. Wells, *The War of the Worlds* (New York: New American Library, 1898 [1986]).

2. R. Buckhout, "Eyewitness Testimony," *Scientific American* 231 (1974): 23–31.

3. E. Loftus, *Eyewitness Testimony* (Cambridge, Mass.: Harvard University Press, 1979); D. F. Ross, J. D. Read, and M. P. Toglia, *Adult Eyewitness Testimony: Current Trends and Developments* (Cambridge: Cambridge University Press, 1994); G. Wells and J. Turtle, "Eyewitness Identification: The Importance of Lineup Models," *Psychological Bulletin* 99 (1986): 320–29.

4. S. E. Asch, "Studies of Independence and Conformity: A Minority of One against a Unanimous Majority," *Psychological Monographs* 70 (1956); D. Krech, R. S. Crutchfield, and E. L. Ballschey, *Individual and Society* (New York: McGraw-Hill, 1962); M. Sherif and O. J. Harvey, "A Study in Ego Functioning: Elimination of Stable Anchorages in Individual and Group Situations," *Sociometry* 15 (1952): 272–305.

5. H. Cantril, *The Invasion from Mars: A Study in the Psychology of Panic* (Princeton, N.J.: Princeton University Press, 1947 [1940]), pp. 94–95.

6. R. E. Markush, "Mental Epidemics: A Review of the Old to Prepare for the New," *Public Health Reviews* 2 (1973): 379.

7. J. Bulgatz, *Ponzi Schemes, Invaders from Mars & More Extraordinary Popular Delusions and the Madness of Crowds* (New York: Harmony Books, 1992), p. 129.

8. E. Loftus and K. Ketcham, *Witness for the Defense: The Accused, the Eyewitness, and the Expert Who Puts Memory on Trial* (New York: St. Martin's Press, 1991).

9. Cantril, *Invasion from Mars*, p. 181.

10. D. Miller, *Introduction to Collective Behavior* (Belmont, Calif.: Wadsworth, 1985); W. S. Bainbridge, "Collective Behavior and Social Movements," in *Sociology*, ed. R. Stark (Belmont, Calif.: Wadsworth, 1987), pp. 544–76; E. Goode, *Collective Behavior* (New York: Harcourt Brace Jovanovich, 1992).

11. Cantril, *Invasion from Mars*, p. 58.

12. Miller, *Introduction to Collective Behavior*, p. 100.

13. Ibid., p. 106.

14. Ibid., p. 107.

15. Goode, *Collective Behavior*, p. 315.

16. N. Z. Medalia and O. Larsen, "Diffusion and Belief in a Collective Delusion," *Sociological Review* 23 (1958): 180–86.

17. Bulgatz, *Ponzi-Schemes*, p. 137.

18. "Mars Raiders Caused Quito Panic; Mob Burns Radio Plant, Kills 15," *New York Times*, February 14, 1949, pp. 1, 7.

19. Telephone conversation between Robert Bartholomew and filmmaker Eric Geringas of Toronto, Canada, August 2001.

20. "Mars Raiders Caused Quito Panic; Mob Burns Radio Plant, Kills 15," *New York Times*, February 14, 1949, pp. 1, 7.

21. Bulgatz, *Ponzi-Schemes*, p. 139.

22. R. Eisler, *Man into Wolf, An Anthropological Interpretation of Sadism, Masochism, and Lycanthropy; A Lecture Delivered at a Meeting of the Royal Society of Medicine* (London: Routledge & Paul, 1951); R. Noll, ed., *Vampires, Werewolves, and Demons: Twentieth Century Reports in the Psychiatric Literature* (New York: Brunner/Mazel, 1992).

23. L. F. Calmeil, *De la Folie, Consideree Sous le Point de vue Pathologique, Philosophique, Historique et Judiciaire* [On the Crowd, Considerations on the Point of Pathology, Philosophy, History and Justice] (Paris: Baillere, 1845); S. Garnier, *Barbe Buvee, en Religion, soeur Sainte-Colombe et la Pretendue Possession des Ursulines d'Auxonne* [Barbe Buvee and Religion, Sister Columbe and the Feigned Possession of the Ursulines at Auxonne] (Paris: Felix Alcan, 1895); A. Huxley, *The Devils of Loudun* (New York: Harper and Brothers, 1952).

24. G. Rosen, *Madness in Society* (London: Routledge and Kegan Paul, 1968); E. Goode and N. Ben-Yehuda, *Moral Panics: The Social Construction of Deviance* (Oxford: Blackwell, 1994).

25. Regarding mass hysteria in schools, see R. E. Bartholomew and F. Sirois, "Epidemic Hysteria in Schools: An International and Historical Overview," *Educational Studies* 22, no. 3 (1996): 285–311; in factories, see R. E. Bartholomew and F. Sirois, "Occupational Mass Psychogenic Illness: A Transcultural Perspective," *Transcultural Psychiatry* 37, no. 4 (2000): 495–524. For discussion of mass hysteria in communities, see M. F. Goldsmith, "Physicians with Georgia on their Minds," *Journal of the American Medical Association* 262 (1989): 603–604; Z. Radovanovic, "On the Origin of Mass Casualty Incidents in Kosovo, Yugoslavia, in 1990," *European Journal of Epidemiology* 11 (1995): 1–13; and Miller, *Introduction to Collective Behavior* and Goode, *Collective Behavior*, both discuss delusions that do not involve psychological illness.

26. J. S. Victor, "The Spread of Satanic-Cult Rumors," *Skeptical Inquirer* 14, no. 3 (1990): 287–91; J. S. Victor, "A Rumor-Panic about a Dangerous Satanic Cult in Western New York," *New York Folklore* 15 (1989): 23–49.

# 3

# THE ROSWELL "FLYING SAUCER" CRASH OF 1947

Stories about a crashed saucer in the New Mexico desert are part of a broader myth dating back at least 85 years before Roswell. What makes this myth so appealing?

An alien spaceship crashes to Earth, killing its occupants. Roswell, New Mexico, 1947? No, a remote Indian Ocean island, 1862. Another ship plunges from the sky above a small town in the southwestern United States, extinguishing the life of its extraterrestrial pilot. Roswell? No, Aurora, Texas, 1897. In July 1947, a flying saucer supposedly crashed in the desert near Roswell, New Mexico, killing or critically injuring its crew. U.S. military personnel are said to have sealed off the area, carted away the evidence, and engaged in a cover-up. Yet stories of crashed UFOs are not new. While dozens of crashed UFOs have been reported at sites around the world since 1947, reports of crashed alien craft date back to at least the middle part of the nineteenth century.[1]

History is a valuable tool in the scientist's arsenal, as it distances observers from events, allowing for a less emotional, more contextual perspective in evaluating incredible claims. For instance, between 1900 and 1950, humanlike aliens typically landed in saucers with protruding exhaust pipes and clumsy disembarking ladders, wore Buck Rogers–style space suits, carried pistol ray guns, and usually hailed from Mars. This caricature is laughable in comparison to present-day depiction of aliens, with large heads and bulbous eyes, who float from their ship and communicate telepathically. The same comparative historical approach can be applied fruitfully to crashed-saucer claims to show that they are part of a broader myth.

In a letter to the *Houston Post* of May 2, 1897, John Leander wrote that an elderly sailor from El Campo, Texas—identified only as "Mr. Oleson"—claimed to have been shipwrecked on a tiny uncharted Indian Ocean island in 1862. He said that during his ordeal, an immense airship sporting gigantic wings crashed into a rock cliff. Inside were the bodies of twelve-foot-tall creatures with dark bronze skin. "Their hair and beard were also long and as soft and silky as the hair of an infant." The surviving sailors lived inside the wrecked airship and eventually "summoned courage to drag the gigantic bodies to the cliff and tumble them over." After building a raft and being rescued by a passing Russian vessel, Oleson retained a ring from the thumb of one of the creatures as the only proof of the events. Two and a quarter inches in diameter, it "[was] made of a compound of metals unknown to any jeweler . . . and [was] set with two reddish stones." As luck would have it, by the time the vessel reached port, his remaining shipmates had died, leaving Oleson as the sole survivor.

This story bears an uncanny resemblance to Roswell: The account is a secondhand narrative of alien creatures in a space vessel crashing at a remote location. The craft was destroyed and foreign writing is found inside. The alien bodies were disposed of and the debris lost. A piece of confirming evidence was retained in the form of an immense ring with unknown properties, but the witness failed to allow public scrutiny. It is important to remember that our interest here in such accounts is in their narrative content and not their truth or falsity per se.

During a wave of phantom airship sightings in the United States between 1896 and 1897, there were several claims of crashed UFOs. On the night of December 3, 1896, a wrecked airship was found in the gully of a cow pasture in a San Francisco suburb, after dairy farmers heard a loud bang followed by cries for help. Rushing to the scene, they found two dazed human occupants staggering near a forty-foot-long, cone-shaped tube of galvanized iron with broken wings and propellers. After causing a local sensation, and under cross-examination by those inspecting the "wreckage," the alleged pilot, J. D. deGear of 538 Fulton Street, confessed that the "ship" had been pulled to the hilltop on a wagon and pushed over.[2] The spot was chosen for its proximity to a nearby saloon, which enjoyed a brisk business during the spectacle.[3] The two men were apparently trying to achieve fame and fortune.

On the night of April 4, 1897, an airship supposedly crashed on the J. D. Sims farm near Bethany, Missouri, killing its pilot.[4] Within a week, a flying machine reportedly plunged into a reservoir near Rhodes, Iowa.[5] No debris was ever found. On April 16, another vessel allegedly crash-landed outside Waterloo, Iowa.[6] In Tennessee, it was rumored that a craft had plunged to Earth in the middle of the night, sinking without a trace into Sycamore Creek.[7]

Finally, there was the Aurora, Texas, hoax where a craft carrying what appeared to be a Martian allegedly crashed, with its pilot supposedly buried nearby.[8] In *UFOs—Explained*, former senior editor of the respected publication *Aviation Week and Space Technology* Philip J. Klass ripped the story to shreds, noting numerous inaccuracies and inconsistencies in the initial press dispatch on the story. Yet, scores of UFO researchers have traveled and continue to travel to the community of Aurora, armed with cameras, Geiger counters, metal detectors, pickaxes, and shovels in hopes of locating the purported grave of the unfortunate alien.

It is also notable that there were theories of government coverups during the airship wave. The *Galveston* (Texas) *Daily News* of April 29, 1897, argued that airship reports were secret U.S. government experiments, noting: "A profound secrecy has been maintained as to what has been accomplished, even army officers themselves only getting vague inklings of what is going on."[9] There were also claims of airships being constructed and hidden in U.S. military installations, including Fort Sheridan near Chicago and Fort Logan in Colorado.[10]

Pre-Roswell crashed-UFO claims have also occurred outside the United States. During 1909, a wave of phantom Zeppelin sightings spread across New Zealand amid rumors that Germany was planning an aerial attack. Within this context, a Zeppelin reportedly crashed at Waikaka,

New Zealand, killing those on board.[11] In Scandinavia during the 1930s, mysterious "ghost aeroplanes" were frequently spotted. On February 5, 1933, several Norwegians became convinced that a "ghost flier" had crashed into Mount Fagar. A police search party revealed nothing.[12] During World War II, the British government was reported to have captured a crashed saucer and tiny aliens.[13] In 1946, dozens of UFOs reportedly crashed in Scandinavia after rumors that the Soviets were test-firing V-rockets. No confirming evidence was ever found, despite intense military investigations.[14]

If there is any mystery surrounding accounts of crashed UFOs, its solution lies not in examining some secret military hangar, but in examining the human mind. We need to ask ourselves, What makes this myth so appealing? Folklorist Jan Brunvand contends that for legends to persist in modern society "as living narrative folklore," they must contain three key elements: "a strong basic story-appeal, a foundation in actual belief, and a meaningful message or 'moral.'"[15] Accounts of crashed saucers and government cover-ups easily meet each of these criteria. They make for fascinating reading and discussion, and are rendered plausible in the many dubious books, pseudoscientific "docudramas," and speculative movies that suggest their existence. These narratives contain a poignant message about a secular age that has used science and reason to expel gods, ghosts, and demons from our minds. These haunting images have been replaced with more plausible contemporary themes: a world of government mistrust, nefarious conspiracies, and alien abductors. Paradoxically, as scientists delve deeper into the mysteries of our universe, they generate more questions. New scientific discoveries continue to reveal a world that is every bit as fascinating as that any pseudoscientist could imagine.[16]

\*          \*          \*

How do these historical stories of extraterrestrial "crash landings" relate to critical thinking? It is important to examine that actual evidence (not second- or thirdhand accounts) and ask penetrating questions, not simply accept accounts at face value. Doing so allows us to view crashed UFO claims within the larger historical context. Critical thinking requires that we look at *all* of the evidence and not just selectively accept what *seems*

Artist Brad Marshall pokes fun at the glut of popular books claiming that aliens are seemingly everywhere. Human perception is dependent upon a person's mental set. Did you see the visual illusion in the alien's head when you first looked at this picture?

# Roswell Daily Record

ROSWELL, NEW MEXICO     TUESDAY, JULY 8, 1947

## RAAF Captures Flying Saucer On Ranch in Roswell Region

### No Details of Flying Disk Are Revealed

Roswell Hardware
Man and Wife
Report Disk Seen

The intelligence office of the 509th Bombardment group at Roswell Army Air Field announced at noon today that the field has come into possession of a flying saucer.

According to information released by the department, over authority of Maj. J. A. Marcel, intelligence officer, the disk was recovered on a ranch in the Roswell vicinity, after an unidentified rancher had notified Sheriff Geo. Wilcox here, that he had found the instrument on his premises.

Major Marcel and a detail from his department went to the ranch and recovered the disk, it was stated.

After the intelligence office here had inspected the instrument it was flown to higher headquarters.

The intelligence office stated, that no details of the saucer's construction or its appearance had been revealed.

Mr. and Mrs. Dan Wilmot apparently were the only persons in Roswell who have seen what they thought was a flying disk.

They were sitting on their porch at 105 South Penn. last Wednesday night at about ten minutes before ten o'clock when a large glowing object zoomed out of the sky from the southeast, going in a northwesterly direction at a high rate of speed.

Wilmot called Mrs. Wilmot's attention to it and both ran down into the yard to watch it. It was in sight less than a minute, perhaps 40 or 50 seconds, Wilmot estimated.

Wilmot said that it appeared to him to be about 1,500 feet high and going fast. He estimated between 400 and 500 miles per hour.

In appearance it looked oval in shape like two inverted saucers, faced mouth to mouth, or like two washbowls placed together in the same fashion. The entire body glowed as though light were showing through from inside, though not like it would be if a light were merely underneath.

From where he stood Wilmot said that the object looked to be about 5 feet in size, and making allowance for the distance it was from town he figured that it must have been 15 or 20 feet in diameter, though this was just a guess.

Wilmot said that he heard no sound but that Mrs Wilmot said she heard a swishing sound for a very short time.

The object came into view from the southeast and disappeared over the treetops in the general vicinity of six-mile hill.

Wilmot, who is one of the most respected and reliable citizens in town, kept the story to himself hoping that someone else would come out and tell about having seen one, but finally today decided that he would go ahead and tell about seeing it. The announcement that the RAAF was in possession of one came only a few minutes after he had decided to release the details of what he had seen.

This press report about a crashed saucer helped give birth to the present-day legend that aliens crashed near Roswell, New Mexico, in 1947.

to support our own position. Twentieth-century accounts of crashed airships with hulking Martians seem incredible today when compared to the Roswell claims, which are more realistic by contemporary standards of technology and science. Nowadays, we expect aliens to travel in metallic saucers, while nineteenth-century stories of Martians in wooden airships sporting propellers seem ridiculous. By not selectively choosing which accounts to accept and reject, we are forced to examine all the accounts, fostering a realization that in the absence of incontrovertible proof of their existence, crashed UFO reports contain key elements typical of urban legends that have circulated for centuries. Just as folklorists study recurrent themes of fairy tales and their underlying meanings, we are compelled to accept the mythical nature of crashed UFO stories, which, when examined on a thematic level, offer an exciting, enchanting universe that is far more seductive than the rather mechanical, godless world portrayed by science.

# REVIEW QUESTIONS

1. Why are crashed saucer stories so appealing in that they have appeared for over 100 years across different cultural settings?
2. What does the persistence of the crashed saucer myth suggest about the likelihood that universal, deep-seated psychological needs are being fulfilled? What might these needs be?
3. Is it possible for "UFOs" (objects in the sky that people cannot readily identify) to exist, but that Earth is not being visited by extraterrestrials? Conversely, is it possible for ETs to be visiting Earth, yet all "UFO" reports to be false? Why is it important to clearly define terms when discussing this topic?
4. Folklorist Jan Brunvand contends that when legends persist over a lengthy time period, they contain which three elements?
5. How does the use of history help the reader to assess sensational claims less emotionally and more accurately?
6. Some press reports from the 1890s claimed that airship sightings were secret U.S. government experiments. What comparisons can be drawn to similar modern stories about crashed saucers being confiscated by the United States military?

# NOTES

1. S. Friedman and D. Berliner, *Crash at Corona* (New York: Paragon House, 1992); K. Randle, *A History of UFO Crashes* (New York: Avon, 1995); M. McGhee and B. Dickeson, *The Gosford File: UFOs over the N.S.W. Central Coast* (Kogarah, New South Wales, Australia: INUFOR, 1996).

2. "An Airship Which Rode in a Wagon Was Planted in a Gulch," *San Francisco Chronicle*, December 4, 1896, p. 5.

3. "Plunged from a Dizzy Height . . . It Landed Suddenly in a Ditch," *The* (San Francisco) *Call*, December 4, 1896, p. 1; "An Airship in the Mud. Night of Weird Whirrings, Cries and Crashes behind Twin Peaks," *San Francisco Examiner*, December 5, 1896, p. 1.

4. "An Inquest Now in Order. Air Ship Falls Near Bethany and One Man Said to be Killed," *St. Joseph* (Missouri) *Daily Herald*, April 6, 1897, p. 5.

5. "Stranger Than Fiction," *Iowa State Register*, April 13, 1897, p. 1.

6. "Is a Clever Fake. Airship Comes Down at Waterloo with One Passenger . . . ," *Cedar Rapids* (Iowa) *Evening Gazette*, April 16, 1897, p. 1.

7. ". . . Hypothetical Fate of the Wonderful Airship," *Nashville Banner*, April 17, 1897, p. 1.

8. "A Windmill Demolishes It," *Dallas Morning News*, April 19, 1897, p. 5.

9. "Airships May be Uncle Sam's," *Galveston* (Texas) *Daily News*, April 29, 1897, p. 10.

10. Ibid.

11. "Testimony by Schoolchildren. A Black Object," (Dunedin, New Zealand) *Evening Star*, July 31, 1909.

12. *Svenska Dagbladet*, February 7, 1934.

13. T. Good, *Beyond Top Secret* (London: Pan, 1997), p. 21.

14. A. Liljegren amd C. Svahn, "Ghost Rockets and Phantom Aircraft," in *Phenomenon: Forty Years of Flying Saucers*, ed. J. Spencer and H. Evans (New York: Avon, 1989), pp. 53–60.

15. J. H. Brunvand, *The Vanishing Hitchhiker* (New York: W.W. Norton, 1981).

16. I am indebted to Thomas E. Bullard for providing most of the press reports.

# 4

# THE MAD GASSER OF MATTOON

## Press Creation of an Imaginary Criminal

*with Robert Ladendorf*

The mass media is often influential in spreading mass hysteria to the public at-large. This is no more evident than in the famous case of the Mad Gasser of Mattoon.

One of best known cases of mass hysteria during the twentieth century is the "mad gasser" of Mattoon (pronounced "MAT-tune") in which a mysterious figure supposedly roamed this small Illinois city, spraying noxious gas into homes and making its terrified occupants ill. Shortly after the publication of a study by Donald Johnson in 1945, in the *Journal of Abnormal and Social Psychology*, the episode became a classic within the social science annals.[1] Since the 1950s, most textbooks on sociology and social psychology that discuss mass behavior cite Johnson's article. Despite its continued popularity among social scientists, virtually nothing has been written about it in the scientific literature. An exception is physicist Willy Smith, who claims there was a real gasser.[2] His argument is based mainly on eyewitness testimony and recollections of the event—both of which are notoriously unreliable, and both of which Smith takes at face value. Meanwhile, in recent years the episode has appeared in many books and articles on mysteries and the paranormal, where it is typically discussed as possibly being an unsolved crime or the work of a supernatural entity.[3] In this chapter, we address critics of the mass hysteria hypothesis, and extend Johnson's original argument on the role of the press by examining this and other factors in greater detail.

## THE PHANTOM ANESTHETIST: A THUMBNAIL SKETCH

The case of the mad gasser began about 11 P.M. Friday, September 1, 1944, as Aline Kearney lay in bed reading the newspaper. Mrs. Kearney was a young housewife whose husband was driving a cab that night in Mattoon, a small city of about 17,000 residents in eastern Illinois. They had a son and two daughters, including three-year-old Dorothy Ellen, who was sleeping in her parents' bed. Also staying with the Kearneys was Mrs. Kearney's sister, Martha Reedy, whose husband was in the war.

Suddenly, Mrs. Kearney smelled a sweet odor that made her sick and she was not able to move, her legs paralyzed. Dorothy Ellen also became sick from the odor. Mrs. Kearney yelled for her sister, who said she smelled the odor coming from an open bedroom window. Mrs. Reedy then contacted a neighbor, Mrs. Earl Robertson, who called police. The police searched and found nothing. Mrs. Kearney recovered in about thirty minutes. As her husband rushed home about 12:30 A.M. after hearing about the incident, he said he saw a prowler at the bedroom window. The police were called again but found nothing. The whole family left to stay with a relative elsewhere that night.

Mattoon's only major paper, the *Daily Journal-Gazette* (hereafter referred to as the *Gazette*) reported the incident on page 1 the next evening with a six-column headline, "'Anesthetic Prowler' on Loose." Two subheads under the headline added, "Mrs. Kearney and Daughter First Victims" and "Both Recover; Robber Fails to Get into Home."

This and other reports described typical symptoms that were brought on by a sickly sweet odor, including lightheadedness, paralysis, upset stomach, and vomiting. All victims either recovered that night or the next morning. On the night of the 5th, Mrs. Carl Cordes picked up a small folded cloth on her porch, saw a wet spot, smelled it and was overcome by an odor. "It was a feeling of paralysis," she told the *Gazette* (September 6, 1944, p. 1). "My husband had to help me into the house and soon my lips were swollen and the roof of my mouth and my throat burned. I began to spit blood and my husband called a physician. It was more than two hours before I began to feel normal again."

For the next week, more and more reports of gassings were reported. Other newspapers began picking up on the story by September 6, and almost daily reports in the *Gazette*, the *Chicago Tribune*, the *Chicago Herald-American*, the *Champaign News-Gazette*, and the (Springfield) *Illinois State Journal* heightened awareness of the mad gasser nationwide. The culprit soon had many names coined by the newspapers: anesthetic prowler, mad anesthetist, mad gasser, phantom chemist, and Will-o'-the-Wisp (*Gazette*); fiendish night prowler, phantom prowler, mysterious prowler, gas fiend, gas prowler, and gas maniac (*Chicago Tribune*); gas phantom, Ape Man, phantom anesthetist, woman gas terrorist, gas madman, and phantom madman *(Chicago Herald-American)*.

Joining the hunt for the mad gasser were two FBI agents, the Illinois State Police, which sent five squad cars and ten officers, and groups of armed citizens roaming the city. A group of fifty armed farmers, members of the Anti-Theft Association, also roamed the city. Meanwhile, the harried Mattoon police, headed by skeptical Police Chief C. Eugene Cole, received veiled criticism in a September 8 *Gazette* editorial about their initial doubts that a prowler existed.

As the police sped off to each new call about a mad gasser incident, armed citizens and farmers quickly followed. Police Commissioner Thomas Wright began ordering officers to arrest the chasers. One woman intending to protect herself loaded her soldier-husband's shotgun and blew a hole in her kitchen wall. Another sighting of demonlike eyes at a woman's bedroom window turned out to be a cat. A woman in the midst of a movie theater audience screamed that she was hit by gas although no one around her was affected! A few suspects were questioned, including a high school student playing a prank on a woman, but no arrests were made.

By September 14, gassing reports had stopped for good. In all there were at least three dozen reported victims, more than one hundred if seventy people in a roaming group claiming to be hit by the smell of gas are included. No prowler was ever identified or arrested, no physical evidence presented (the Cordeses' cloth proved negative for any unusual substances at a state crime lab), and there was no medical substantiation of a gas being used. In fact, none of the victims ever reported having eye problems from the alleged gas. If it were a poisonous gas, the eyes would most certainly be affected.

## MEMORY RECONSTRUCTION AND EMBELLISHMENT

The Mattoon *Gazette* practically created the entire mad gasser scare. We know that the first few gassing reports were not taken seriously by police. This was noted in a September 8 *Gazette* editorial criticizing police who had not taken Aline Kearney seriously. Neither did they place much credence in the three reports that quickly followed by residents who reported "gassings" only after learning of the Kearney case. According to the *Gazette*, police concluded that these early reports were "just imagination." They did not begin to become concerned until about September 5, after Mrs. Cordes found the strange cloth on her porch. But this police skepticism is not reflected in the early press reports. On Saturday, September 2, the *Gazette* carried the first report on the incident: "Anesthetic Prowler on Loose." Not only was the gasser's existence treated as absolute fact, but there was an implication that more gassings might follow: Recall the sub-headline that read "Mrs. Kearney and Daughter *First* Victims . . . Robber Fails to get into Home" (emphasis added).

Sensationalism by the *Gazette* prompted a series of retrospective gassing reports that supposedly had occurred before or during Mrs. Kearney's "attack." In reporting these cases, there is no hint of police skepticism or of the possibility of the gasser being imaginary. Only after reading or hearing of the *Gazette* story did several local families report similar home attacks. Mrs. George Rider said that the gasser had struck her Prairie Avenue home about the same time Mrs. Kearney and her daughter were made ill. At about the same time, a few blocks from Mrs. Rider, a woman and her children awoke and began vomiting. It was later assumed that the gasser had been there. Mr. and Mrs. Orban Raef of Grant

Avenue said the night before Mrs. Kearney was gassed, they were asleep at 3 A.M. when fumes came through the bedroom window. Both experienced "the same feeling of paralysis" and felt unwell for about ninety minutes. Curiously, friends staying at the house and sleeping in another room reported no ill effects. Finally, Mrs. Olive Brown on 22nd Street told police that several months earlier, she and her daughter had been gassed, but did not report the incident thinking no one would believe them. These incidents were mentioned in the next *Gazette* article about the gasser on September 5 (" 'Anesthetic Prowler' Covers City"). (No reports appeared on September 3 and 4 because the newspaper was not printed on Sundays and holidays.)

Smith states because there were gassing reports prior to Mrs. Kearney's on September 1, and they occurred late at night, it is "very unlikely that word of the incidents could have spread so quickly. As they were not reported in the newspaper until two days later, they simply had to be real events."[4] By his own admission, Smith says, "I am a physicist, not a psychologist."[5] He makes no mention of studies on the fallibility of human memory and perception.[6] These earlier reports are dubious. At the time of the supposed gassings, no one reported these incidents to police, bothered to contact friends or relatives to share their concern, or even fled their house. Just imagine—you suspect someone has sprayed poison gas into your home making you and your family ill; you experience dizziness, burning lips, vomiting, partial limb paralysis. It was well known that poison gas could cause permanent disabilities or even prove lethal. And what do these pre–September 1 "gas victims" do? They remain in the house and soon go back to sleep without telling a soul! This behavior only makes sense if, after learning of the mad gasser, these "victims" began redefining recent ambiguous incidents during which they had noticed a strange smell and embellished upon it. Knowledge of poison gas was widespread at this time due to fears that the Germans might use it during World War II.

This brings to mind a story discussed by UFO investigator Philip Klass.[7] Early on the evening of June 27, 1959, the Rev. William Gill and a small group watched an illuminated object in the sky near Boianai, Papua New Guinea. They became excited after thinking they could see humanlike figures waving back at them. The exchange of waves continued and a flashlight was turned on and off toward the "craft," which seemed to respond by moving in a pendulum fashion. With the object still in view, and having witnessed what he was certain was an alien spaceship for only about thirty minutes, what did Father Gill and the group do at this potentially historic juncture in history? He and the entire group went to dinner! They resumed watching at 7 o'clock. This makes for an exciting story, but human memory does not recall events as they happened, but as we *think* they happened. Often the details get changed after the fact. It brings to mind the saying, "The older I get the better I was." If we had been convinced an alien craft were hovering nearby, we would likely have called the police and every friend and relative, and told them to get there—fast. We certainly would not have gone to dinner. Such stories sound exciting after the event, but logic and common sense suggest otherwise.

## PRESS RECONSTRUCTION

Let us re-examine the report by Mrs. Kearney in the *Gazette* on September 2. The newspaper quoted Mrs. Kearney at length. Neither she nor her sister mentioned any prowler, although her sister mentioned an open window. Mrs. Kearney is quoted saying that her sister contacted the neighbor, Mrs. Earl Robertson, who called police. The newspaper then indicated that Mr. Robertson searched the yard and neighborhood "but could find no trace of the prowler. Police also searched without success." After being notified, Mr. Kearney arrived home about 12:30 A.M. and saw a prowler who was "tall, dressed in dark clothing and wore a tight fitting cap." He gave chase but the "prowler" escaped.

No one is directly quoted actually seeing a "prowler" until Mr. Kearney arrived and reported seeing a figure at the bedroom window. In the article's lead and a following reference to Mrs. Kearney's parched and burned lips from "whatever was used by the prowler," the unidentified newspaper reporter conjectures that there is a prowler spraying gas through the bedroom window. After quoting Mrs. Kearney, the reporter then refers to Mr. Robertson, the police, and Mr. Kearney, who is reported as seeing a man at the window. That sighting, though, was a second incident. Apparently, all involved assumed or reinterpreted the first incident as one caused by a prowler spraying an anesthetic substance.

The "anesthetic prowler" was thus a creation of the *Gazette* by combining the first incident involving Mrs. Kearney's paralysis and an odor with the second incident, Mr. Kearney's alleged sighting of a prowler. A close reading of this initial public report shows that no one involved is quoted as saying that an "anesthetic prowler" was seen. That phrase is an invention of the headline writer. In addition, the "anesthetic prowler" now conveys the impression of retrospective rationalization, which was also evident in the next three reports of a "prowler" by the Rider, Raef, and Brown families.

The *Gazette* then immediately added fuel to the fire by suggesting that there would be more victims; the subhead under that first headline was, "Mrs. Kearney and Daughter First Victims." The headline was "'Anesthetic Prowler' *on Loose*.'" The other newspapers soon followed with coverage, and the whole country was being made aware of the "mad gasser of Mattoon."

## CONTEXT: THE POISON GAS SCARE

Willy Smith correctly states that mass hysteria "usually stems from a single case, or a trigger event." Yet, he goes on to say that in "the Mattoon case there was no event that could have triggered a mass hysteria."[8] Nothing could be further from the truth. By the fall of 1944, when an Allied victory seemed inevitable in World War II, the fear of gas attacks was evident. Even though poison gas was not known to have been used in World War II for fear of retribution that could devastate civilians, during the year of the "gassings" in 1944, there were no less than 112 articles in the *New York Times Index* under the heading "chemical warfare." Dozens of popular and scientific periodicals around this time also discussed the poison gas peril in publications such as *Newsweek*, *Popular Science*, and the *American Journal of Public Health*.[9] As the tide of World War II turned increasingly in favor of the Allies, so did concern that desperate German commanders might resort to gas warfare.[10] In fact, the Allies were so concerned that the Germans might use poison gas during their June 6, 1944, D-Day invasion of Normandy, that they had a plan to retaliate within forty-eight hours with two bombing raids of 400 planes each, all loaded with chemical weapons designed to hit selected targets.[11] Gas warfare expert Frederic Brown states that D-Day was the "most dangerous period for German [gas] initiation"—a credible threat that was widely discussed in the press during later 1944.[12] The mad gasser appeared just two and a half months after D-Day. There was even discussion as to whether the United States should be the first to use gas. This view received a firestorm of criticism by many readers and commentators, fearful that the Axis powers would think that the use of gas was imminent and initiate a first strike. Following editorials favoring the idea of using gas first in the *Chicago Tribune*, the *New York Daily News*, and the *Washington Times-Herald*, noted *Saturday Review* editor Norman Cousins branded their editors as "incredibly irresponsible."[13]

About the time of the first gassing report in Mattoon by Aline Kearney, newspapers in Champaign, Chicago, and Springfield carried wire service articles about gas use. The August 30 *Champaign News-Gazette* included a page 1 article: "Believe Nazis Prepared to Use Gas." On August 31 the *Chicago Herald-American* had one on page 2 ("Report Nazis Plan Poison Gas Attack") and another report in the September 1 issue on page 2 ("Allies Ready if Nazis Use Gas"); and an Associated Press article in the (Springfield) *Illinois State Journal* on September 1 ("Unlikely Gas to Be Used in War") appeared on the day of Mrs. Kearney's alleged gassing. The Associated Press article stated: "If Nazi extremists bent on ruling or ruining should employ gas against civilian populations in a bitter end resistance, the allies would be in a position through air strength to drench German cities. . . . Recurrent rumors that the Germans are preparing to initiate gas warfare bring no official reaction here."

While Mattoon's *Gazette* did not carry news of the potential German use of gas, knowledge of the threat, whether perceived as domestic or foreign, would have been widespread. Many state newspapers were read by Mattoon citizens, as Johnson pointed out, and the gas fears were almost certainly discussed on radio and by word-of-mouth. In addition, during that same time, a Nazi prisoner had escaped from Camp Ellis in the Mattoon area and was reported to be seen in the city ("Hunt Escaped Nazi Here," *Gazette*, August 31, 1944). He was captured the following night in another city. If this were not enough, at the same time there was a wave of robberies in Mattoon ("Two Homes Entered," *Gazette*, August 31, 1944; "Robbery Wave Continues," *Gazette*, September 1, 1944).

Another mad gasser sighting was reported by Mattoon fortune-teller Edna James, who said she was sprayed by an ape-like man with long, hairy arms. The September 16 *Chicago Herald-American* reported on it with the headline, "Ape Man Clue at Mattoon." What movie was playing in Chicago at that time? *The Hairy Ape*, starring William Bendix and Susan Hayward. Was Mrs. James drumming up business?

## CONCLUSION

In revisiting the famous case of the mad gasser of Mattoon, we have sought to bolster Johnson's original argument with further information that has come to light about the pre–September 1 gassing claims, and the context. The episode was clearly triggered by a confluence of factors: sensational press coverage, ignorance of human perceptual fallibility and memory reconstruction, fear of Nazi poison gas attacks, an escaped Nazi in the city, and a robbery/break-in wave. When interpreting the significance of mysterious events, it is not necessary to embrace exotic explanations when they are readily explainable using mainstream scientific theories. It is also a good practice to stick to your area of expertise.

It is essential to understand the overall context of what happened in Mattoon within the social and historical context as it was experienced by Mattoonites and reported by the media at the time. People of the period lived under the specter of massive poison gas attacks on civilian targets. While certainly unusual, given the war scare context, the case of the mad gasser of Mattoon is not so bizarre after all. Indeed, during the twentieth century a strange odor is the most common trigger of epidemic hysteria in both job and school settings.[14] It is a sign of our present times which are dominated by occupational safety legislation and environmental fears.

Episodes such as the mad gasser of Mattoon may be set to recur. Given the increase in terrorist fears coinciding with the dawn of the third Christian millennium, we can expect more outbreaks of epidemic hysteria in communities and public places. For instance, in Japan during 1995, the use of Sarin nerve gas on the Tokyo subway by the Aum Shinrikyo cult killed 12 people. It also triggered a wave of mass collapses from pseudo attacks after commuters detected strange smells.[15] Like a chameleon, outbreaks of anxiety and delusion mirror the times, thriving on fear and uncertainty.

Since the September 11, 2001, terrorist attacks on the United States, Americans have been inundated with reports of mass hysteria and social delusion. In one instance, a man was wrestled down by police after squirting a strange substance at a Maryland subway station. Thirty-five persons in the vicinity were overcome by what was widely assumed to have been a toxic chemical, and were treated for symptoms ranging from nausea to sore throats. The substance was later identified as a common window cleaner.[16] Similar episodes of psychogenic illness prompted by the chemical and bioterrorism scare were reported from California to the Philippines.[17] In the latter case, a flu outbreak coupled with rumors of a mysterious "airborne virus" prompted thousands of college students to deluge local physicians.[18] At the height of the anthrax mail scare which claimed several lives, CNN reported that more than twenty-three hundred anthrax false alarms occurred over a two-week span in early October 2001.[19]

The blame for the "mad gasser" episode seems to lie squarely on the shoulders of the reporters and editors of the Mattoon *Daily-Journal Gazette,* who literally created an imaginary chemical weapons attack. The reporters, swept away by their assumptions and emotions, failed to inform their readers during the early days of the investigation that the Mattoon police were skeptical of the initial gasser claims. As a result, readers got a distorted view of evidence and opinions on the subject. The reporters failed to examine the evidence factually, instead jumping to speculation and making assumptions that reflected their wartime worldview, which held that German chemical weapons attacks on America were possible, if not likely. These early reports in the *Gazette* were based on fear, which in turn generated more fear, encouraging citizens to over-scrutinize their surroundings. This state of affairs led to the reinterpretation of mundane objects, odors, and circumstances as gasser related.

# REVIEW QUESTIONS

1. Cite other examples where the media has fueled community outbreaks of mass hysteria or general panic.
2. The "mad gasser" would appear to be an isolated, rare instance of mass hysteria. Yet mass hysteria may be far more common. Do you agree or disagree? Support your position.
3. How did the nature of human memory reconstruction contribute to the widespread folk belief of the gasser's reality?

4. Cite examples of Mattoon citizens (including the police, press, and community leaders) becoming carried away with their emotions, and how this either prolonged or lent credibility to the "mad chemist" scare.

5. Even before the first gasser reports appeared in the Mattoon *Journal-Gazette*, what pre-existing factors contributed to citizens expecting that a sinister figure might be loose in the city? What does this indicate about the accuracy of eyewitness testimony?

## NOTES

1. D. M. Johnson, "The 'Phantom Anesthetist' of Mattoon: A Field Study of Mass Hysteria," *Journal of Abnormal and Social Psychology* 40 (1945): 175–86.

2. W. Smith, "The Mattoon Phantom Gasser," *The Skeptic* 3, no. 1 (1994): 33–39.

3. J. Clark, *Unexplained!* (Farmington Hills, Mich.: Visible Ink Press, 1999); M. T. Shoemaker, "The Mad Gasser of Botetourt," *Fate* 38, no. 6 (June 1985): 62–68; W. Smith, "The Mattoon Gasser: A Modern Myth," *International UFO Reporter* 9, no. 6 (1984): 7, 9, 14; L. Coleman, *Mysterious America* (Winchester, Mass.: Faber & Faber, 1983).

4. Smith, "Mattoon Phantom Gasser," p. 35.

5. Ibid., p. 39.

6. E. Loftus and K. Ketcham, *Witness for the Defense: The Accused, the Eyewitness, and the Expert Who Puts Memory on Trial* (New York: St. Martin's, 1991).

7. P. J. Klass, *UFOs Explained* (New York: Vintage, 1974), pp. 283–84.

8. Smith, "Mattoon Phantom Gasser," p. 34.

9. E. K. Lindley, "Thoughts on the Use of Gas in Warfare," *Newsweek* 22 (December 20, 1943): 24; E. W. Scott, "Role of the Public Health Laboratory in Gas Defense," *American Journal of Public Health* 34 (March 1944): 275–78; V. Sanders, "Our Army's Defense against Poison Gas," *Popular Science* 146 (February 1945): 106–11.

10. J. Marshall, "We Are Ready with Gas if the Axis Turns on the Gas," *Collier's* 112 (August 7, 1943): 21.

11. F. J. Brown, *Chemical Warfare: A Study in Restraints* (Princeton, N.J.: Princeton University Press, 1968), p. 244.

12. Ibid.

13. N. Cousins, "The Poison Gas Boys" [editorial], *Saturday Review of Literature* (January 22, 1944): 12.

14. R. E. Bartholomew and F. Sirois, "Epidemic Hysteria in Schools: A International and Historical Overview," *Educational Studies* 22, no. 3 (1996): 285–311; M. Olkinuora, "Psychogenic Epidemics and Work," *Scandinavian Journal of Work, Environment and Health* 10, no. 6 (1984): 501–15.

15. S. Wessely, "Hysteria after Gas Attacks," *The Times* (London), July 4, 1995, p. 14a.

16. L. Lellman, "Suspicious Incident Forces Subway's Closing," *Rutland* (Vt.) *Daily Herald*, October 10, 2001, p. A3.

17. H. Becerra and E. Malnic, "Complaints of Dizziness Shut Down Subway," *Los Angeles Times*, September 27, 2001.

18. R. L. Villanueva, M. C. Payumo, and K. Lema, "Flu Scare Sweeps Schools," *Business World* (Philippines), October 3, 2001, p. 12; Reuters News Service, October 2, 2001.

19. "Special Report Live with Aaron Brown," CNN, broadcast October 16, 2001, 10–11 P.M.

# 5

Sometimes people want to believe something so much that they let their emotions get carried away, see only what they want to see, and selectively ignore contrary evidence. One such instance occurred near the turn of the twentieth century when New Englanders began seeing imaginary inventions in the sky. The event is best described as an episode of mass wish-fulfillment.

# NEW ENGLAND'S GREAT AIRSHIP HOAX

*with Dr. Stephen R. Whalen*

### What ardently we wish, we soon believe. [1]

—Edward Young

There are times when bad examples are good teachers. This chapter tells the story of an incident where the public and the press failed to exercise good critical thinking, and as a result became the victims of a hoax. The perpetrator of the hoax was a man who took advantage of the times, an era when people expected new developments in airplane technology, and when the newspapers cared more about headlines than accuracy. The questions at the end of the chapter will help you to analyze the event with a critical eye, so keep this in mind as you read.

As the old year of 1909 drew to close and the new year began, residents of the New England seaboard participated in a mass delusion that reflected the exciting times in which they lived. For a period of about six weeks, the Yankee press covered a story that a local businessman had invented the world's first practical heavier-than-air flying machine. With the Wright brothers' first experiment occurring only six years earlier, New Englanders anticipated this event as one that would revolutionize aviation. In doing so, they temporarily suspended their normal healthy skepticism and replaced it with a natural wish fulfillment that met its inevitable disappointment.

The airship hoax of 1909–1910 cut a wide swath across the northeastern United States between December 13 and January 23. Large portions of entire states temporarily believed the rumors reported by the papers, and thousands of otherwise responsible citizens reported sighting the vessel as it sailed through the frosty night skies. The rumors and subsequent sightings triggered an extensive search to uncover the airship's whereabouts. An army of inquisitive reporters canvassed the land, surveying abandoned farmhouses and interviewing local eccentrics. Journalists from across the United States and as far away as Europe converged on eastern Massachusetts, the locus of the majority of the sightings. At the height of the excitement, the story of the great airship fostered expectations of great accomplishments and writers predicted a wondrous future.

Mass delusions grow on their own momentum, and the airship story was no exception. The number of reported sightings grew rapidly with the highest concentration in the state of Massachusetts (61), with other observations in Rhode Island (10), Connecticut (7), Vermont (6), Maine (1), and New York (1). These sightings often involved large numbers of people in towns and cities who believed that a prominent local entrepreneur, Wallace E. Tillinghast, was making secret nocturnal flights in his new flying machine. Tillinghast did little to dispel their belief, and it was a time of such rapid social and technological change that rumors of perfected air flight were credible.

As all hoaxes must, this event progressed to its logical end. Intense press scrutiny and investigation of the reported sightings revealed that the story of the great airship was a grand deception, but its success stemmed from the desire of people who wanted to believe that they were participating in a new age of technical marvels. Before the hoax ended, scores of eyewitnesses—including police officers, businessmen, prominent politicians, and even judges—came to believe that they had really observed the vessel. Many were certain that they could discern the roar of its powerful engine churning in the distance, and a few even emphatically claimed to be able to distinguish the outline of the pilot maneuvering the airship through the night sky. Of course, these same witnesses experienced considerable embarrassment and anger once the truth of the hoax became evident. The stories ended with the same speed they began, the hoax became yesterday's news and quickly forgotten, and the development of air flight continued with the same deliberate pace it had before the incident.

# AN ERA OF ANTICIPATED SUCCESSES

One factor that contributed to the airship hoax was the plausibility of practical heavier-than-air travel. In the generation preceding the episode, powered heavier-than-air flight went from a dream to reality, but inventors still had not achieved a serviceable means of achieving this goal. Public enthusiasm first waxed and then waned with each of five attempts at piloted powered flight between 1874 and 1899. These flights were crude, erratic, and brief, with more failures than successes.

The dawn of the twentieth century saw rapid and dramatic aeronautical advances, and the newspapers provided coverage of powered flight attempts, leading to a spectacular climax just prior to the airship delusion event. After the Wright brothers' first success in December 1903, progress on powered air flight was slow over the next three years. By October 1905 their *Flyer III* was able to cover 24.2 miles in thirty-eight minutes, but they did no flying in 1906. In September of that year, Alberto Santos-Dumont of France made the first officially recorded airplane flight in Europe, a flight that lasted only eight seconds.[2]

Progress in powered flight became rapid and dramatic in the two years immediately preceding the airship hoax. In July 1908 Glenn Curtis made the first official public flight of more than one mile, and in September Orville Wright made a demonstration flight for the U.S. Army at Fort Myers, Virginia. In August 1909, Curtis won a speed test in France at 46.5 m.p.h. over a 12-mile course. In November 1909 the Wright Company incorporated with a capitalization of $1,000,000.[3] British aviation historian

Charles H. Gibbs-Smith noted that in 1909 "the aeroplane came of age" and achieved practicality for two reasons: Louis Bleriot's flight across the English Channel on July 25, followed by the world's first aviation meeting in France during the week of August 22 to 29. Gibbs-Smith observed:

> If the Channel crossing made the greatest impact on the public, it was the Reims aviation week which provided the greatest technical and governmental stimulus to aviation, and proved to officialdom and the public alike that the airplane had indeed "arrived." . . . Reims marked the true acceptance of the airplane as a practical vehicle, and as such was a major milestone in the world's history.[4]

The significance of these events is that in the two years immediately before the airship hoax, two trends prepared the public to accept rapid advances in aviation. First, technical developments appeared to be proceeding very fast, and second, the press provided full coverage of these events. In 1907 there were only fourteen powered flights, but this number increased in a meteoric rise to forty-seven in 1908.[5] As the number of flights grew, so did media interest and public exposure. The *New York Times Index* for the years 1900–1909 shows that under the listing "aeronautics" for 1900, only one article appeared. This increased to 58 articles for 1905, 138 for 1907, 466 in 1908, and 964 in 1909, the year of the hoax.

By the end of 1909, powered flight had reached a point where the technical advances in aviation promised a dependable, practical means of navigating the skies. Full press coverage of these developments meant that the public was aware of these advances and knowledgeable people could anticipate even further successes. Within this historical context, the airship hoax is perfectly understandable as a desire to believe that Wallace Tillinghast had broken the barriers to practical flight. It is only a short step from mass belief to mass delusion.

## THE AIRSHIP DELUSION

The airship hoax started with one newspaper article. The *Boston Herald* of December 13, 1909, published a lengthy interview with prominent local businessman Wallace Tillinghast in which he claimed to have perfected and flown the world's first sophisticated airship, one that far exceeded any of the period. Tillinghast also stated that he was continuing his experimental flights. The *Herald* published the account with a front page headline: "Tells of Flight 30 Miles in the Air." The article detailed that Tillinghast had built an airplane that carried three passengers with a total weight of 600 pounds. Tillinghast described his machine as "of the monoplane type, with a spread of 72 feet, a weight of 1550 pounds, and furnished with a 120 horsepower gasoline engine." The inventor said that he had made a night trip from Worcester, Massachusetts, to New York on September 8, a distance of about 300 miles, and at a speed of 120 miles per hour.

Tillinghast's claims fit the time period well. His "machine" had capabilities that were beyond those of current reported flights, but not so far as to generate disbelief among the public. All that was necessary to propagate the hoax was an air of mystery, and Tillinghast provided that as well. The *Herald* article reported that Tillinghast refused to give the location of his airplane because he wished "to enter into Boston contests next year as a sure winner." He also declined to give the details of where the machine was built "because it is the business of no one but myself and my mechanics. . . . The machine is no experiment, as it has been thoroughly tested. All of the tests have been under the cover of night and have been considered successful." The desire for secrecy and clandestine experiments were normal for the time as inventors competed for fame and fortune. Tillinghast's assertions and prudence in disclosing information made him appear to the reading public as a credible and exciting new force in airplane development.

There is a strong probability that Tillinghast intentionally propagated the hoax based on an earlier newspaper article. On the same day that Tillinghast's article appeared, both the *Boston Herald* and the *Boston Post* ran stories that a lifeguard on Fire Island in New York claimed to have heard a noise like an airplane engine in the distance on one evening in early December. Perhaps seizing on knowledge of this, Tillinghast claimed that he had circled the Statue of Liberty on December 8 before returning to his secret airstrip, and that motor trouble had caused him to fly near the beach on Fire Island. Before giving his interview, he would probably have been aware of press reports appearing several days earlier, in which Fire Island lifeguard William Leach stated that he heard the sound of "an aeroplane pass high above him while he was doing patrol duty."[6]

While Tillinghast's story was a hoax, it appeared plausible considering his reputation as an inventor and businessman, coupled with the recent rapid progress in flight technology, and the expectant social climate. Still, not everyone accepted his claims. Within two days of his published interview, news of Tillinghast's purported feats made headlines in virtually every New England-area newspaper, and many throughout the world. The heavy press coverage included conflicting opinions concerning the legitimacy of his claims by aviation experts, local authorities, and press editors. Wilbur Wright scoffed at the report, and aviator Glenn Curtis declared Tillinghast's claims to be "extraordinary if facts can be improved."[7] The ensuing newspaper debate provided a degree of legitimacy to the initial hoax interview. As newspaper stories continued to cover the topic, many residents of the area, believing in the likelihood of the claims, began to redefine various past and contemporary events to coincide with their collective wish fulfillment. By connecting their own unusual or unexplained experiences to the current controversy, these "observers" became participants in a great new technical achievement, and added fuel to the hoax.

It did not take long for the first "believer" to add to the credibility of the hoax. The day after Tillinghast's interview, Mr. E. B. Hanna of Willimantic, Connecticut, reported that on the same night that Tillinghast claimed to circle the Statue of Liberty, he observed a "bright light" crossing the night sky for about an hour. After reading the Tillinghast interview, Hanna concluded that the light was most likely the flying machine. Despite the ambiguous nature of Hanna's sighting, the *Willimantic Chronicle* printed a speculative headline: "What Mr. Hanna Saw May Have Been the Worcester Airship!"[8]

The hoax smoldered for almost a week before the next sighting. Immigration inspector Arthur Hoe reported seeing an airship flying rapidly through the clear night sky in the early morning of December 20, over Boston Harbor. This incident illustrates how the media's desire for sensational news contributed to the hoax. The *Boston Globe* published Hoe's sighting on the front page of its evening edition with the headline "Sailed over the harbor. Unknown airship makes a flight at night." The following day, the *Boston Herald* printed an explanation on page 12 that Hoe "mistook the lights and masts of a ship in the harbor for the mysterious airship."[9] Despite the vagueness of Hoe's observation, the *Globe* published the account, reporting as fact that Hoe had seen an airship, most likely Tillinghast's. In light of the widespread press coverage of Tillinghast's spectacular claims, Hoe's sighting, and the earlier accounts of the sightings by Mr. Hanna and lifeguard William Leach, the vessel's existence began to gain credibility. New England-area residents started to reinterpret recent events as airship-related, and they scrutinized the skies for confirming evidence of their preconceived ideas.

Reinterpretations attributed earlier phenomena to Tillinghast's airship. On December 23, 1909, the *Boston Globe* published a letter from Cyril Herrick in which he assumed that a "Double Meteor" he had sighted the previous August was in reality the airship. Originally, Herrick thought that "only the great speed of the lights marred our belief that it was an aircraft." He questioned this when he heard the next day of reports from two other vacationers who saw the lights traveling in the opposite direction, but Herrick did not dismiss his meteor theory until "this news from Worcester as to Tillinghast offers itself as a refreshing possible hypothesis in explanation of the strange sight we saw that night."[10] Meanwhile, several Connecticut residents told a reporter from the *Hartford Daily Times* that one night in early September they had spotted an unusual aerial object. In light of recent events and revelations, they assumed that it must have been the airship. [11]

Along with these "reinterpretations" of past events, the first new mass observations of an airship occurred. In the vicinity of Worcester on the evening of December 22, over 2,000 people reported an airship "circling" Boston several times and remaining visible for over three hours. This incident began at about 5:40 P.M. when a squad of police officers noticed an unusual aerial light. By about 6:30 P.M. a crowd of Christmas shoppers and several policemen reported a light they estimated to be 1,000 feet aloft to the southeast, and steadily growing in size. By 7 o'clock, observers reported that the "airship" had "sailed over the city," and it remained stationary for several minutes over the State Mutual Life Insurance building.[12] Hundreds of reports also came in from residents of nearby Marlboro, Cambridge, Revere, Greendale, Nahant, Maynard, Fitchburg, Leominster, and Westboro, many of whom were in communication by telephone.[13]

As with previous stories, the press reported the airship's existence as factual. One story said that Tillinghast "was seen by fully a thousand residents here tonight repeatedly circling the city in a huge airship." Another account stated that "there is no doubt that some person was navigating a heavier-than-air machine here." In this manner, the press fueled the credibility of the airship's existence. Only the *Berkshire* (Mass.) *Evening Eagle* described the perceived phenomenon as a "fire balloon," which of itself was also a fanciful and speculative conclusion.[14]

The mass sightings, concentrated in the vicinity of Boston and Worcester, continued for several days. On December 23, the vessel purportedly reappeared above Worcester and several nearby communities between 6:00 and 7:30 P.M. An estimated 50,000 residents of Worcester poured into the streets and nearly brought the city to standstill.[15] The *Boston Globe* reported that "In the main thoroughfares people with bundles stood agape. . . . Men and boys poured from the clubrooms and women rushed from the houses to view this phenomenon. The streets were thronged."[16] The *Globe* suggested that the Worcester sightings were Venus, but mass observations in Boston, Revere, Cambridge, and Willimantic received less skepticism.[17] Other press accounts continued to add plausibility to the airship stories, such as the *Boston Herald*'s headline, "Mysterious Air Craft Circles about Boston for Nearly Six Hours."[18]

In this growing atmosphere of mass belief and official acceptance, individuals began to report details that confirmed the aircraft's existence. Alex Randell of Revere claimed to distinguish "the frame quite plainly," while Baltic resident P. D. Donahue stated that he could discern two men in the vessel as it passed over. When many Willimantic residents saw the strange light, the city's mayor, Daniel Dunn, stated that "there was no doubt but that it was an airship."[19]

The great airship episode peaked in a frenzy on Christmas eve, 1909. On that night there were thirty-three separate reports, spreading from Massachusetts to Rhode Island and Connecticut, northward to Vermont and Maine, and as far west as New York. In Boston, "thousands upon thousands of people . . . stood on sidewalks, street corners and squares from soon after dark till well on toward midnight" hoping for a glimpse of the airship. It was at this point that people suspended disbelief and convinced themselves that they were viewing a phenomenon of the age. When one observer "expressed doubt whether the airship was really moving . . . he was assured in gentle but firm tones by another that undoubtedly the operator had temporarily shut off his power, but that the machine had been moving unmistakably a few minutes before."[20]

By Christmas, the airship hoax had reached its peak, fueled by the press and a receptive public, but also by its perpetrator. Tillinghast certainly enjoyed the notoriety of being the center of attention. He continually noted that he had never sought the initial publicity for his invention, and that an industrious journalist had hounded him for the initial interview. However, a reporter for the rival *Boston Globe* subsequently learned that the *Boston Herald* reporter who obtained the first story "with the great inventor, didn't have to spend any sleepless nights running down Mr. Tillinghast." In fact, the day prior to his interview, Tillinghast telephoned the *Herald* and requested to meet with a journalist the following day, "as he had an item to get out."[21]

Many of Tillinghast's actions were deliberately ambiguous in an obvious effort to solidify the rapidly emerging consensus that he was the inventor and operator of the airship. The press reinforced this perception by closely monitoring his movements. The *Boston Journal* reported that

> people who saw the airship took it for granted that Tillinghast was the aviator, and a Journal reporter, with others, at once made inquiries and learned that Mr. Tillinghast was away from home and that he telephoned his house at 4 o'clock in the afternoon that he would not be home tonight. Further, [he] usually goes to where he says his aeroplane is hidden in automobile but his auto is now out of repair, and he was seen taking a train shortly after 4 o'clock this afternoon. At 11 o'clock tonight he had not returned to his home and he was not expected until morning. All this taken into consideration, together with the . . . thin black form of the airship hovering about the city from almost every point . . . leaves no doubt in the minds of all who witnessed it that Mr. Tillinghast was the operator and the airship was his own invention.[22]

On the following evening, December 24, the *Journal* reported that when Tillinghast returned home in the morning, "his eyes were terribly bloodshot and his face was cut and wind tanned, showing every evidence of having been out in a strong high and cold wind for a long while." On the basis of this description, the reporter concluded that it was "almost certain that Mr. Tillinghast is the mysterious aviator of the marvelous airship."[23]

While the press and the public were willing consumers of the hoax, Tillinghast's careful manipulation of the situation allowed the deception to reach its widest acceptance. He maintained an aura of secrecy that enhanced his claims and allowed the press and the public to associate him with other inventors of the time, many of whom jealousy guarded their technical secrets. As a result, reporters searched the countryside for the location of Tillinghast's airship, investigating scores of sheds and buildings in remote locations in the hope of discovering the elusive machine. Police arrested one reporter for trespassing on private property while checking a country shed owned by a business associate of Tillinghast. While he did not actually see the vessel, the reporter concluded that his arrest confirmed that he must have found the secret machine shop that housed the airship.[24]

The hoax deflated with almost the same speed with which it began. There were six sightings on December 27, but in general, after Christmas the press and the public became increasingly skeptical. Newspaper editors began to cite the popular theories of French psychologist Gustav LeBon, which were well known during the period, in attributing the sightings to individual "primitive" impulses activated within emotional situations, producing a form of temporary irrationality or madness.[25] As early as December 23 a *Boston Globe* reporter described the city of Marlboro as "airship crazy."[26] Two days later a reporter in nearby Rhode Island depicted the city as "airship mad," comparing it to LeBon's contagious mental disease model:

> The epidemic of infected vision that has turned Massachusetts upside down struck town with a bang late yesterday afternoon. From the time that the sun went down until the last shopper had found his way home this morning all kinds of aerial craft circled over the city. . . . On the streets the greeting wasn't "Merry Christmas." It was "Did you see it?"[27]

By December 26, a deluge of skeptical press accounts appeared. The *Boston Globe* expressed concern that residents of Worcester and its environs would soon become the laughingstock of the world as reporters representing newspapers from around the globe wired information that there was apparently little basis for the "fantastic stories." The *Boston Sunday Herald* reported that a Mr. C. D. Rawson of Worcester confessed to sending up large owls with lanterns and a reflector attached to their legs. A letter to the editor noted that most observations coincided with misidentifications of Venus, which was prominent in the western sky in the early evening. One press correspondent wired back to his West Virginia office, noting the growing doubts of the remarkable claims: "Go where you will in New England today and you will hear them talk about Tillinghast and his mysterious airship. The majority of New Englanders don't believe in Tillinghast."[28]

By December 27, the press began to sense that the story line had changed from covering a marvelous new airship to uncovering a hoax as local citizens became concerned about the area's reputation. Journalists criticized colleagues who had a vested interest in keeping the story alive. One editor noted that the mysterious light was seen on three consecutive evenings in the same position in the sky, corresponding exactly with the position of Venus. A Connecticut newspaper ran a story with the headline, "Willimantic Laughs at the Airship Faking."[29] The *Providence* (Rhode Island) *Journal* reported on December 27 that the people of Worcester were angry at the ridicule they were receiving in the national press. The sensational airship stories annoyed "the staid folks who are proud of the commercial reputation of their city. They have awakened to the fact that the weird stories of flying marvels are not simply local in their effect and therefore are planning to take action." Negative press coverage led to businessmen of Worcester to demand that Tilllinghast provide proof of his airship. Failing that, they would declare the whole episode a hoax, for they wanted to "settle the thing once and for all."[30]

Attempts to coerce proof from Tillinghast failed, but the public acclaim he sought earlier became overwhelming. He and his family became prisoners in their home, and Tillinghast was under constant surveillance wherever he went. The situation seemed to accomplish what the local business community desired, to silence Tillinghast:

> Tillinghast . . . is absolutely incommunicado. Even his closer friends don't say airship to him these days. When he hears the word he is apt to say things that don't sound charitable at Christmas time. The notoriety that has followed him since the mysterious lights were seen has seriously interfered with his business and with his home life. He has not been permitted an hour's peace. At his office there are constantly two or three persons who want to know something. At the door of his place of business and at his home he is closely watched by mysterious men. When he is at home his telephone rings constantly. . . . The constant clang is not conducive to his good nature.[31]

And so the great airship hoax of 1909 quickly faded from the public interest. There were four sightings reported during January, but these brought only derision. When several Willimantic residents, including a police officer, noted an unusual light in early January, the press restricted its coverage to two small paragraphs and there was no credible suggestion that they actually saw an airship. One newspaper proclaimed, "Willimantic people have been 'seeing things' again."[32] When a resident of East Poultney, Vermont, reported a sighting on the evening of January 6, a local press account began sarcastically: "The expected has occurred, the inevitable has come to pass. Rutland county has seen the airship."[33] On the evening of January 19, several residents of Fair Haven Heights, Connecticut, reported observing the airship. The local newspaper responded by prominently offering the opinion of an astronomer who had observed the object through a telescope, and identified it as the star Sirius.[34] At this point, the reports ceased.

Like a meteor, the Great Airship Hoax of 1909–1910 flared across the sky of public interest, burning brightly, and disappearing in the space of a few weeks. There were three factors contributing to the episode: Tillinghast, the press, and the public.

Every hoax needs a perpetrator and Tillinghast's role is evident, but not unusual. A study of his background might expose some interesting psychological data, but it would not be as significant as understanding the era. The turn of the century was an exciting time of technical advancement, social adjustments, and commercial competition, and Tillinghast was only one of many people with the potential to become the source for what became a mass delusion. The airship hoax needed an instigator, yet the scope and speed of the incident depended on the media and the public's wish-fulfillment.

During the last quarter of the nineteenth century the popular press expanded rapidly. Mass production of daily newspapers coupled with a growing literacy meant that the average citizen had access to immediate information. In a free market system, the newspapers provided a product that the public demanded, and the tabloid press and "Yellow Press" developed to challenge the established media. In this atmosphere of cut-throat competition, the publisher who delayed or procrastinated lost readership. With this in mind, it is understandable that the New England press immediately placed the airship story on the front page. As the hoax became

# MYSTERIOUS LIGHTS ON HIGH SEEN BY 50,000 WORCESTER PEOPLE ALL TALKING AIRSHIP

On the evening of December 23, an estimated 50,000 Worcester residents poured into the streets and nearly brought the city to a standstill as they gazed skyward at a mysterious light thought by many to have been Wallace Tillinghast's airship. Reprinted with permission of the Associated Press.

apparent, this too was a story, but it lacked the sensationalism of the original, so the papers relegated these accounts to interior pages of later editions. The media was the vehicle and the catalyst for the rapid diffusion of the hoax, and without this easy access the public could never have reached such a wide and certain belief of the airship's existence.

The significance of the airship episode is that it fits into a pattern of mass delusion and collective wish-fulfillment. This pattern is symptomatic of a modern society that must constantly adjust to new scientific knowledge and technical advancements. Ever since Jules Verne published *From the Earth to the Moon* in 1865, Western civilization has been caught in a conflict between the fantastic and the possible. Thirty years later, H. G. Wells published *The Time Machine, The Invisible Man,* and *The War of the Worlds* in the space of just three years, 1895 to 1898. It was also in this decade that the respected astronomer Percival Lowell asserted that he could discern canals on the face of the planet Mars. Coupled with the very real advancements of this time period in communication, power generation, medicine, transportation, and many other areas of scientific and technical research, it is not surprising that the general public had difficulty in differentiating between reality and science fiction. This produced a fertile arena for the great airship hoax of 1909–1910.

The people of New England who participated in the airship delusion were not uniquely gullible or credulous. One newspaper editor commented that "These must, indeed, be times sorely troublesome to the

Lowell (Ma.) Courier
Citizen

Dec. 23, 1909

# MYSTERIOUS AIRSHIP HOVERS OVER WORCESTER'S HOUSETOPS

## Thousands Watch the Flight in the Glare of Its Searchlight---Believed to Be That of Worcester Inventor.

Worcester, Dec. 22.—Flying through the night at an average speed of 30 to 40 miles an hour, a mysterious airship tonight appeared over Worcester shortly before 8 o'clock, hovered over the city a few minutes, disappeared and then returned to cut four circles above the gaping city, meanwhile sweeping the heavens with a searchlight of tremendous power.

The news of its presence spread like wildfire and thousands thronged the streets to watch the liner in the sky.

The airship remained over the city for about 15 minutes, all the time at a height that most observers set at about 2000 feet, too far to enable even its precise shape to be seen.

The glaring rays of its great searchlight, however, were sharply defined by reflection against the light snow-fall which was covering the city at the time. The dark mass of the ship could be dimly seen behind the light, which flashed in all directions.

At the time of the airship's visit, Wallace E. Tillinghast, the Worcester man who claims to have invented a marvellous aeroplane capable of almost incredible feats, was absent from his home and could not be found in Worcester.

The visitor from the clouds was first sighted from Marlboro at 5.20, about the same time that reports say it has been seen on other nights this week and last. The 16 miles between this city and Marlboro was covered in 30 minutes.

In the heart of the city it was first sighted by an employe of a prominent restaurant, who shouted out the news of his discovery. The 75 diners at the restaurant, many of them prominent business men of the city, deserted their tables and rushed into the street.

Coming up from the southeast, the sky voyager veered to the west, remained in sight a few minutes and then disappeared to the northwest. Meanwhile the streets filled with thousands of people, all with faces upturned to the sky.

In five minutes the searchlight was again seen glowing in the distance like a monster star and the ship came up, hovered over the city a short time and then disappeared to the south-east.

At 5.40 an eager shout from the crowds announced its return. Slowly its light sweeping the heavens, it circled four times above the city and then disappeared for the night, heading first southeasterly and then to the east.

Its searchlight appeared to the watching thousands about the size of the bucket.

Although Wallace E. Tillinghast

claims to have made over 100 successful aeroplane trips in machines of his own construction, of which a score have been made in the machine in which, it is believed, he navigated the air over Worcester and vicinity tonight, it was not until December 12 that the story of his achievements became public.

On that day aeronauts and others were surprised by the announcement that Mr. Tillinghast had on September 8, made a trip in his aeroplane to the statue of Liberty in New York harbor, thence to Boston and back to his starting point, in the vicinity of Worcester, a distance of 400 miles, without once alighting.

In connection with this statement, Mr. Tillinghast asserts that when near Fire island one of the cylinders missed fire, the motor stopped while the machine was 400 feet in the air and his two mechanics repaired it while it remained 45 minutes in the air without motive power.

This statement is in wide contradiction of all the established records of such machines.

Mr. Tillinghast says that he will make his first competitive test during the airship exhibition in Boston next summer.

He describes his machine as being of the monoplane type, with a spread of 72 feet, and weighing 1550 pounds, furnished with a gasolene engine of 120 horse power, made from particular specifications. An average speed of 20 miles an hour has been gained from its power, he says.

Three passengers are usually carried—two mechanics and Mr. Tillinghast. He claims that its performances exceed the best announced records for speed and altitude.

Mr. Tillinghast is a business man of good standing in this city. He is an experienced mechanic and has invented several devices which are the foundation of the company for which he is vice president. He has made a specialty of airships for 11 years, he says.

New York Tribune

Dec 23 1909 P.1

AIRSHIP STIRS CITY.

# AIRSHIP STIRS CITY.

## Twice Appears Over Worcester—Tillinghast Suspected.

Worcester, Mass., Dec. 22.—Flying through the night at an average speed of from thirty to forty miles an hour, a mysterious airship to-night appeared over Worcester, hovered over the city a few minutes, disappeared for about two hours and then returned to cut four circles above the gaping city, meanwhile sweeping the heavens with a searchlight of very high power. The news of its presence spread like wildfire and thousands thronged the streets to watch the mysterious visitor.

The airship remained over the city for about fifteen minutes, all the time at a height that most observers set at about two thousand feet, too far to enable even its precise shape to be seen. After a time it disappeared in the direction of Marlboro, only to return later.

Coming up from the southeast, the sky voyager veered to the west, remained in sight a few moments, and then disappeared to the northwest. In five minutes the searchlight was again seen glowing in the distance like a monster star, and the ship came up, hovered over the city a short time and disappeared to the southeast.

Two hours later an eager shout from the waiting crowds announced its return. Slowly, its light sweeping the heavens it circled four times above the city and then disappeared, finally heading first southerly and then to the east.

At the time of the airship's visit Wallace E. Tillinghast, the Worcester man who recently claimed to have invented a marvellous aeroplane in which he said he had journeyed to New York and return by way of Boston, was absent from his home and could not be located.

Marlboro, Mass. Dec. 22.—An airship was sighted over Marlboro early to-night, going northwest at thirty or more miles an hour. Persons in all sections of the city reported having had a glimpse of it. Its general course, they say, was in the direction of Clinton.

These front-page press reports of the Tillinghast airship are typical of the period, mixing speculation with fact and irresponsibly describing the aerial lights as a flying machine.

human imagination." He concluded that rapid progress in knowledge and technology "have no doubt brought the popular mind under no little strain and made it more susceptible than common to seeing phantoms in the air if not ghosts on the earth."[35]

While the editor was justly skeptical, the times were not "sorely troublesome." The public's desire for a practical means of heavier-than-air flight was worldwide. Between May and June 1909 British newspapers reported a wave of phantom airship sightings, one of which involved a man named M. B. Boyd who closely paralleled Tillinghast's claims.[36] Thousands of New Zealanders claimed to have observed Zeppelin-type ships in July and August of the same year, and the mania spread to Australia where in August there was a brief outbreak of sightings on the east coast.[37] The common thread connecting these cases to Tillinghast's is the Western faith in technology. The public's eager anticipation of the next logical advancement provided fertile ground for mass delusion and for anyone who wished to take advantage of the situation.

It is also possible to place the 1909 airship hoax in a broader chronological context. In many respects it is of the same genre as Orson Welles's *War of the Worlds* broadcast in 1938 and the national mania over UFOs in the decade after the Roswell incident in 1947. In all three cases, the general public was receptive to accepting new circumstances based on improved communication systems—newspapers, radio, and television, respectively—and leaps in technical developments—internal combustion engines, liquid fueled rockets, atomic energy.

The Great Airship Hoax of 1909 as a singular event quickly faded from the public consciousness, but it was part of a greater phenomenon of the twentieth century. The clash of technical advances and the public's perception of their significance sometimes produced mass delusions. As a hoax, the Tillinghast affair depended on an active media and a collective public optimism for rapid progress, and in this respect it was similar to other incidents of the era. As an example of self-delusion, the Tillinghast hoax provides an excellent opportunity to examine the process of critical thinking.

The Great Airship Hoax cannot simply be blamed on one person, the sly Wallace Tillinghast. There is plenty of blame to go around. Many New Englanders, giddy with the prospect that one of their own had achieved a world's first, let their emotions, at least for a short time, cloud their judg-

# SAILS TWO HOURS OVER CITY IN HIS AEROPLANE

## Tillinghast Makes Amazing Flight in Worcester, Circling City, Stopping Machine in Mid-Air, While Crowds in Streets Look On in Amazement

### Two Men in Machine—Great Searchlight Flashed on People in Streets Below

-- WORCESTER, Dec. 22.—Wallace E. Tillinghast silenced to an extent the sceptics who have scoffed at his claims for a marvellous aeroplane he invented when he circled over Worcester in his mysterious airship for two hours tonight.

During his flight he swept the heavens and city with a searchlight of tremendous power, the glaring rays of which were sharply defined by reflection against the light snow covering the ground.

Thousands of persons in various parts of the city saw the big aeroplane as it sped rapidly through the air at a height judged to be from 1500 to 2000 feet.

The searchlight appeared to the watching thousands to be about the size of a bucket.

Since Tillinghast claimed recently that he had made a flying trip from Worcester to New York, then to Boston and back to Worcester, the night of Sept. 8, his pretensions have come in for much ridicule, and it is believed the flight tonight was planned to put to blush his critics.

#### TWO MEN IN AIRSHIP

The mysterious airship was first sighted tonight in the southwest, bound for Worcester, and it was at first thought that the headlight on the front of the machine was a star.

As the machine approached the centre of the city, those standing on the streets, including the relief squad of the police department, could plainly see a long object trailing behind it, with two dark forms, believed to be men, in the centre near the searchlight.

Tillinghast put in his first appearance about 6:40 tonight, coming over the city from the direction of Millbury. He then sailed over City Hall, State Mutual building, and then out toward Greendale, where he was seen by the farmers and the men working on the Boston & Maine railroad at that place.

Then he circled about the city several times and speeded toward Spencer at a good rate of speed.

It was thought that Tillinghast has probably gone off for another record trip.

*Boston Post*
*December 23, 1909*

The power of the press to influence belief is evidenced by this *Boston Post* article of December 23, 1909 (continued on the next page). While this report describes the airship's existence as an absolute fact, almost certainly they had been gazing at Venus.

# People Laughed When Inventor Told of Trip to New York

**Continued from First Page**

It was reported at Spencer and at Marlboro that Tillinghast and his aircraft were seen sailing over that town and city respectively tonight shortly before 9 o'clock, and it is thought that when he speeded off toward Millbury he made a circle about Worcester, this time keeping out of sight of the residents of the city.

Tillinghast left his office in the Central Supply building on Commercial street shortly after 4 o'clock this afternoon and did not go home, nor had he arrived there up until midnight.

When a Post representative called on Mrs. Tillinghast tonight to find out the inventor's whereabouts, she stated that he had not been home to dinner, but had telephoned her he was going out of town for the night and did not know when he would return.

Tillinghast did not take his automobile tonight, as has been the custom on the night trips, but evidently slipped quietly out of town by way of the Union station.

For five nights a record of Tillinghast's auto-speedometer has been kept by a Post representative and several others interested, and it was found that on three nights it registered over 130 miles each night, or at the rate of 65 miles to a trip, and it is thought by this Tillinghast probably has his machine housed either near Litchfield, Conn., or somewhere over the Rhode Island line.

### One Thousand Viewed Flight

It is thought that at least 1000 persons in this city had a view of Tillinghast and the machine he was steering through the air, and several of the business men, who happened to be on Main street at the time in their motor cars made an attempt to follow in the direction that Tillinghast disappeared.

It is now believed by those who doubted his story of the flight to New York and Boston in one night, that he has a real aeroplane or monoplane, and one capable of making such a trip.

Although Wallace E. Tillinghast claims to have made over 100 successful aeroplane trips in machines of his own construction, of which a score have been made in this machine which navigated the air over Worcester and vicinity tonight, it was not until Dec. 12 that the story of his creative interest became public.

On that day aeronauts and others were surprised by the announcement that Mr. Tillinghast had on Sept. 8 made a trip in his aeroplane to the Statue of Liberty in New York city, thence to Boston and back to his starting point in the vicinity of Worcester, a distance of 600 miles, without once alighting.

In connection with this statement, Mr. Tillinghast asserted that, when near Fire Island, one of the cylinders missed fire, the motors were stopped while the machine was 4000 feet in the air, and his two mechanics repaired it while it remained 45 minutes in the air without motive power. This statement is in wide contradiction of all the established records of the gravity of such machines.

Mr. Tillinghast says that he will make his first competitive test during the airship exhibit in Boston next summer. He describes his machine as being of the monoplane-type, with a spread of 72 feet, and weighing 1550 pounds, furnished with a gasoline engine of 120 horse-power, made from particular specifications.

An average speed of 120 miles an hour has been gained from its power, he says. Three persons are usually carried, two mechanics and Mr. Tillinghast. He claims that its performances exceed the best announced records for speed and altitude.

Mr. Tillinghast is a business man of good standing in this city. He is an experienced mechanic and has invented several devices which are the foundation of the company of which he is vice-president. He has made a hobby of airships for 11 years, he says.

### BRING AIRSHIP TO STANDSTILL

In less than an hour the inventor with his machine was back over the again, circling about. The airship finally stopped over the State, Mutual build and here the mysterious craft could be seen quite plainly. A porter, sweeping sidewalk in front of Putnam & Thurston's restaurant on Main street, sighted object and called to his employer, Paul McHale, who rushed to the street and the machine hovering in the air.

At the time 60 people were dining in the Italian room, and as many in the down stairs lunch room of the restaurant, and Mr. McHale rushed in called his patrons out into Main street in time to see Tillinghast sail off a towards Greendale, make another circle in the air and sail back over the buil and on towards Spencer.

Arthur Nichols and A. M. Wyman, prominent automobile owners, the mer the proprietor of the Pilot garage, while coming down Main street to W ster square, sighted Tillinghast's mysterious machine and tried to rush toward city to beat him out and announce the news, but found the air pilot speedier they were.

### ROSE TO GREAT HEIGHT

A peculiarity of Tillinghast's flight over the city tonight was the heigh which the aviator rose and remained, and it is thought that his object in d this was to keep out of sight as much as possible. In this he was quite succe for it was almost impossible to distinguish any lines of his mysterious cra appearing only as a long dark object with a bright light at its head, but at t it could be seen that there was more than one human form in the centre of craft, and the noise of the eight-cylinder engine which he claims to in the aeroplane or monoplane of his own invention, could be heard on the st

Continued on Page 2—Fourth Column

*Boston Post*
*Dec. 23 1909*
*Continued*

ment. They failed to adequately assess the evidence for Tillinghast's claims, including their own biases and assumptions. The evidence was based mostly on sightings of vague nocturnal lights. Indeed, near the end of the wave, when press accounts had turned overwhelmingly negative, it was pointed out that most sightings coincided with the appearance of

Venus. Such observations were rarely reported during the first several days of sightings. The possibility of Venus and other astronomical bodies being mistaken for an airship *was* mentioned, but was either dismissed or given little credence in most papers, whose editors and reporters were writing based on their emotions and not the evidence. At the top of the list for guilt, is the editor of the *Boston Herald*, who placed Tillinghast's initial interview of December 13 on the front page despite his sensational claims and the fact that no one could verify his story with "hard" facts.

# REVIEW QUESTIONS

1. Why did people convince themselves that they actually saw Tillinghast's airship? Who were the only people who challenged Tillinghast's claims when he first made them? Did their background experiences make them better critical thinkers?

2. How did Tillinghast's reputation as a prominent businessman and inventor contribute to the hoax? Why was his secretive behavior not immediately questioned as suspicious?

3. How did the response of the newspapers contribute to the hoax? What responsibilities does the media have in reporting events? Is it proper for the media to offer assumptions as well as facts?

4. When and how did the hoax begin to unravel? Why do you suspect that this happened when it did?

5. How did people of the era understand the meaning of "airship"? How did Tillinghast's claims fit within this definition?

6. Explain how the press and the public crossed the line between facts and conclusions. Give specific examples.

7. How did the public's preconceived notions contribute to the hoax's success?

8. Why did individuals interpret their experiences as part of the "great airship viewing"? Respond for both those who claimed to have seen the airship months earlier and those who claimed to have seen it in a large group.

9. How many other explanations were there for the sightings? Why did these receive little acceptance at first?

10. In accepting the idea of the "great airship," did people keep an

open mind to new ideas, or did they view it as an absolute truth? Is it possible to do both?

## NOTES

1. K. L. Roberts, ed., *Hoyt's New Cyclopedia of Practical Quotations* (New York: Funk and Wagnalls, 1940), p. 67.

2. AIAA, "History of Flight, 1900s" [online], http://flight100.org/history/1900s.html, accessed April 4, 2001.

3. Ibid.

4. Charles Gibbs-Smith, *Aviation: An Historical Survey from Its Origins to the End of World War II* (London: Her Majesty's Stationery Office, 1985), pp. 145–46.

5. Ibid., pp. 231–36.

6. "Noise Like an Airplane. Fire Island Surfman Heard It in the Air; Sure It Was Not Geese," *Boston Herald*, December 13, 1909, p. 1.

7. "Tillinghast to His Story Clings," *Berkshire* (Mass.) *Evening Eagle*, December 14, 1909.

8. "What Mr. Hanna Saw May Have Been the Worcester Airship," *Willimantic* (Conn.) *Chronicle*, December 14, 1909, p. 8.

9. "Sailed over the harbor. Unknown airship makes a flight at night. . . . Immigration inspector Hoe able to distinguish part of the framework of the craft," *Boston Globe*, Evening Edition, December 20, 1909, p. 1; and "Boston airship a boat's masts. Inspector Hoe mistook towering sticks of the James S. Whitney for framework of mysterious night flier," *Boston Herald*, December 21, 1909, p. 12.

10. "Air Ships Seen at Night," *Boston Globe*, December 23, 1909, p. 6.

11. "Light seen in Hartford, also," *Hartford* (Conn.) *Daily Times*, December 24, 1909, p. 3.

12. "Worcester agape at airship lights. Wallace E. Tillinghast may have been flying above city," *Boston Herald*, December 23, 1909, p. 1; and "Worcester palpitating. . . . Tillinghast generally given credit for being the man," *Boston Globe*, Evening Edition, December 23, 1909, p. 1.

13. *Boston Herald*, December 23, 1909, p. 1.

14. "Thousands See Big Airship over Worcester," *Boston Journal*, December 23, 1909, p. 1; "Worcester Palpitating," *Boston Globe*, Evening Edition, December 23, 1909, p. 1; and "Light Caused by a Toy Balloon," *Berkshire Evening Eagle*, December 23, 1909, p. 1.

15. "Mysterious Air Craft Circles about Boston," *Boston Herald*, December 24, 1909, p. 1.

16. "Airship Is Just Venus," *Boston Globe*, December 24, 1909, p. 1.

17. Refer to the following press accounts in the *Boston Globe*, December 24, 1909, p. 1: "Seen in Boston. Many persons positive they saw the light of some mysterious navigator of the air"; "Revere sees its wings. Several observers say they were able to make out outlines of the airship"; "Cambridge also sees it. Airship described as moving from west to east and then in opposite direction"; "Again the searchlight."

18. "Mysterious Air Craft Circles about Boston," p. 1.

19. "Skyship of Mystery Flies above Boston," *Boston Journal*, December 24, 1909, p. 1; and "Mystery Airship Just Like Venus. Machine Hovers over Willimantic," *Daily Times*, December 24, 1909, p. 3.

20. "Certain as the Stars. Airship Again on Route. Even Skeptics See Its Charging Lights," *Boston Globe*, December 25, 1909, p. 1.

21. "Tillinghast Very Modest," *Boston Globe*, December 20, 1909, p. 14.

22. "Mr. Tillinghast Absent," *Boston Journal*, December 23, 1909, p. 1.

23. "Skyship of Mystery Flies above Boston," *Boston Herald*, December 24, 1909, p. 1.

24. "Craft of Mystery Finally Tracked to Its Lair," *Willimantic Daily Chronicle*, December 24, 1909, p. 1.

25. Gustav LeBon, *Psychologie des Foules*, 2d ed. (Paris: Felix Alcan, 1896).

26. "Marlboro Has It, Too," *Boston Globe*, Evening Edition, December 23, 1909, p. 1.

27. "City Is Airship Mad," *Providence Journal*, December 25, 1909, p. 2.

28. "Airship Story Worries Them," *Boston Globe*, December 26, 1909, p. 14; "Airship Owl Is Worcester Tale," *Boston Sunday Herald*, December 26, 1909, p. 15; "Venus and the Public Eye," *Providence Sunday Journal*, December 26, 1909, Section 2, p. 5; and "Tillinghast in His Shop, Not His Airship. New Englanders Probably Mistake Venus for a Soaring Flying Machine and Get Excited," *Wheeling* (W.Va.) *Register*, December 26, 1909. The "Owl" story is as amusing as Tillinghast's. Rawson, a member of the Order of Owls, claimed to have ordered three stuffed owls from North Carolina. When the owls arrived alive, he decided to contribute to the excitement by releasing the owls with a small lantern attached to their legs with a light string. That anyone would expect to confuse these birds with an airship indicates the absurd nature of the hoax.

29. *Hartford Daily Times*, December 27, 1909, p. 11.

30. "Worcester Angry over Airship," *Providence Journal*, December 27, 1909, p. 11.

31. Ibid.

32. "The Inky Sky, and Not a Star in Sight," *Willimantic Daily Chronicle*, January 7, 1910, p. 1; "Willimantic Men See Things Again," *Hartford Courant*, January 8, 1910, p. 1.

33. "The Inevitable Airship," *Rutland* (Vermont) *Daily Herald*, January 10, 1910, p. 4.

34. "Fair Haven Sees Phantom Airship . . . Astronomer Has Solution," *Hartford Daily Times*, January 19, 1910, p. 9.

35. (Editorial), *Springfield* (Massachusetts) *Republican*, January 2, 1910, p. 6.

36. David Clarke, "Scareships over Britain: The Airship Wave of 1909," *Fortean Studies* 6 (1999): 39–63; *The Aero*, July 13, 1909.

37. Many newspapers covered the New Zealand sightings. One example is "Close View of the Craft," *Auckland Star*, July 31, 1909. An example of the Australian incident is "Lights in the Air," *Melbourne Argus*, August 9, 1909, p. 7. The Australian press exercised a healthy skepticism about the sightings and attributed them to overactive imaginations.

# PART 3

# THE CROSS-CULTURAL PICTURE

# 6

# WHAT
# IS
# NORMAL?

After briefly surveying the extreme variation in beliefs and customs that have become institutionalized in certain cultures or time periods, we ask, "What is normal?" The answer is far from clear.

Humankind has reaped enormous rewards by adhering to scientific principles. This is most evident in the physical and biological sciences that seek to uncover universal laws. The same experiment conducted under identical conditions should yield the same outcome regardless of historical or cultural context. But in the social sciences such as psychology, sociology, and psychiatry—typically those disciplines whose role it is to determine what is normal—the outcome is often more controversial. Why? Because these fields deal with something less predictable and more difficult to measure: human behavior. When we throw in the mix normative values in assessing, for example, whether a behavior is normal or abnormal, we are faced with a daunting task if we wish to maintain that we are doing science.

At the heart of the matter is how to reconcile that what is right, rational, healthy, moral, and legal for one culture, subculture, or time period may be wrong, irrational, sick, immoral, and illegal in another. Are there universal norms and behavior standards, and if so, how do we determine this? If we use science we face another dilemma—the social sciences are dominated by Western norms and values. What may seem clearly right or wrong when viewed through Western eyes is often a political product of the social and cultural *zeitgeist* (spirit of the times). The problem is compounded when social scientists classify certain behaviors as abnormal because many people might assume what they say is an absolute fact when the social scientists are really only reflecting popular beliefs. Classification schemes of abnormal behavior are not elements in nature awaiting description like a zoologist might classify a group of animals.[1]

## HUMAN DIVERSITY

Scientific methods have been used to justify classifying behaviors into such categories as normal and abnormal, moral and immoral, legal and illegal. Yet these designations often reflect the evaluators' norms, values, and beliefs about health at any time and place.[2] The ethnographic record shows that across cultures and historical eras, the variation in norms, values, practices, and beliefs is dynamic and extreme. Examples include cannibalism, head-hunting, and polyandry (having multiple husbands at one time) as established cultural traditions among certain peoples. On the other hand, some scientists have used Western medicine to justify colonization, slavery, and blood-letting based on prevailing folk beliefs. Of course, these mistakes were not the fault of science. Science itself does not determine what is moral or legal—it's the so-called scientists who use science improperly.

Normality is not an objective given from which simple assessments of behavior can be made independent of historical era, culture, subculture, or social group. Not surprisingly, many of the earliest challenges to narrow universalist views of normality were from cultural anthropologists familiar with many behaviors that were accepted within their respective settings. Ruth Benedict observed that normality "within a very wide range, is culturally defined," and therefore psychiatrists should resist using a set list of symptoms in determining abnormality, but should instead examine how a certain constellation of behaviors align with the deep structural values, beliefs, and mores of the people in question.[3]

The ethnographic record of acceptable or institutionalized behaviors is extraordinary. In parts of Indonesia, it is acceptable for close male friends to greet each other by grabbing the other's testicles. A survey of 185 cultures revealed that polygyny (having more than one wife at a time) was allowed in 84 percent of them.[4] Yet this is a jailable offense in many modern Western countries. Psychiatrists Silvano Arieti and Johannes Meth state that suicide is viewed as an indication of emotional disturbance in the West, whereas for Japanese samurai it is normal in certain situations. Further, in Dobu, Melanesia, "no sane woman leaves her cooking pots unguarded for fear of being poisoned. To us this behavior would indicate paranoia. Among the Papuans it is traditional for an uncle and nephew (mother's brother and son) to practice homosexuality. It is not unusual for an Arapesh of Papua New Guinea to marry simultaneously a mother and her daughter."[5]

Cultural relativism holds that criteria for judging the behavior of other cultures is relative and varies according to circumstance. Anthropologist Richard Shweder notes that, as there are few if any standards of universal conduct, for cultural relativists to ask what is the proper way to classify the world or design a society "is like asking what is the proper food of man or what is the best language to speak."[6] Indeed. Indonesians eat rat, Indians relish a meal of mouse meat; Australian Aborigines eat ants and moths.

Historian Robert Darnton documents how medieval European carnivals commonly involved what was then considered an amusing pastime—torturing cats:

> Crowds made bonfires . . . and threw into them . . . cats—cats tied up in bags, cats suspended from ropes, or cats burned at the stake. Parisians liked to incinerate cats by the sackful . . . [others] preferred to chase a flaming cat through the streets. . . . In the Metz region [of northeastern France] they burned a dozen cats at a time in a basket on top of a bonfire. The ceremony took place with great pomp in Metz itself, until it was abolished in 1765. . . . Although the practice varied from place to place, the ingredients were everywhere the same: *a feu de joie* (bonfire), cats, and an aura of [the] hilarious. . . .[7]

The problem of cultural relativity poses difficult dilemmas for mental health professionals—psychiatrists, psychologists, psychoanalysts, social workers. In acknowledging that psychiatric classification systems often reflect popular and professional fads and fashions, anthropologist Arthur Kleinman urges caution in accepting these schemes, given the historical tendency to incorporate them as part of reality. He remarks that "Psychiatric diagnoses are not things, though they give name and scope to processes . . . [they] . . . derive from categories . . . [which] are outcomes of historical development, cultural influence, and political negotiation."[8]

# PSYCHIATRY AS UPHOLDER OF THE WESTERN MORAL STATUS QUO

The brief history of psychiatry is replete with instances where observations of people behaving different from prevailing social, cultural, political, and ethical standards of American and European conduct have inappropriately been labeled disordered or diseased. Examples include illness designations for such deviant acts as prostitution, homosexuality, political dissent, masturbation, polygamy, gambling, lying, and holding minority religious beliefs. In this regard psychiatrist Thomas Szasz observes that psychiatry more closely resembles religion and politics than science and medicine: "In religion and politics we expect to find conflicting systems or ideologies. Broad consensus concerning the practical management of human affairs, and the ethical systems utilized in governing . . . are regarded merely as a measure of the political success of the dominant ideology."[9] This point is poignant when one reads the American Psychiatric Association's *Diagnostic and Statistical Manual of Mental Disorders* (DSM), the "bible" of the psychiatric community. In flipping through this influential manual, it appears that some violations of Western norms and values are misclassified as mental disorders. For example, if one strays below modern Western norms regarding frequency of sexual intercourse, he or she may be classified as having "hypoactive sex drive." The excessive participation in games of chance becomes "pathological gambling" under the general heading of "impulse-control disorders not elsewhere classified." The consistent exhibition of irritating behavior patterns is "antisocial personality disorder." The problem is, there are no tests for these so-called disorders—the diagnosis of abnormal behavior is based solely on a list of vague criteria. It's a judgment call.

While the concept of mental disorder varies across cultures and history, sociologist Craig Little provides a culturally and historically sensitive definition. He states that "in most times and places a person has been classified as mentally disordered when . . . [exhibiting] what seems to be uncontrolled, irrationally motivated behavior considered by most others to be sufficiently abnormal and irresponsible in its sociocultural context to require special treatment, isolation, or social control."[10] This definition tries to account for the motivation of actions, their context, and their perception by others. It also recognizes that the psychologically disordered "behave with unclear motives and, upon being judged irresponsible, require treatment or exclusion from everyday social situations in which their behavior is upsetting or potentially dangerous to others."[11]

Psychiatrists and other mental health workers face a tougher task in making accurate diagnoses than medical doctors because the former must rely almost exclusively on their judgment, with little recourse to diagnostic tools such as blood tests or X-rays. Thus they are prone to transmitting stereotypes of their popular culture. There are examples of the tendency for psychiatrists and other social scientists to employ prevailing social and cultural norms in their practice of "objective" science. These include the incorporation of popular nineteenth- and early twentieth-century racist stereotypes of indigenous peoples, minority groups, and nonconformists, to support so-called value-free scientific theories of degeneration, European intellectual superiority, and the genetic basis of behavior.[12] In parts of the southern United States during the middle nineteenth century, rebellious Negro slaves who tried to escape plantation servitude were popularly believed to be suffering from a mental disease ("drapetomania"). At the time this position was widely rationalized on the grounds that slavery provided advantages to the Negro over their "primitive" African existence, and their inferior psychological constitution was typified as ideally suited for bondage.[13] The support by many in the white-dominated psychiatric and medical professions for the continued enslavement of Negroes on plantations in the southern United States during the nineteenth century, by diagnosing dissatisfied slaves as psychologically sick, underscores the ambiguity of psychiatric diagnoses, their political nature, and the potential for popular social beliefs to become superimposed as "scientific" realities.

# PSYCHIATRY AND POLITICS

The politics of psychiatric diagnoses is evident in the first two editions of the DSM,[14] which, for example, classified homosexuality as a mental disorder ("sexual orientation disturbance"). A campaign by the Sexual Preference Rights Movement, including disrupting psychiatric conferences and public protests, prompted negotiations with the American Psychiatric Association, culminating in removal of the disorder status after a reassessment of the literature and a subsequent unanimous vote by the APA board of trustees.[15] In 1974 nearly 60 percent of 10,000 votes cast in an APA-member referendum to formally approve the change agreed.[16]

There are many modern instances where actions and beliefs exhibited by a particular group or social movement have been labeled as hysterical or sick because they vary with those of mainstream social scientists. One prominent example involves claims by scientists that the Nazi movement during the first half of the twentieth century was a form of mass mental disorder among the German people, ignoring the literature on conformity and cultural context in shaping Nazi beliefs.[17]

Clearly, many behaviors in the world are abnormal and dangerous. Yet when it comes to determining what is acceptable (and thus normal) and what is not, there is a fine and ever-shifting boundary that more often than not reflects the social world of the interpreter than the mental state of those being interpreted. The difference between which side of the line one stands often depends on who is holding the chalk and has the political power to draw the line. Social scientists must be more aware of human diversity, and the realization that there are often many different ways of doing things—each falling within a broad spectrum of what can be called "normal."

When trying to assess what is normal, being aware of our own biases and assumptions helps to foster a greater appreciation for customs and beliefs outside our own culture. Often we judge behavior as sick or bizarre just because it is different and unfamiliar and does not fit within the narrow Western view of what is normal or rational. Critical thinking fosters an awareness of the temptation to oversimplify our complex world and to consider other viewpoints or lifestyles as equally valid. The use of critical thinking will most likely lead to the "discovery" that the social sciences can be interpreted in many ways. The United States may be at present more technologically advanced than the world, but this does not give it moral superiority when it unwittingly superimposes its values and folk beliefs as scientific facts. One of the most notorious examples occurred when the American Psychiatric Association defined homosexuality as an abnormality, and exported this baseless assumption throughout the world in the form of influential textbooks.

## REVIEW QUESTIONS

1. How can you determine whether a particular behavior is normal or abnormal?
2. How have Western cultural stereotypes held by psychiatrists resulted in erroneous diagnoses?
3. What is the ethnographic record and why is it important to be familiar with it?
4. Psychiatry has been used in the history of the United States to support existing prejudices and stereotypes. Explain.
5. In Morocco men sometimes walk arm in arm or holding hands. How might this be interpreted in other countries? Give other examples of behavior that might be considered normal in one culture but not another.
6. List behaviors that are common today and accepted as normal, that one hundred years ago might have been deemed sick or abnormal.
7. List positive and negative aspects of cultural relativism.

## NOTES

1. R. Clark, *The Survival of Charles Darwin* (New York: Random House, 1984), p. 23.

2. J. Wing, *Reasoning about Madness* (Oxford: Oxford University Press, 1978), p. 16.

3. R. Benedict, "Anthropology and the Abnormal," *Journal of General Psychology* 10, no. 2 (1934 [1959]): 59–82.

4. C. S. Ford and F. A. Beach, *Patterns of Sexual Behaviour* (New York: Harper & Row, 1951), p. 108.

5. S. Arieti and J. M. Meth, "Rare, Unclassifiable, Collective, and Exotic Psychotic Syndromes," in *American Handbook of Psychiatry*, ed. S. Arieti (New York: Basic Books, 1959), p. 560.

6. Richard A. Shweder, "Anthropology's Romantic Rebellion against the Enlightenment, or There's More to Thinking Than Reason and Evidence," in *Culture Theory: Essays on Mind, Self and Emotion*, ed. Richard A. Shweder and Robert A. LeVine (New York: Cambridge University Press, 1984), p. 49.

7. R. Darnton, *The Great Cat Massacre and Other Episodes in French Cultural History* (New York: Basic Books, 1984), pp. 83, 85.

8. A. Kleinman, *Rethinking Psychiatry: From Cultural Category to Personal Experience* (New York: The Free Press, 1988), p. 12.

9. Thomas S. Szasz, *The Myth of Mental Illness* (New York: Harper and Row, 1974), p. 95.

10. Craig B. Little, *Deviance and Social Control: Theory, Research, and Social Policy* (Itasca, Ill.: F. E. Peacock, 1995), p. 106.

11. Ibid.

12. J. Edward Chamberlin and Sander L. Gilman, *Degeneration: The Dark Side of Progress* (New York: Columbia University Press, 1985); R. Castel, "Moral Treatment; Mental Therapy and Social Control in the Nineteenth Century," in *Social Control and the State*, ed. S. Cohen and A. Scull (Oxford: Blackwell, 1985); Daniel Pick, *Faces of Degeneration* (Cambridge: Cambridge University Press, 1989).

13. A. Thomas and S. Sillen, *Racism and Psychiatry* (New York: Brunner/Mazel, 1972).

14. American Psychiatric Association, *Diagnostic and Statistical Manual of Mental Disorders* (Washington, D.C.: American Psychiatric Association, 1952); American Psychiatric Association, *Diagnostic and Statistical Manual of Mental Disorders*, 2d ed. (Washington, D.C.: American Psychiatric Association, 1968).

15. Ronald Bayer, *Homosexuality and American Psychiatry: The Politics of Diagnosis* (New York: Basic Books, 1981).

16. D. Greenberg, *The Construction of Homosexuality* (Chicago: University of Chicago Press, 1988).

17. F. Cartwright and M. Biddiss, *Disease and History* (New York: Thomas Y. Crowell, 1972); G. Kren, "Psychohistory and the Holocaust," *Journal of Psychohistory* 6 (1978–1979): 409–17; H. Asher, "Non-Psychoanalytic Approaches to National Socialism," *Psychohistory Review* 7, no. 3 (1979): 13–21; Erich Goode, *Collective Behavior* (New York: Harcourt Brace Jovanovich, 1992), pp. 46–47.

# 7

# *LATAH*

## Strange Mental Disorder or Exotic Custom?

The curious and bizarre behavior known as *latah* has been classified as an exotic syndrome, but evidence indicates it is more likely to be a culturally based deception.

For the past one hundred years anthropologists and psychiatrists have debated the origin and nature of a curious behavior, confined almost exclusively to the Southeast Asian neighboring cultures of Malaysia and Indonesia. Upon being startled, ordinarily timid, exceedingly polite women sometimes respond with vulgar obscenities and outrageous sexual gestures. Severe cases experience "automatic obedience," doing whatever they are told, afterward claiming amnesia and thus not held responsible for their actions. Episodes of this type last from a few minutes to several hours. Victims of *latah* are almost always middle-aged women of Malay and Javanese descent, and it is very rare among those of other nationalities, despite nationalities often living next door. Scientists have been divided as to whether it is a disease, disorder, or form of unconscious symbolic cultural expression.[1] None of these traditions has been able to account for all of the characteristic features of *latah*, which is typically classified in medical textbooks as a culture-bound psychiatric syndrome.

In January 1990, I (Robert Bartholomew) married into a Malay extended family where *latah* is prevalent, and over the next three and a half years, was able to gain the confidence of family members. While having no intention of studying *latah* despite it landing at my anthropological doorstep, the more I observed, the more a number of contradictions became evident. Of ninety-nine living family members surveyed, twenty-nine were classifiable as mild cases and two were severe, according to classic textbook definitions of the condition. The two latter subjects, elderly women of sixty-one and seventy, claimed to respond involuntarily and with total amnesia.

I first observed a severe case of *latah* while attending my brother-in-law's wedding and was astounded to observe my wife's shy, decrepit, seventy-year-old aunt who has considerable difficulty even walking, intentionally startled by a relative. The aunt, Sembok, suddenly leaped to her feet, lost all inhibition, and for the next ten minutes followed each of her teaser's commands and mimicked his every gesture. During the episode, she was made to cry like a baby, perform *silat* (Malay self-defense), dance vigorously, and partially disrobe, all to the hilarity of an entire wedding party which crowded around her inside the bride's parents' home. She would occasionally improvise gestures, such as lifting her sarong in a sexually suggestive manner and uttering the most repulsive words and phrases. Throughout the episode, after some outrageous display she would immediately and profusely apologize for her vulgarity, then launch into another series of behaviors, apologizing more than thirty times during this particular "fit." The next day at a crowded wedding reception at the groom's home, I was able to tease her into a similar, less dramatic episode by suddenly slapping my hands onto the floor next to her. She responded with a ten-minute display, mimicking my every action, from dancing to slapping her face repeatedly. Other family members also joined in the teasing.

A few days later I visited Sembok at her residence in the presence of two relatives. I startled her by melodramatically throwing crumpled paper onto the floor next to her. She responded with a short vulgar phrase.

Immediately afterward, I slapped my hands to the floor next to her, exactly as I had done at the wedding, but this time there was no response. I slapped the floor, then my face—hard, but again, no response. I was perplexed. Just a few days earlier in the presence of about sixty people, even minor startles sent her into prolonged "fits." On both occasions she was sitting on the floor next to me, and I executed the same sequence—I startled her, slapped the floor, then my face. Family elders later explained emphatically that unless there is a large social gathering, "severes" *never* exhibit anything beyond "mild" symptoms, responding only with a blasphemous word or phrase. They also report that "teasers" are always close relatives—ensuring that the "victim" does not do anything too outrageous, such as being asked to stab someone with a knife. While such "teasing" seems cruel and juvenile to outsiders, the behavior is not what it appears to be, as we will find out.

In the course of a month, I observed Sembok teased into ten-minute "fits" at separate weddings where she sat in the main crowded room of the groom's house, despite claiming to dread being teased. If Sembok genuinely fears teasing, she could simply tell family members not to tease her, and easily avoid wedding crowds; or visit privately, instead of prancing onto center stage. "If you suffer amnesia during 'attacks,' how can you apologize if you are unaware of your actions?" I later asked. She had no explanation. Psychiatrist Ronald Simons is the leading proponent of the theory that *latah* is a disorder of the universal human propensity to startle in response to a sudden fright, akin to Westerners swearing after a fright, the extent of which varies according to cultural conditioning. Simons takes subjects at their face value, assuming their truthfulness in claiming that the reaction is involuntary.

I was also surprised to learn that Sembok, who would commonly drop and throw objects while *latah*, was frequently allowed to cradle babies in her arms, with a perfect record of holding onto them! Since there remain many "severe" cases in Malaysia, one wonders why there are no newspaper headlines: "Another Malay Drops Baby!" or "Latah Claims Two in Yet Another Car Mishap." Both "severe" cases that I investigated claimed to hate being "teased," yet both the "victim" and onlookers seemed to heartily enjoy it. This denial of self-control is necessary for perpetration of the *latah* deception since it "sets the stage" for the ensuing performance which allows for the violation of Malay norms, and under which the subject enjoys complete immunity from blame. No "victim" can willingly invite the *latah* condition since it would be tantamount to admitting that they enjoy violating strict taboos. If the victim's protestations were genuine and not perfunctory—well, mothers, sons, and grandchildren would certainly not torment their elder loved ones, who are always treated with the utmost dignity and respect in Malayo-Indonesian culture. From this perspective, the *latah* startler unwittingly serves as a coach, orchestrating and dictating the transgressions. This ritual also allows for the release of individual expressions in that while the subject is required to perform the coach's choreography, the foul language and obscene body gestures are improvisations conducted entirely by the *latah* performer. The performance is almost always terminated by both physical and verbal cues by the teasers that they are tired. Yet, in this ritual of deception, while family members recognize the *latah* subject is not ill, teasers do believe they have temporary and complete control over the *latah*'s mind, and are careful to keep knives and sharp objects away from them during episodes.

## DISCUSSION

*Latah* has been an enigmatic "ailment" in that its classification has curiously eluded a number of competent researchers. In fact, in the *American Handbook of Psychiatry*, Arieti and Brody place it under "Rare, Unclassifiable, Collective, and Exotic Psychotic Syndromes."[2] To date, outsiders have been able to catch only fleeting glimpses of the mysterious world of *latah*s. They have noted considerable difficulty in gathering detailed case histories from informants, as with the late, prominent psychiatrist Pow Meng Yap, despite his fluency in the Malay language.[3] Anthropologist Michael Kenny remarks that only a single case of *latah* has been observed and studied in sufficient context and depth to provide some insights into the processes involved—that gathered by anthropologist Clive Kessler.[4] Coincidentally, the woman in his case study possesses a marked exhibitionistic personality.

A histrionic perspective best fits the evidence, explaining why *latah* is not considered an illness by participants and their families, and the reluctance of informants to provide detailed information. It explains its almost exclusive restriction to social subordinates—lower class women and servants, and their conspicuous tendency to startle in the presence of higher-status peers.[5] It has been observed that "severe" subjects typically lead solitary and reclusive lives, so as to avoid teasing.[6] Yet, it is equally plausible that these subjects become performers *because* they are lonely and desire attention. Previous observers have presented primarily anecdotal evidence that the onset of severe symptoms coincides with depression, financial dependence, and loneliness following the death of a close family member.[7] Some anthropologists even argue that *latah* symbolizes the plight of such people and is a means of conveying that something is amiss to others.[8] Sembok first exhibited severe symptoms at public gatherings a few months after the death of her daughter followed in close succession by the death of her husband, while another relative displayed a similar pattern following her husband's death. Both were unemployed, in social isolation, and dependent upon their children for support. Researchers have focused their attention on the conditions which are likely to prompt the *latah* illness, largely ignoring the question of under what conditions people are likely to feign or exaggerate for attention.

It cannot be overemphasized that "severe" *latah*-like behavior is exceedingly rare, including in Malayo-Indonesia. One reason researchers have chosen to downplay the obvious exhibitionistic nature of "severe" cases are reports that it once affected the majority, if not the entire population of Malaya and parts of Indonesia.[9] Some anthropologists reasoned that certainly not everyone could be feigning; therefore *latah* must possess some unconscious ritualistic or symbolic quality. Hence, while prominent Hong Kong psychiatrist Pow Meng Yap was convinced that *latah* is a mental disease of hysterical dimensions, he remarks that "it is often difficult to separate the genuine cases from those which are basically histrionic and exhibitionist in nature."[10] Like Yap, psychiatrists Arei Kiev[14] and H. B. M. Murphy each assume that this behavior characterizes its hysterical aspects and dissociative nature, especially since most of those affected are female.[11] A prominent Malaysian physician, Eng-Seng Tan, makes a similar observation:

> Although there has not yet been any systematic scientific study of the latah phenomenon from a psychological viewpoint, the hysterical nature of the condition is inescapable to the psychiatric observer. The condition invariably occurs in the presence of an audience, the behavior of the sub-

ject has a marked theatrical quality about it, often provoking spasms of laughter among the audience, and the subject pleads amnesia for her buffoonery when she comes out of her altered state of consciousness.[12]

Upon closer scrutiny, the argument that *latah* cannot be fraud due to its pervasiveness dissolves. Of the ninety-nine living members of my wife's family surveyed, only two are "severe" (100 percent female) and twenty-nine are "mild" (86 percent female). Since "milds" do not consider themselves to be suffering from a disorder, upon explaining the common psychiatric definition of "mild," I was told that "everyone is a little *latah*." There is no evidence that "severe" cases were any more common in the previous century than they are today. Its habitual form persists in certain families, although it has no major social significance, except as a prerequisite for performers to emulate and elaborate. "Mild" *latah*s simply respond to startle in a manner comparable to Western swearing. There is no exaggeration, mimicking, amnesia, or involuntary expression. Then how to explain its appearance in women from certain Malay families? In its "mild" form, *latah* can be viewed as an infrequent habit formed almost exclusively by post-pubescent females in certain Malay households with cultural traditions of such behavior, while emulating elders. Since it is considered a feminine trait, most males do not engage in the habit, but if they do, it is infrequent and typically denied. In a similar vein, smoking cigarettes was once considered a solely masculine trait, and women who smoked usually denied it. The view of "mild" *latah* as habit is consistent with Canadian psychiatrist H. B. Murphy's enigmatic observations that the condition was extremely rare in Malayo-Indonesia during the first half of the seventeenth century, reported on virtually every street corner and common among men by the 1890s, scarce during the 1920s, and diminishing in frequency today and almost exclusive to women.[13]

The status of *latah* as a disorder is reminiscent of social scientists mislabeling other habits and fashions as pathological. Penrose considered the playing with yo-yos and crossword puzzles to be a mild form of psychopathological crowd behavior.[14] In his enduring classic on collective folly, *Memoirs of Extraordinary Popular Delusions and the Madness of Crowds,* journalist Charles Mackay discusses the common nineteenth-century social science view that the habitual use of the words "flare up" and "Hookey Walker" by Londoners to describe virtually any behavior exemplified herd suggestibility.[15] Child psychiatrist W. Burnham makes a similar evaluation of the brief "craze" of tickling residents with feather dusters in Worcester, Massachusetts, during the early 1900s,[16] while epidemiologist Robert Markush considers the worldwide proliferation of the cigarette smoking habit to be a form of "epidemic hysteria."[17]

Recently, psychiatrist Jack Jenner reportedly discovered seemingly indisputable evidence that *latah* is an abnormality of the human startle mechanism which varies with cultural conditioning.[18] He treated a forty-year-old Dutch woman who would swear profusely, become abusive, and act oddly upon being startled. It is claimed that subject has no ties to Malayo-Indonesian culture, and was successfully treated with "flooding" therapy consisting of her husband and son startling her dozens of times daily. Yet, it is an amazing coincidence that the sole documented case of the individual spontaneous severe *latah* was to occur to someone from a culture with a large population of Malaysian and Indonesian descendents, both countries being former Dutch colonial outposts. Jenner's case study notes that the woman startled several times daily for twenty years, yet had not sought help. Only after her startling nearly resulted in a car accident did the husband seek psychiatric assistance. Unaddressed are such fundamental questions as to whether the woman had Malaysian or Indonesian companions—an excellent likelihood given their large population in Holland—or if she was previously aware of *latah*. Jenner also notes that startling enabled the woman to receive a variety of benefits: avoiding household chores; getting her way in deciding holiday destinations; and serving as "her most effective weapon in marital conflicts."[19] A fraud perspective is equally plausible and best conforms to historical and contemporary evidence. I would argue that upon commencement of "flooding," the subject rebelled, intensifying malingering to demonstrate the ineffectiveness of treatment. Upon realizing the determination of her husband and psychiatrist to continue this strategy, "symptoms" rapidly disappeared and have never returned. Since continuance of startling would only elicit negative responses, the performances suddenly ceased.

# CONCLUSION

There are numerous historical precedents to individual malingering for social gain, or institutionalized feigning. Anthropologist Michael Kenny contends that "severe" *latah* subjects do not enter an altered state of consciousness, but are engaged in *latah* "performance" and "theater"—a culture-specific idiom expressing marginality.[20] Never are the words "fraud," "fakery," or "deception" used. Yet anthropologists appear guilty of employing double standards. A number of researchers have exposed fakery and deception in group settings: the Salem witch trials of 1692; spiritualism during the early twentieth century; epidemic demonic possession in medieval European nunneries; and channeling associated with the contemporary New Age movement. However, anthropologists and psychiatrists tend to use different language in scrutinizing similar non-Western traditions. The study of a Western faith healer is often viewed as fraudulent, but place an exotic label on essentially the same behavior involving a shaman in some African tribe and anthropologists are quick to point out the "symbolic" qualities. Yet, there is also symbolism in fraud, quackery, and channeling. For example, Carlos Castaneda's fictional writings are filled with a seductive, adventurous quality that was ideal for captivating popular American culture during the 1960s and '70s, blending "the use of psychedelic drugs, a belief in real magical (or paranormal) powers, and a thoroughgoing mysticism."[21] The discovery of a "stone age" tribe in the Philippines during 1971 captured the imagination of the world due in large part to its ultrapacifist symbolism—a community of "Noble Savages" living in unspoiled isolation from the decadence of twentieth-century civilization.[26] The media heavily touted that the Tasaday people did not even have a word for war. It was later uncovered by Swiss journalist Oswald Iten to be a hoax after he gained access to the Tasadays' restricted preserve and found the "lost tribe" "living in houses, wearing Western clothing, and saying they had faked the whole thing."[23] The conspiracy was apparently perpetrated by the the government of Filipino president Ferdinand Marcos in order to deceive the world for political and economic gain.[24]

Social scientists do an injustice by using such words as "malingering," "histrionic," "sick role," "performance," and "symbolic action" in describing attempts to achieve social gain in the absence of an organic

Sembok, pictured above wearing a cap, would exhibit wild outbursts of outrageous behavior after being startled or poked in the ribs. While many psychiatrists view these reactions as a mental disorder, the author's investigation suggests that she is perfectly normal and engaging in a form of local ritual.

illness. But stripped of these euphemisms, the underlying content involves conscious deception for personal gain. The entire notion of the perpetration of fraud in non-Western cultures needs to be reevaluated regardless of whether the perpetrators express a belief in their partial ability to heal. In this regard they are culture-bound idioms of deception that are couched in semi-legitimizing scientific labels. At the present rate, we will soon be classifying the propensity of preachers to defraud their flocks as the Jim Bakker Syndrome, or "psychics" who perform magic tricks for financial gain as the Uri Geller Disorder, when in fact there is no illness, only fakery and deception. Anthropologists have an unfortunate tendency to emphasize, idolize, and glorify the exotic, while psychiatrists are often too eager to place a convenient and unitary disorder or disease label on deviant or deceptive behavior.

In the case of *latah*, initially Robert Bartholomew, upon marriage into his wife's Malay family, failed to practice good critical thinking. Instead he accepted what the psychiatric textbooks said about *latah*—that it was a mental disorder peculiar to Malaysian-Indonesian society. After observing family members who exhibited *latah*, he was able to put aside his Western assumptions and biases, after which he began to slowly unravel the complex conduct code of *latah* as a local custom and habit, not a disorder. Prior to this point, considering other interpretations seemed to be a waste of time, because everyone knew and assumed that the textbooks were correct—most everyone, that is, except the anthropologists at the University of Malaya, who suggested to him that he should consider viewing *latah* as a kind of performance.

## REVIEW QUESTIONS

1. What biases did scientists in the nineteenth and early twentieth centuries have that led them to assume that *latah* was a disorder?
2. What evidence is there that *latah* is an illness?
3. What did Robert Bartholomew do to determine whether Sembok was truthful or faking her *latah* symptoms?
4. List the different theories put forward to explain *latah*. Which do you support and why?
5. Tourette's Syndrome causes sufferers to exhibit tics (involuntary muscle spasms) and utter words that are often obscene. *Latah* was once thought to be a form of Tourette's, but no longer. Why do you think scientists no longer consider these two behaviors to be the same?
6. Can you think of any parallels to *latah* in Western culture? Can you think of excuses people may use to allow themselves to break rules, such as claiming to be sick to have extra time to take a test?

## NOTES

1. On the belief *latah* is a disease, see M. K. Opler, *Culture and Psychiatry* (New York: Atherton Press, 1967), p. 133; D. Rosenthal, *Genetic Theory and Abnormal Behavior* (New York: McGraw-Hill, 1970). Discussion that *latah* is a disorder can be found in the following: R. Howard and R. Ford, "From the Jumping Frenchmen of Maine to Post-Traumatic Stress Disorder: The Startle

Response in Neuropsychiatry," *Psychological Medicine* 22 (1992): 695–707; R. Simons, "Latah II—Problems with a Purely Symbolic Interpretation," in *The Culture-Bound Syndromes*, ed. R. Simons and C. Hughes (Dordrecht, The Netherlands: D. Reidel, 1985), pp. 77–89; R. Simons, "A Feasible and Timely Enterprise: Commentary on Culture-Bound Syndromes and International Disease Classifications by Raymond Prince and Francoise Tcheeng-Laroche," *Culture, Medicine and Psychiatry* 11 (1987): 21–28. For discussion regarding *latah* as a type of cultural expression, see M. Kenny, "Latah: The Symbolism of a Putative Mental Disorder," *Culture, Medicine and Psychiatry* 2 (1978): 209–31; R. L. Lee and S. E. Ackerman, "The Sociocultural Dynamics of Mass Hysteria: A Case Study of Social Conflict in West Malaysia," *Psychiatry* 43 (1980): 78–88.

2. S. Arieti and E. B. Brody, *American Handbook of Psychiatry* (New York: Basic Books, 1974).

3. P. M. Yap, "The Latah Reaction. Its Pathodynamics and Nosological Position," *Journal of Mental Science* 98 (1952): 537.

4. M. Kenny, "Paradox Lost: The Latah Problem Revisited," in Simons and Hughes, *The Culture-Bound Syndromes*, p. 74; C. Kessler, "Conflict and Sovereignty in Kelantanese Malay Spirit Seances," in *Case Studies in Spirit Possession*, ed. V. Crapanzano and V. Garrison (New York: Cambridge University Press, 1977), pp. 295–329.

5. H. Geertz, "Latah in Java: A Theoretical Paradox," *Indonesia* 3 (1968): 96; J. B. M. Murphy, "History and the Evolution of Syndromes: The Striking Case of Latah and Amok," in *Psychopathology: Contributions from Social, Behavioral, and Biological Sciences*, ed. M. Hammer et al. (New York: John Wiley, 1973), pp. 33–35; J. Murphy, "Notes for a Theory on Latah," in *Culture-Bound Syndromes, Ethnopsychiatry, and Alternate Therapies*, ed. William P. Lebra (Honolulu: East-West Center Press, 1976), pp. 3–21; Kenny, "Latah," p. 213.

6. L. L. Langness, "Hysterical Psychosis: The Cross-Cultural Evidence," *American Journal of Psychiatry* 124 (1967): 149.

7. Yap, "Latah Reaction," pp. 536–37; T. Chiu, J. Tong, and K. Schmidt, "A Clinical Survey of Latah in Sarawak, Malaysia," *Psychological Medicine* 1 (1972): 159; Kessler, "Conflict and Sovereignty," p. 313; Kenny, "Latah," p. 210.

8. Kenny, "Latah," p. 217.

9. H. Clifford, *Studies in Brown Humanity* (London: Grant Richards, 1898), p. 195; Murphy, "Notes for a Theory," p. 11.

10. Yap, "Latah Reaction," p. 537.

11. A. Kiev, *Transcultural Psychiatry* (New York: The Free Press, 1972), pp. 72–75; Murphy, "Notes for a Theory."

12. E. S. Tan, "The Culture-Bound Syndromes Among Overseas Chinese," in *Normal and Abnormal Behavior in Chinese Culture*, ed. A. Kleinman and T. Lin (Dordrecht, Holland: D. Reidel, 1980), p. 380.

13. Murphy, "Notes for a Theory."

14. L. S. Penrose, *On the Objective Study of Crowd Behavior* (London: H. K. Lewis, 1952).

15. C. MacKay, *Memoirs of Extraordinary Popular Delusions and the Madness of Crowds*, vol. 2 (London: Office of the National Illustrated Library, 1852), pp. 623–24.

16. W. H. Burnham, *The Normal Mind* (New York, D. Appleton-Century, 1924), pp. 337–38.

17. R. E. Markush, "Mental Epidemics: A Review of the Old to Prepare for the New," *Public Heath Reviews* 2, no. 4 (1973): 375.

18. J. Jenner, "Latah as Coping: A Case Study Offering a New Paradox to Solve the Old One," *International Journal of Social Psychiatry* 36 (1990): 194–99; J. Jenner, "A Successfully Treated Dutch Case of Latah," *Journal of Nervous and Mental Disease* 179 (1991): 636–37.

19. Jenner, "Latah as Coping," p. 195.

20. Kenny, "Latah," p. 209.

21. T. Hines, *Pseudoscience and the Paranormal* (Amherst, N.Y.: Prometheus Books, 1988), p. 277.

22. L. E. Sponsel, "Ultraprimitive Pacifists: The Tasaday as a Symbol of Peace," *Anthropology Today* 6, no. 1 (1990): 3–5.

23. O. Iten, "Die Tasaday: Ein Philippinischer Steinzeit Schwindel," *Neue Zurcher Zeitung* (Zurich) (April 12–13, 1986): 77–79; M. Willson, "Two Films about Truth and Falsehood," *Anthropology Today* 5, no. 5 (1989): 18.

24. J. Dumont, "The Tasaday, Which and Whose? Toward the Political Economy of an Ethnographic Sign," *Cultural Anthropology* 3, no. 3 (1988): 261–75.

# 8

Western norms and values continue to be placed onto minority, unpopular, or unfamiliar religious beliefs and expressions. Judgments as to what are acceptable forms of expression and worship are often made under the "neutral" label of science. But science is dominated by Western notions of what is normal. We must be more aware of the global human experience.

# EXPLORING TOLERANCE

## Religious Devoutness or Bizarre Ritual?

### with Dr. Julian O'Dea

Scientists are often portrayed as value-neutral. In other words, scientists follow the scientific method and arrive at unbiased assessments of human behavior. While this sounds good on paper, in reality, nothing could be further from the truth. Scientists are like everyone else. They are subject to political influences and diagnostic fashions which lead them astray from the scientific process. As a result, prevailing Western social and cultural norms and values are often unwittingly placed onto minority groups—especially religious movements. A classic example of this process occurred during the mid-1800s, when one particular "strange" religious movement in the United States became widely feared. The group's leaders were painted as authoritarian and immoral, and female devotees were characterized as sex slaves. Many Americans felt this "cult" had to be stopped and there were moves in Congress to bar any member from working for the government. There were all sorts of wild rumors that the group was secretly plotting with Native Americans to violently overthrow the government. Several protests broke out and some erupted into fatal riots. Yet, despite all of this opposition, this unpopular group—Roman Catholics—is now considered a mainstream religion in the United States.[1]

This chapter provides a brief survey of how some scientists have placed labels of illness or disorder onto unpopular or unfamiliar religious expressions. Group suggestibility and imitation are well documented among various religious movements whose members characteristically exhibit extreme emotional zeal in the course of expressing reverence and devotion. Such phenomena can affect virtually any mentally healthy person exposed to the appropriate circumstances.[2] Many studies suggest that the participation in the search for meaning through religious experience, including the cathartic release of emotions during ceremonies, can produce positive psychological effects.[3] It was not long ago, however, that expressions of religious fervor in group settings were considered by the general scientific community to represent a form of mental disorder, and this opinion persists in some psychiatric quarters today.

Since its inception as a formal profession, psychiatry has used medical labels to control deviant behaviors. At the beginning of the nineteenth century, Christian revivalism in America grew in popularity, with adherents primarily comprised of the lower socioeconomic classes, ethnic minorities, and females. Emotional zeal and ecstatic phenomena accompanying this movement were at variance with the rational linear model of human progress, and characterized as exemplifying "degeneration" due to the influence of the "maddening crowd." Congregants were portrayed as temporarily regressing to the unconscious mental level that was believed to typify "primitive" peoples, who were widely believed to be prone to emotional outbursts due either to inherent degeneracy or lack of integration with "superior" European civilization.[4] The nineteenth-century U.S. medical profession was almost exclusively composed of conservative Caucasian males of high socioeconomic status, adhering to a doctrine of rational scientism. Consequently, religious fervor was relabeled as a medical problem and emotional excitement associated with various deviant, unpopular, or unfamiliar religious groups was pathologized within mainstream psychiatry.

During the nineteenth century the notion of "religious insanity" became popular in the United States, as emotional excitement associated with so-called deviant religious groups was believed to precipitate psychological illness.[5] Collective reactions among revivalist movement members were typically viewed as contagious hysteria,[6] which was separated into one of two categories, religious hysteria or secular hysteria. Sociologist Walter Bainbridge documents how the theory of religious insanity was promulgated by distinguished social scientists and psychiatrists, reified by the mass media and incorporated into the United States census.[7]

The common nineteenth-century association between group religious expression and abnormality was based on the prevalent view that extreme emotional arousal could affect permanent mental disturbance. Influential physician Amariah Brigham wrote that extended emotional excitement "is likely to injure the brain and nervous system."[8] Conversely, exposure to peaceful surroundings was believed to heal damaged nerves. It is within this context that pathological labels were evoked to describe various ritualized behaviors that were either learned and acted out, or which would often engender involuntary muscular spasms (what contemporary physicians term "psychomotor agitation"), and various imitative movements in hypersuggestible congregants, whose members became appropriately labeled as the Shakers, Quakers, Leapers, Jumpers, Rollers, and Barkers. During the Kentucky Revivals of the early nineteenth century, congregation members would roll on the ground to the point of exhaustion. This was called "the rolling exercise" and participants were correspondingly known as "Holy Rollers."

> At one meeting not less than a thousand persons fell to the ground apparently without sense or motion. . . . Towards the close of this commotion, viz. about the year 1803, convulsions became prevalent. . . . The rolling exercise consisted in doubling the head and feet together, and rolling over and over like a hoop. . . . The jerks consisted in violent twitches and contortions of the body in all its parts. . . . When attacked by the jerks, the victim of enthusiasm sometimes leaped like frogs, and exhibited every grotesque and hideous contortion of the face and limbs. The barks consisted in getting down on all fours, growling, snapping the teeth, and barking like dogs. Sometimes numbers of the people squatted down, and looking in the face of the minister, continued demurely barking at him while he preached to them. These last were particularly

gifted in prophecies, trances, dreams, rhapsodies, visions of angels, of
heaven, and of the holy city.

Men and women fell in such numbers that it became impossible for
the multitude to move about without trampling them, and they were hur-
ried to the meeting-house. At no time was the floor less than half covered.[9]

Intense laughter, which first appeared during the Kentucky Revivals,
grew in popularity, until in 1803 the Holy Laugh was systematically
introduced as a form of worship.[10] In recent years there has been a resurgence in laughter as a religious expression, especially among members of
the Toronto Blessing revivalist movement in Canada, which has been
controversial since its beginnings in the Toronto Vineyard Church in
1994. Writer Tony Payne presents a critical treatment of this movement,
in part because of its unconventional features such as laughter.[11]

During the early Quaker movement, members were known to walk or
run naked through public streets. Recently, public nudity has characterized
the more radical members of the anarchistic Doukhobor ("spirit-wrestler")
Christian sect of Canada, posing a challenge for authorities, as has their
recourse to arson.[12] While philosophically opposed to civil laws, one particularly contentious point is the practice of members concealing school-age
children from truant officers. Numerous government raids on their premises
have been met by non-resistance and immediate disrobing. During the
1950s, when representatives of the Province of British Columbia forcibly
removed their children, the Doukhobors engaged in widespread arson,
bombings, and parades of nudity. Their use of arson continues, and three
female members were recently incarcerated for such acts.[13]

As strange as these religious behaviors may appear to those removed
from the historical, social, or cultural dynamic, and no matter how
tempting it is to pathologize these actions, they represent recognized religious expressions, accepted within their particular subculture as a means
of penance, worship, or divine favor. Medical historian George Rosen
reports that those experiencing the condition of psychomotor agitation
known as "the jerks," induced through prolonged dancing, singing, and
zealous orations, were often considered divinely possessed. Collective
barking was used "as a means of chastisement for sins" as participants
occasionally surrounded a tree while on all fours, barking and yelping to
"tree the devil."[14] It was subsequently considered an act of piety or a sign

of divine favor. The rationale for prancing naked in public was seen by Quakers as a form of truthfulness.[15] The history of stripping naked as a religious expression includes a famous case involving St. Francis Assisi, as he expressed his rejection of the world of his wealthy father that he wanted to leave behind in order to pursue a life of ascetic holiness.

Near Nelson, British Columbia, Canada, in August 2001, the small Doukhobor religious sect made news when one of its members, eighty-one-year-old Mary Braun, appeared in court naked to answer charges that she set fire to a community college computer room. The Doukhobors, who emigrated to Canada in the 1890s to escape persecution in Russia, believe in complete equality and have often been charged with going naked in public and arson in their attempts to help make everyone equal. During the 1950s the group burned down their own homes and marched naked in the streets to highlight a "purity" campaign. The group wants the British Columbia government to apologize for placing their children in an internment camp in the 1950s to force them to attend public school— something their parents are set against.[16]

There is clearly a fine line between what behavior social scientists label as a cult, with its pejorative, fanatical connotations, and what is considered to be mainstream and acceptable. The difference is often based on the number of followers, and reflects changing diagnostic fashions and assumptions that are molded by the *zeitgeist* and professional ideology. It is typically asserted, without substantiating evidence, that "cult" members are either psychologically deviant, mentally ill, or the victims of coercion or "brainwashing." The determination of deviance is often based solely upon the exotic nature of the social realities, and the assumption that no one in their "right mind" would act in a particular manner. Hence, when certain practices appear strange or unpopular, writer Jerimiah Gutman notes:

> A religion becomes a cult; proselytization becomes brainwashing; persuasion becomes propaganda; missionaries become subversive agents; retreats, monasteries, and convents become prisons; holy ritual becomes bizarre conduct; religious observance becomes aberrant behavior; devotion and meditation become psychopathic trances.[17]

An example of this point is the common label of "crazy" being placed on the mass suicide of approximately 900 People's Temple members, followers of Jim Jones, at Jonestown, Guyana, on November 18, 1978. Almost universally, the mass media and psychiatric professionals portrayed those who participated in the event as mentally disturbed, based solely on the acts per se. Yet, given the relative isolation with outside contact, autocratic social hierarchy, a sense of persecution, and belief in the existence of a utopian life after death, the event can be viewed as an exemplifying conformity to group norms like *hara-kiri* among Japanese pilots during World War II, or the Indian *suttee* throwing herself onto her husband's funeral pyre.[18] There is also evidence that some members refused to commit suicide and were shot by other followers or forced to drink the poison. Hence, certain types of suicide can be viewed as rational. A classic example is altruistic suicide by a police officer in the line of duty.

Collective suicide is often interpreted as psychopathological behavior.[19] For instance, R. B. Ulman uses a Freudian model to analyze the Jonestown event as exemplifying "collective pathological regression" that resulted in "mass madness."[20] Such authors tend to overemphasize the significance of the actions per se, without seriously evaluating the symbol system context of the social actors. One writer in the *British Medical Journal* discusses the frequent occurrence of suicide "epidemics" within the Russian Empire, and their scarcity elsewhere. Mass suicide by live burial by at least twenty-five members of a Russian religious sect is described as an example of "mental pathology."[21] However, the author fails to consider the social realities of the so-called victims in their morbid decision. The particular incident in question occurred within a small, isolated, Siberian religious community, the members of which were convinced by a charismatic leader "that the Antichrist had descended, and the end of the world was at hand, so that whoever sought death now gained a heavenly crown."[22] There are abundant examples of culturally condoned voluntary ritualistic suicides, such as among certain groups in Germany, Russia, and ancient Greece.[23] Clusters of suicides by self-incineration, particularly by Buddhists protesting the Vietnam War, do not necessarily indicate psychopathology when viewed from the symbolic universe of the "victims."

> . . . self-sacrifice by suicide brings secondary gains to the victim in the personal attainment of a "divine" state (e.g., Nirvana for the Buddhists), posthumous glorification which often immortalizes a martyr, or win-

ning honor or glory for the individual's family or group. Religious or political figures, as exemplified by the Buddhists, may identify at times so completely with a cause that they perceive their lives solely as instruments for attaining the goals of the group, allowing total submission to control. Thus, a command or even a suggestion to commit a sacrificial suicide would provide sufficient motivation for a person with such extreme zeal or devotion.

The Buddhist self-incinerations may thus be characterized as an epidemic which resulted from the confluence of several conditions: (1) a conducive atmosphere of open conflict and emotional tension; (2) a dramatic and powerful expression of a widely shared emotion—a passionate expression laden with complex symbolic meaning which served to intensify and focus the ubiquitous emotional tension; and (3) a population of individuals whose religious devotion, personal commitment, and unquestioning obedience perhaps made them particularly susceptible to suggestion from their leaders who may have encouraged the sacrifices for political purposes.[24]

Medieval millenarian participants are often viewed as exhibiting signs of group pathology precipitated by the stress of rapid social change.[25] Historian Norman Cohn in *The Pursuit of the Millennium* describes medieval flagellant movements (people who whip and beat themselves) in pathological terms, viewing them as collective paranoid fantasies.[26] Self-flagellation in expectation of divine reward in the afterlife quickly gained widespread acceptance across Europe during the twelfth century, not only becoming a "normal feature" of monastic Latin Christendom, "but one of the commonest of all penitential techniques" in general.[27] Cohn provides a graphic account of a fourteenth-century flagellant by a friar, who writes about a man who

shut himself up in his cell and stripped himself naked . . . and took his scourge with the sharp spikes, and beat himself on the body and on the arms and on the legs, till blood poured. . . . One of the spikes . . . was bent crooked, like a hook, and whatever flesh it caught it tore off. He beat himself so hard that the scourge broke into three bits and the points flew against the wall. He stood there bleeding and gazed at himself. It was such a wretched sight that he was reminded in many ways of the appearance of the beloved Christ, when he was fearfully beaten. Out of

pity for himself he began to weep bitterly. And he knelt down, naked
and covered in blood, in the frosty air, and prayed to God to wipe out
his sins from before his gentle eyes.[28]

Self-flagellation as part of monastic and devout lay life has continued into
modern times. As recently as the 1980s, Trappistine nuns of Holy Cross
in Dorset, England, were still using a small whip to inflict penance on
themselves once daily.[29] Self-flagellation continues to be a feature of certain Islamic groups.[30] So-called self-torture with the expectation of
receiving spiritual reward has occurred in northern New Mexico among
the Los Hermanos Penitentes de Sangre de Christo, and been classified as
"collective mental disorders" by Faguet and Faguet.[31] The ranks of members have experienced a recent resurgence, with some predictions that it
may spread to Western urban centers.[32]

# WITCH-HUNTS AND POSSESSION AS PATHOLOGY

In explaining the witch-hunts and fear of demons which spread through
Western society between the sixteenth and seventeenth centuries, the
behavior of those persecuted, the persecutors themselves, or their social
structure have traditionally been labeled by social scientists as resulting
from a dysfunctional social order triggered by the stresses of rapid social
changes. Such evaluations are primarily based on the fantastic, implausible nature of the beliefs and their cruelty per se, relative to the conduct
of scientists assessing the behavior. However, since reality is socially
constructed,[33] intelligent, educated, rational, and mentally healthy people,
through social and cultural conditioning, can consensually support virtually any idea. Examples include the belief in headhunting, cannibalism,
slavery, and Nazism. Those evaluating the witch "mania" typically reason
that such actions are "sick," and that no normal group of persons would
torture, hang, or burn alive suspected witches on such flimsy evidence as
hearsay, coerced confessions, and ambiguous body marks (for example,
birth marks supposed to be a sign of the Devil). Yet those involved were
behaving in a logical pattern of conduct that was consistent with the prevailing religious beliefs of their milieu.

Italian author Scipio Sighele viewed crowd behavior as unleashing "primitive" impulses within susceptible individuals, a conclusion formulated from Jean Charcot's psychopathological notion of hypnotic suggestibility.[34] In addition to Gustav LeBon's influential work on the study of crowd "madness," many other social theorists of the period utilized and modified these earlier concepts of suggestibility and mass behavior, including Fournial and Tarde.[35] Recent works, particularly by psychologists and psychiatrists, draw on similar intellectual roots relative to collective hypnosis in explaining the fear of witches and mass demon possession. Bliss states that much of the "insane" idea about demonophobia (a fear of witches that spread across Europe in the latter Middle Ages) is attributable to spontaneous "self hypnosis," disregarding more prosaic and plausible explanations: deviance, labeling, conformity dynamics, and symbol system analysis.[36] Schmidt holds a similar "group trance" interpretation.[37] Freud viewed demon possession states psychopathologically.[38]

Anthropologist John Conner emphasizes the significance of understanding the cultural codes and belief structures of late medieval and post-Reformation Europe to contextually explain the preoccupation with witchcraft, and the consequences of such convictions (torture, exorcisms, stake burning, imprisonment). By evaluating the witch "mania" in its historical, social, and cultural context, "not only was a belief in witchcraft not irrational and a delusion, but also it did in fact make good sense."[39] Prior to this period, the perception of God in Europe was that he permitted good and bad events. However, in the context of the high mortality associated with the Black Death, a new worldview emerged, attributing misfortunes and disasters to the work of Satan or his human cohorts:

> Everywhere there were deserted towns, empty villages, abandoned homes, and a dreadful silence that seemed to hang over the world. Furthermore, no remedy appeared to work, no amount of piety was sufficient, and no amount of flagellation or other extreme form of penance had the slightest effect in reducing the severity of the plague. It is little wonder, then, that the preachings of the Church on the infinite mercy and compassion of Christ had a hollow ring and were less and less heeded. . . .
>
> . . . Whereas earlier theodicies had attempted to explain anomic phenomena in terms of visitations of the wrath of God, the present hor-

rors appeared to be of such magnitude that they could only be the work of Satan. A new world view had begun to emerge—that is, all that was horrible, terrifying or evil would henceforth be attributed to the work of Satan and his cohorts. . . .

Thus, both the laity and the clergy had now accepted a full-blown Manichean heresy: All that was good, productive, holy and enabling was the work of God, but all that was evil, destructive, terrifying and obscene could only be the work of Satan.[40]

It is with this understanding that various misfortunes—miscarriages, crop failures, illness—were attributed to the Devil or his worldly agents: witches. This worldview led to the famous bull of Pope Innocent VIII in 1484, which encouraged the identification of witches and exemplifies the degree to which an actively evil universe was legitimized and institutionalized. The papal decree served as the authority for the notorious *Malleus Maleficarum* written by Germany's chief witchcraft inquisitors, Heinrich Kramer and Jakob Sprenger, and is credited with causing the ensuing inquisiton.[41]

Instead of labeling accused witches or the persecutors as being mentally ill or deviant, a culturally relativistic, contextual view can be useful in understanding their motivations.[42] In the case of the 1692 Salem witch trials, historians James Davidson and Mark Lytle view as essential an evaluation of the events relative to their Massachusetts social setting.[43] Such behavior does not appear in a social vacuum during periods of social stress. Boyer and Nissenbaum concur:

When "Salem witchcraft," like some exotic cut flower, is plucked from the soil which nurtured it—or, to change the image, when the roles assigned to the actors of 1692 are shaped by a script not of their own making . . . [it] cannot rise above the level of gripping melodrama. It is only as we come to sense how deeply the witchcraft outbreak was rooted in the prosaic, everyday lives and how profoundly those lives were being shaped by powerful forces of historical change . . . the more we have come to know these men for something like what they really were, the more we have also come to realize how profoundly they were shaped by the times in which they lived. For if they were unlike any other men, so was their world unlike any other world before or since. . . .[44]

Shamanic possession states have been commonly portrayed in the anthropological literature as involving the mentally disturbed. A description by Bogoras is typical, describing shamans among the Arctic Chukchee, as possessing "lunatic" characteristics, being "extremely excitable, almost hysterical, and not a few were half crazy."[45] Silverman typifies shamans as possessing nonparanoid schizophrenia.[46] While pathological interpretations remain among some contemporary social scientists, Heinze challenges this assumption, contending that there is no compelling evidence to suggest that shamans in general suffer from psychopathology:

> [T]he 122 shamans I worked with over the last twenty-seven years, go regularly and professionally into trance, and lead a productive life which bears no indication of any pathology. Furthermore, the conditions of a hysteric or schizophrenic will, at times, be uncontrollable and, in many countries, be diagnosed as spirit-possession which requires exorcism. The trances of shamans, on the other hand, take place in a culturally acceptable framework and are controlled. These are important differences. With different geographic, climatic, and cultural circumstances we find different forms of shamanism corresponding to local needs . . . shamans function well in their community.[47]

Under the predominant eighteenth- and nineteenth-century conceptions, individual hysteria was typically classified as a disease. However, psychiatrist Thomas Szasz, in *The Myth of Mental Illness*, argues that "witches" experiencing conversion symptoms or dissociated states are not mentally ill but use a form of nonverbal communication which utilizes a specific set of signs.[48] The pathological classification was popularized in psychiatry by influential psychiatrist Gregory Zilboorg, who considered most persons defined as medieval witches as mentally ill.[49] This view of witches and participants of collective medieval flagellation, dancing mania, lycanthropy, and demonology continues, particularly in psychiatry and psychology.[50] Schoeneman demonstrated this several years ago in an examination of twenty abnormal psychology textbooks published between 1978 and 1981, noting that while psychopathological models of individuals "misidentified as witches and demoniacs . . . has been discredited,"

Almost all authors endorsed at least one aspect of the psychopathological interpretation, and only three books included contradictory opinions. Textbooks that presented the psychiatric model seem to have
derived it primarily from the work of Gregory Zilboorg, and there is
also evidence of unreferenced internal borrowing among textbooks.
Authors generally ignored prominent historical and anthropological
research on witchcraft and possession; in addition, they also gave min-
imal attention to more recent, socioculturally oriented histories of psychiatry and to critiques of the older psychiatric paradigm.[51]

It is important to recognize that a broad spectrum of beliefs that are
considered implausible or ridiculous by modern Western standards of
what is normal have been held by intelligent, educated people. There is a
tendency to ignore and suppress the evidence of such beliefs among pre-
sumably "enlightened" figures including famous scientists, although the
prevailing view in the history of science is being increasingly challenged.
Such renowned scientific thinkers as Robert Boyle and Francis Bacon
were unable to completely liberate their writings from the popular superstitions of their milieu. Boyle suggested the interviewing of English
miners to determine whether they "meet with any subterraneous
demons," while Bacon held that "malign spirits" may be responsible for
witchcraft. Sir Isaac Newton devoted considerable time to studying what
are now regarded as fringe areas (such as alchemy), while John Locke, in
his famous *Essay Concerning Human Understanding*, wrote that "spirits
can assume bodies of different bulk, figure or configuration."[52]
    Human religious expression is remarkably diverse. Attempts by some
social scientists to place foreign, unfamiliar, or minority religious beliefs
into categories of psychiatric disorder reflects the increasing tendency to
place labels onto behaviors that do not fit within narrow Western notions
as to what actions are rational or normal. In doing so we risk mistrans-
lating conviction into obsession; devoutness into fanaticism. The most
fascinating "document" in human history is not the Bible or Koran, but it
encompasses these and all other religious writings. It is the ethnographic
record. The natural tendency toward ethnocentricity can only be reduced
by becoming knowledgeable of and sensitive to the remarkable breadth
and scope of human diversity. If we do not, we risk misunderstanding
those with different beliefs and modes of expression.

It is beyond the realm of science to prove the existence of God, although use of the scientific method has disproved many religious claims—from how the world was created to miraculous cures. When we examine various religious expressions around the world and try to assess their normality, it is absolutely essential to practice good critical thinking by being aware of our biases. Why? Throughout the relatively brief history of science, Western values and science have frequently become intermingled, such as the notorious case in the United States during the eighteenth century of labeling Catholics as bizarre cultists simply because they were unpopular and relatively few in number. In the future, we need to avoid simplistic, emotional labels for religious deviants using such terms as "cult" and "cultists," and instead assess their rationality and normalcy in terms of the context of seemingly unconventional behaviors and their meaning.

# REVIEW QUESTIONS

1. Many religions today might be considered cults: the Jehovah's Witnesses, the Church of Jesus Christ of Latter-Day Saints (Mormons), the Church of Scientology. Should they be? But who decides?
2. Today in some religious communities, followers speak in strange languages and handle poisonous snakes. Do you consider this to be abnormal? Why or why not?
3. Should Jehovah's Witnesses be allowed to refuse a live-saving blood transfusion? What if a three-month-old baby is the one requiring the transfusion?
4. A recent controversy about cults involves the Falun Gong movement in China. The Chinese government labels the group a dangerous cult, while followers claim it is simply a peaceful philosophy. How might the Chinese benefit from publicly labeling Falun Gong as a cult?
5. Regardless of whether the group led by David Koresh in Waco, Texas, was a cult or not, did the U.S. government have a vested interest in portraying it as one in the media?
6. Why is it important to be tolerant of different religious beliefs and expressions?

7. Should government tolerate the Doukhobors of Canada? Where does the line between religious freedom end and the need to enforce community morals and act in the public good begin?

8. Why do you think that the idea of "religious insanity" became popular in the United States in the nineteenth century?

9. Why is it important to judge behavior within its context?

10. How can we reduce the natural human tendency of being ethnocentric?

## NOTES

1. D. G. Bromley and A. Shupe, "Public Reaction against New Religious Movements," in *Cults and New Religious Movements: A Report of the American Psychiatric Association from the Committee on Psychiatry and Religion*, ed. M. Galanter (Washington, D.C.: American Psychiatric Association, 1989), pp. 305–34.

2. W. Sargant, *Battle for the Mind: A Physiology of Conversion and Brainwashing* (London: Windmill Press, 1957).

3. W. Sargant, *The Mind Possessed: A Physiology of Possession, Mysticism and Faith Healing* (London: Heinemann, 1973); J. T. Richardson, "The Psychology of Induction: A Review and Interpretation," in Galanter, *Cults and New Religious Movements*, pp. 211–38; S. G. Post, "DSM-III-R and Religion," *Social Science and Medicine* 35 (1992): 81–90.

4. S. Fernando, *Mental Health, Race and Culture* (Hampshire, England: Macmillan Education Ltd., 1991), p. 33.

5. W. Bainbridge, "Religious Insanity in America: The Official Nineteenth Century Theory," *Sociological Analysis* 45 (1984): 223–40.

6. M. Melcher, *The Shaker Adventure* (Princeton, N.J.: Princeton University Press, 1941), p. 61; A. F. C. Wallace, "Mass Hysteria," in *The Encyclopedia of Mental Health*, ed. A. Deutsch and H. Fishman (New York: Franklin Watts, 1963), vol. 3, p. 991.

7. Bainbridge, "Religious Insanity," p. 224.

8. A. Brigham, *Observations on the Influence of Religion upon the Health and Physical Welfare of Mankind* (Boston: Marsh, Capen & Lyon, 1835), p. 284.

9. R. A. Knox, *Enthusiasm: A Chapter in the History of Religion* (London: Oxford University Press, 1950), pp. 560–61.

10. Ibid.

11. T. Payne, *No Laughing Matter* (Sydney: Matthias Media, 1995).

12. M. Bach, *Strange Sects and Curious Cults* (New York: Dorset Press, 1992).

13. S. Brook, *Maple Leaf Rag* (London: Picador, 1989); the Doukhobor Collection, Electronic Document Centre, Simon Fraser University, Burnaby, British Columbia, online at: edocs.lib.sfu.ca/projects/Doukhobor-Collection.

14. G. Rosen, "Psychopathology in the Social Process: Dance Frenzies, Demonic Possession, Revival Movements and Similar So-Called Psychic Epidemics. An Interpretation," *Bulletin of the History of Medicine* 36 (1962): 35.

15. Ibid., p. 27.

16. Reuters, "Woman Accused of Arson Goes to Court Naked," August 29, 2001.

17. J. Gutman, "Constitutional and Legal Aspects of Deprogramming," in *Deprogramming: Documenting the Issue*, ed. H. W. Richardson (New York: ACLU/Toronto School of Theology, 1977), pp. 208–15.

18. P. Conrad and J. Schneider, *Deviance and Medicalization: From Badness to Sickness* (St. Louis, Mosby, 1980), p. vi.

19. W. S. Tseng and J. F. McDermott Jr., *Culture, Mind and Therapy: An Introduction to Cultural Psychiatry* (New York: Brunner/Mazel, 1981), p. 69; R.A. Faguet and K. F. Faguet, "La folie a deux," in *Extraordinary Disorders of Human Behavior*, ed. C. T. H. Friedmann and R. A. Faguet (New York: Plenum Press, 1982), p. 11; R. B. Ulman and D. W. Abse, "The Group Psychology of Mass Madness: Jonestown," *Political Psychology* 4, no. 4 (1983): 637–61.

20. Ulman and Abse, "Group Psychology."

21. "Collective Suicide," *British Medical Journal* 2 (1896): 1181–82.

22. Ibid., p. 1182.

23. G. Rawlinson, *History of Herodutus* (London: John Murray, 1880), vol. 3, p. 213; H. Yule and A. Burnell, *Hobson-jobson delhi* (Delhi, India: Munshiram Manoharlal, 1968), p. 879; W. Brooke, *The Popular Religion and Folklore of Northern India* (Westminster: Archibald Constable, 1806), p. 185.

24. K. Crosby, J. O. Rhee, and J. Holland, "Suicide by Fire: A Contemporary Method of Political Protest," *International Journal of Social Psychiatry* 23, no. 1 (1977): 65–66.

25. P. Worsley, *The Trumpet Shall Sound: A Study of "Cargo" Cults in Melanesia* (London: MacGibbon & Kee, 1957).

26. N. Cohn, *Pursuit of the Millennium* (Fair Lawn, N.J.: Essential Books, 1957), p. 73.

27. Ibid., p. 127.

28. Ibid.

29. G. Moorhouse, *Against All Reason* (London: Weidenfeld & Nicolson, 1969).

30. R. Cardoza, "The Ordeal of Moharram," *Natural History* 99 (September 1990): 50–57.

31. K. A. Menninger, *Man against Himself* (New York: Harcourt, Brace & World, 1938); Faguet and Faguet, "La folie a deux," p. 16.

32. W. Larson, *Larson's New Book of Cults* (Wheaton, Ill.: Tyndale House Publishers, 1989).

33. P. Berger and T. Luckmann, *The Social Construction of Reality* (New York: Anchor Books, 1967).

34. S. Sighele, *La foule criminelle, essai de psychologie collective,* trans. by P. Vigny (Paris: Felix Alcan, 1892).

35. G. LeBon, *La psychologie des foules* (Paris: Felix Alcan, 1896); G. Tarde, *L'opinion et la foule* (Paris: Felix Alcan, 1901); H. Fournial, *Essai sur la psychologie des foules: considerations medico-judiciaires sur les responsabilites collectives* (Paris: G. Masson, 1892).

36. E. L. Bliss, *Multiple Personality, Allied Disorders, and Hypnosis* (New York: Oxford University Press, 1986), p. 224.

37. C. G. Schmidt, "The Group-Fantasy Origin of AIDS," *Journal of Psychohistory* 12, no. 1 (1984): 37–78.

38. S. Freud, "A Seventeenth-Century Demonological Neurosis," in *Collected Works* (London: Hogarth Press, 1961).

39. J. W. Conner, "Social and Psychological Reality of European Witchcraft Beliefs," *Psychiatry* 38 (1975): 366.

40. Ibid.

41. E. Maple, *Witchcraft: The Story of Man's Search for Supernatural Power* (London: Octopus, 1973), p. 45.

42. N. P. Spanos, "Witchcraft in Histories of Psychiatry: A Critical Analysis and an Alternative Conceptualization," *Psychological Bulletin* 85 (1978): 417–39; T. J. Schoeneman, "The Role of Mental Illness in the European Witch Hunts of the 16th and 17th Centuries: An Assessment," *Journal of the History of the Behavioral Sciences* 13 (1977): 337–51; R. Neugebauer, "Treatment of the Mentally Ill in Medieval and Early Modern England: A Reappraisal," *Journal of the History of the Behavioral Sciences* 14 (1978): 158–69.

43. J. W. Davidson and M. L. Lytle, *After the Fact: The Art of Historical Detection* (New York: McGraw-Hill, 1982).

44. P. Boyer and S. Nissenbaum, *Salem Possessed* (Cambridge, Mass.: Harvard University Press, 1974), pp. xii–xiii.

45. W. Bogoras, *The Jesup North Pacific Expedition*, vol. 2, *The Chukchee* Leiden, 1907), p. 415.

46. J. Silverman, "Shamans and Acute Schizophrenia," *American Anthropologist* 69 (1967): 21–31.

47. R. Heinze, "Who Are the Shamans of the Twentieth Century?" *Association for the Anthropological Study of Consciousness* 4 (1988): 7.

48. T. S. Szasz, *The Myth of Mental Illness* (New York: Harper & Row, 1974).

49. G. Zilboorg, *The Medical Man and the Witch during the Renaissance* (Baltimore: Johns Hopkins University Press, 1935); G. Zilboorg and G. W. Henry, *A History of Medical Psychology* (New York: Norton, 1941). See also T. S. Szasz, *Myth of Mental Illness*, p. 184.

50. R. G. Meyer and P. Salmon, *Abnormal Psychology* (Boston: Allyn and Bacon, 1988), p. 17; M. P. Duke and S. Nowicki, *Abnormal Psychology* (New York: Holt, Rinehart and Winston, 1986), p. 47.

51. T. J. Schoeneman, "The Mentally Ill Witch in Textbooks of Abnormal Psychology: Current Status and Implications of a Fallacy," *Professional Psychology Research and Practice* 15, no. 3 (1984): 299.

52. M. Wolf, "Witchcraft and Mass Hysteria in Terms of Current Psychological Theories," *Journal of Practical Nursing and Mental Health Services* (March 1976): 24.

# 9

# GENITAL-SHRINKING SCARES

At first glance it's one of the world's most bizarre delusions, but upon closer inspection it may reveal just how vulnerable we all are to mass deception.

It sounds like something from a grade-B movie. It might even make the 1978 cult film *Attack of the Killer Tomatoes* seem plausible. I'm referring to scares where communities are swept up in fear that their sex organs are rapidly shrinking. In parts of Asia and the Orient entire regions are occasionally overwhelmed by terror-stricken men who believe that their penises are shriveling up or retracting into their bodies. Those affected often take extreme measures and place clamps or string onto the precious organ or have family members hold the penis in relays until an appropriate treatment is obtained, often from native healers. Occasionally women are affected, believing their breasts or vulva are being sucked into their bodies. Episodes can endure for weeks or months and affect thousands. Psychiatrists are divided as to the cause of these imaginary scares. Some believe that it is a form of group psychosis triggered by stress, while others view it in nonpathological terms as mass hysteria. How can groups of people come to believe that their sex organs are shrinking? We will try to unravel this mystery by briefly describing several genital-shrinking scares, their similarities, and the factors involved in triggering them.

While genitalia shrinking is known by a variety of names in different cultures, psychiatrists refer to it with the generic term *koro*. A Malay word of uncertain derivation, "koro" may have arisen from the Malay word *keruk*, meaning to shrink,[1] although it is more likely a reflection of the Malaysian-Indonesian words for "tortoise" (*kura, kura-kura,* and *kuro*). In these countries, the penis, especially the glans or tip, is commonly referred to as a tortoise head. This led Dutch scientist P. M. Van Wulfften-Palthe to conclude that this is how the modern term *koro* most likely arose: "The fact that a tortoise can withdraw its head with its wrinkled neck under its shell literally into its body, suggested . . . the mechanism . . . in 'Koro' ('kura') and gave it its name."[2]

The first well-documented outbreak in modern times of genitalia shrinking occurred in October and November 1967, when hospitals on the tiny Southeast Asian island nation of Singapore were inundated by frantic citizens who were convinced that their penises were shrinking and would eventually disappear, at which time, many believed, death would result. "Victims" used everything from rubber bands to clothes pins in desperate efforts to prevent further perceived retraction. These methods occasionally resulted in severe organ damage and some pretty sore penises. At the height of the scare the Singapore hospital treated about seventy-five cases in a single day. The episode occurred amid rumors that eating pork vaccinated for swine fever prior to slaughter could trigger genitalia shrinkage. One erroneous report even claimed that a pig dropped dead immediately after inoculation when its penis suddenly retracted!

The panic abruptly ended when the Singapore Medical Association and Health Ministry held public news conferences to dispel fears. Writing in the prestigious *British Journal of Psychiatry*, Singaporian doctor C. I. Mun described two typical cases. In one, a pale sixteen-year-old boy rushed into the clinic clutching his penis and accompanied by his parents. After providing reassurance and a sedative, there was no recurrence. The frightened boy said that he had heard the rumors of contaminated pork at school, had eaten pork that morning, and upon urinating, his penis appeared to have shrunk. At that point he hung on for all he was worth and shouted for help. In a second case, a mother dashed into the clinic clutching the penis of her four-month-old baby and frantically asking help. Dr. Mun said that "The child had not been well for two days with cold and a little diarrhoea. The mother was changing his napkin . . . when the child had colic and screamed. The mother saw the penis getting smaller and the child screamed and [she] thought he had koro. She had previously heard the rumours. The mother was first reassured, and the baby's cold and diarrhoea treated. The child was all right after that."[3]

Most Singaporeans are of Chinese origin, and on the Chinese mainland there is a common belief in the reality of shrinking genitalia. Chinese medical texts from the nineteenth century even describe such cases as caused by an actual disease. Pao Sian-Ow's book, *New Collection of Remedies of Value*, published in 1834, states that episodes occur when "the penis retracts into the abdomen. If treatment is not instituted at once and effective, the case [patient] will die. The disease is due to the invasion of cold vapors and the treatment is to employ the 'heaty' drugs."[4]

At least 5,000 inhabitants in a remote area of southern Guangdong province, China, were affected by a genital-shrinking panic between August 1984 and the summer of 1985.[5] Male residents of the region are reared to practice restraint in matters of sexual desire and activity, as excessive semen discharge is believed to cause poor physical and mental health, even death. If that wasn't enough to worry about, many residents believe that certain spirits of the dead, especially female fox maidens, wander in search of penises that will give them powers. Each of the 232 "victims" surveyed by University of Hawaii psychiatrist Wen-Shing Tseng and his colleagues were convinced that an evil female fox spirit was the culprit, while 76 percent of those affected had witnessed others being "rescued." Most of these cases occurred at night following a chilly sensation which would appear before a feeling of penile shrinkage. Tseng and his researchers reported: "Thinking this [chill] to be a fatal sign and believing that they were affected by an evil ghost, they [the *koro* "victims"] became panic stricken and tried to pull at their penises, while, at the same time, shouting for help."[6] Interestingly, several children reported shrinkage of their tongue, nose, and ears, reflecting the prevalent ancient Chinese belief that any male (yang) organs can shrink or retract. Tseng investigated a separate episode in 1987, affecting at least 300 residents on the Leizhou Peninsula of Guangdong province. Genital shrinking is well known in southern China, with genital-shrinking panics recorded in 1865, 1948, 1955, 1966, and 1974, all involving at least several hundred residents.[7]

Dr. Tseng has sought to determine why episodes repeatedly occur in the vicinity of Leizhou Peninsula and Hainan Island, but have never spread to the principal section of Guangdong province or other parts of China, and why is it that only certain residents in a region report *koro*. A survey showed that those affected held the more intense *koro*-related folk beliefs relative to a control group from the adjacent nonaffected area,[8] helping to explain "why each time the koro epidemic spread from the Peninsula, it would cease when it reached the urban area of Guangzhou, where the people are more educated and hold less belief in koro." While recognizing the importance of rumors and traditional beliefs in precipitating episodes, Tseng considers *koro* outbreaks in southern China to be a psychiatric disorder ("genital retraction panic disorder") which primarily affects susceptible individuals, such as the poorly educated and those possessing below normal intelligence who are experiencing social crisis or tension.[9]

Another *koro* episode occurred in northeast Thailand between November and December 1976, affecting about 2,000 people, primarily rural Thai residents in the border provinces of Maha Sarakham, Nakhon Phanom, Nong Khai, and Udon Thani. Symptoms included the perception of genitalia shrinkage and impotence among males, while females typically reported sexual frigidity with breast and vulva shrinkage. Other symptoms were panic, anxiety, dizziness, diarrhea, discomfort during urination, nausea, headaches, facial numbness, and abdominal pain. Some patients temporarily lost consciousness, and many were fearful of imminent death. Of 350 subjects studied in detail, irrespective of whether they sought treatment from native healers or physicians, "most patients had recovered within one day and all within one week."[10]

The episode began at a technical college in Udon Thani province, with rumors that Vietnamese immigrants had deliberately contaminated food and cigarettes with a *koro*-inducing powder. During this time, there was a strong anti-Vietnamese sentiment throughout Thailand in conjunction with communist victories in Southeast Asia in 1975, the growing influence of the Communist party of Thailand, and the perceived control of Cambodia and Laos by the Vietnamese. Anti-Vietnamese sentiments in the region were especially strong in the month before the episode,[11] with allegations by Thailand's Interior Minister that there was "solid evidence" of a plot whereby "Vietnamese refugees would incite rioting in northeast Thailand, providing Vietnam with an excuse to invade" on February 15.[12] As the episode continued, the poisoning rumors became self-fulfilling as numerous Thai citizens recalled that previously consumed food and cigarettes recently purchased from Vietnamese establishments had an unusual smell and taste. However, an analysis of suspected sources by the Government Medical Science Department "detected no foreign substance that could possibly cause sexual impotence or contraction of the male sex organ."[13]

*Koro* rumors, combined with preexisting awareness of the "disease," served to foster and legitimate its plausible existence. Sangun Suwanlert and D. Coats found that 94 percent of "victims" studied "were convinced that they had been poisoned."[14] Negative government analysis of alleged tainted substances was undermined by contradictory statements by authority figures in the press. Security officials attributed the tainting substances believed responsible for causing the *koro* in food to a mixture of vegetable sources undetectable by medical devices.[15]

Another outbreak occurred in northeastern India from July to September 1982. Cases numbered in the thousands, as many males believed their penises and testicles were retracting while women felt their breasts "going in." Indian psychiatrist Ajita Chakraborty said the panic reached such proportions that medical personnel toured the region, reassuring with loudspeakers those affected.[16] Some parents tied string to their sons' penises to reduce or stop retraction, a practice that occasionally produced penile ulcers. Authorities even went to the extent of measuring penises at intervals to allay fears. A popular local remedy was drinking lime juice and also to have the "victim" tightly grasp the affected body part while being dowsed with buckets of cold water.[17] While there was evidence of preexisting *koro*-related beliefs among some residents, the episode spread across various religious and ethnic groups, social castes, and geographical areas by way of rumors. Based on interviews with thirty "victims," investigating physicians were unable to identify obvious signs of psychological disturbance.[18]

# MAGICAL GENITALIA LOSS IN AFRICA

If *koro* panics now top your list of the most bizarre human delusions, after reading this section you may have to juggle your list. In parts of Africa, there is an even stranger behavior—*vanishing* genitalia! "Magical" genitalia loss in Nigeria has also been interpreted as an exotic, unambiguous example of isolated individual mental disturbance. The influence of socio-cultural context is evident in collective episodes of magical genitalia loss in Nigeria that have been reported for at least twenty years. While working at a teaching hospital in Kaduna, northern Nigeria, in 1975, psychiatrist Sunny Ilechukwu writes in the *Transcultural Psychiatric Research Review* that he was approached by a police officer who was accompanied by two men. One of the men made the startling claim that the other had caused his penis to vanish; the officer, acting on orders from his superior, was to obtain a medical report to settle the dispute. The patient explained that he was walking along a street and "felt his penis go" after the robes worn by the other man had touched him. Incredulous, Ilechukwu initially refused to handle the case, but later agreed to conduct a physical exam, which transpired in full view of the concerned parties. The patient stood and stared straight ahead until it was announced that his genitals were normal. Reacting in disbelief, the patient glanced down at his genitals and suggested that they had just reappeared! The policeman then indicated that charges would be filed against the man for falsely reporting an incident.[19]

This may appear to be a clear case of isolated individual mental disturbance, as it is beyond Western credulity that people could believe that entire body parts were missing when clearly they were not. Yet, Ilechukwu reports on "epidemics" of temporary magical penis loss in Nigeria during the mid-1970s, and again in 1990. A major Nigerian episode of "vanishing" genitalia in 1990, affected mainly men, but sometimes women, while they were walking in public places. Accusations were typically triggered by incidental body contact with a stranger that was interpreted as intentionally contrived, followed by unusual sensations within the scrotum. The affected person would then physically grab his genitals to confirm that all or parts were missing, after which he would shout a phrase such as "Thief! My genitals are gone!"[20] The "victim" would then completely disrobe to convince quickly gathering crowds of bystanders that his penis was actually missing. The accused was threatened and usually beaten (sometimes fatally) until the genitals were "returned." While some "victims" soon realized that their genitalia were intact, "many then claimed that they were 'returned' at the time they raised the alarm or that, although the penis had been 'returned,' it was shrunken and so probably a 'wrong' one or just the ghost of a penis."[21] In such instances, the assault or lynching would usually continue until the "original, real" penis reappeared.

Ilechukwu reports that incidents quickly spread like wildfire across the country. "Men could be seen in the streets of Lagos holding on to their genitalia either openly or discreetly with their hands in their pockets. Women were also seen holding on to their breasts directly or discreetly by crossing the hands across the chest. It was thought that inattention and a weak will facilitated the 'taking' of the penis or breasts. Vigilance and anticipatory aggression were thought to be good prophylaxis."[22]

The role of socio-cultural traditions in triggering episodes is evident, as many Nigerian ethnic groups "ascribe high potency to the external genitalia as ritual and magical objects to promote fecundity or material prosperity to the unscrupulous. Ritually murdered persons are often said to have these parts missing."[23] The reality of vanishing genitalia is institutionalized to such an extent that during the 1990 episode, several influential Nigerians, including a court judge, protested vehemently when police released suspected genital thieves, and many knowledgeable citizens "claimed that there was a real—even if magical—basis for the incidents."[24] One Christian priest supported cultural beliefs in genital theft by citing a biblical passage where Christ asked "Who touched me?" because the "power had gone out of him," claiming that it was a reference to genital stealing.[25] Ilechukwu concludes that socio-cultural beliefs related to magical genitalia loss in Nigeria render sexually maladjusted individuals susceptible to "attacks."

## UNRAVELLING THE MYSTERY

There have been a few sporadic reports of individual penis-shrinking occurring in widely separated cultural settings, but there is little doubt that most of these people are seriously disturbed. Common themes among victims include preoccupations with masturbation and nocturnal emissions, perceived sexual inadequacies or excesses, and ignorance, sexual inexperience, or insufficient confidence in sexual relationships. These factors may be reinforced by social and cultural beliefs about sexuality. Unlike "epidemics," individual cases can persist for months or years in people with obvious psycho-sexual problems and psychiatric disturbance. Psychiatrist R. A. Emsley describes the case of a man who became mentally traumatized and developed a great fear of impotence after being unwillingly circumcised in a tribal ritual. He then failed to get an erection while trying to have sex—at which point he could feel his penis shrinking.[26] Many disturbed men who believe their penis is shrinking suffer from schizophrenia, a condition where overvalued notions or delusions regarding damaged or impaired sexual organs can occur.[27] In one case recorded by psychiatrists Edward Kendall and Peter Jenkins while they were working in a Columbia, South Carolina, hospital, a thirty-five-year-old schizophrenic man was hospitalized after experiencing delusions of having "the largest penis in the world." A few days later, he tied cloth around his penis to prevent retraction, believing he was changing into a woman![28]

Large-scale genitalia-shrinking episodes are typified by the symptoms of anxiety persisting for a few minutes to several days and those affected *always* experience a complete "recovery" upon being convinced they are no longer in danger. Isolated singular cases experience more severe symptoms and may never recover. For instance, British psychiatrist Anne Cremona treated a man who at age eighteen was unable to get an erection while attempting intercourse on three different occasions. He came to believe that his penis was abnormal and experienced great anxiety, violence, drug abuse, began hearing voices, and became a hypochondriac. In 1977 at age twenty-one, while walking down the street, he suddenly felt his penis shrink half an inch, and after two years of such delusions, Dr. Cremona reported that his *koro* symptoms were "as frequent and distressing as ever" and were unresponsive to drug treatment.[29] In another case, an Englishman with *koro* was afraid to urinate in public, fearing that friends might spot him being "unable to find his penis when using a urinal" and tease him. His symptoms persisted for twenty years but disappeared after he received psychotherapy and drugs.[30] With cases like these on record, it's no wonder that some psychiatrists have assumed

that epidemic *koro* is also triggered by similar psychological disturbances. Yet a closer look at mass outbreaks reveals that they result from
an entirely different process.[31]

The few isolated, individual cases often take years to recover, and do
so only after the underlying sexual problems are addressed. Drug treatment can also sometimes be helpful. "Victims" of genitalia-shrinking
panics recover within hours or days after being convinced that the "illness" is over or never existed, and most clearly lack any psychosexual
problems. Episodes also share similar symptoms: anxiety, sweating,
nausea, headache, transient pain, pale skin, palpitations, blurred vision,
faintness, insomnia, and a false belief that body parts are shrinking. These
symptoms are normal body responses to extreme fear. The penis, scrotum,
breasts, and nipples are the most physiologically plastic external body
parts, regularly changing size and shape in response to various stimuli
ranging from sexual arousal to temperature changes. Studies also reveal
that stress, depression, illness, and urination can cause small but discernible penis shrinkage.[32] Another key factor is the nature of human perception, which is notoriously unreliable.[33] Perception is also precondi-
tioned by a person's mental outlook and their social and cultural reference
system. In each of the countries reporting epidemic *koro*, there were preexisting beliefs that genitalia could shrivel up under certain circumstances.

Far from exemplifying group psychosis, disorder, or irrationality,
penis-shrinking panics are a timely reminder that no one is immune from
mass delusions and that the influence of culture and society on individual
behavior is far greater than most of us would like to admit. This is a valuable lesson to remember at the dawn of a new millennium. It is all too
easy to think of past or non-Western delusions with a wry smile as if we
are somehow now immune or that those involved were naive and gullible.
Yet, the main reason for the absence of penis-shrinking epidemics in
Western societies is their incredible nature. It is simply too fantastic to
believe. But any delusion is possible if the false belief underlying it is
plausible. So while we may laugh at the poor "misguided" Indian or Chinese for believing in penis and breast-shrinking panics, we are haunted by
our own unique delusions: crashed saucers, alien abductors, and CIA
coverups of just about everything.

Until recently, the psychiatric community viewed genital-shrinking
scares along the lines of anorexia, as a body image disorder. In this case,

various parts of the body related to sexuality—the breasts and vulva in females, the penis and scrotum in males—become the focus of undue scrutiny. According to this view, certain people become preoccupied with the size of their sex organs and body parts, leading to a distortion in their perception of themselves. Only recently has this paradigm begun to shift by viewing evidence in a new light, through the lens of the "victims." Robert Bartholomew has been at the forefront of this shift, noting that large-scale "genitalia-shrinking" outbreaks are *always* temporary, affecting people with folk beliefs of their reality. In each episode, the symptoms simply mimic anxiety and persist for no more than a few days—at which point they make a complete "recovery" once they are convinced they are no longer in danger. This becomes obvious after several days as their genitals clearly have not shriveled away or retracted out of sight! In each of the countries reporting epidemics, there were preexisting beliefs that genitalia could shrivel up under certain conditions. The evidence for genital-shrinking scares simply resulting from local folk beliefs and anxiety has always been there, but it was through asking questions and exploring preexisting biases that the "disorder" was understood.

# REVIEW QUESTIONS

1. What is it about the people affected by genital-shrinking scares that renders them susceptible?
2. How should we regard those involved in genital-shrinking scares: as ignorant, irrational, or normal?
3. What is the difference between isolated individual cases of men who report that their genitals are shrinking and group outbreaks?
4. Assuming that genital-shrinking scares occur to normal people and result from beliefs that foster extreme anxiety about one's genitals, how have scientists been so wrong for so long about episodes, in that most psychiatric texts continue to carry definitions of genital-shrinking outbreaks in terms of psychological disturbance?
5. What factors contribute to vanishing genitalia scares in Africa?

# NOTES

1. A. L. Gwee, "Koro—It's Origin and Nature as a Disease Entity," *Singapore Medical Journal* 9, no. 1 (1968): 3.

2. P. M. Van Wulfften-Palthe, "Psychiatry and Neurology in the Tropics," in *Clinical Textbook of Tropical Medicine*, ed. C. de Langen and A. Lichtenstein (Batavia: G. Kolff and Company, 1936), p. 536.

3. C. I. Mun, "Epidemic Koro in Singapore," *British Medical Journal* 1 (March 9, 1968): 640–41.

4. Pao Sian-Ow, "New Collection of Remedies of Value, cited in A. L. Gwee, "Koro—A Cultural Disease," *Singapore Medical Journal* 4 (1963): 120.

5. W. G. Jilek, "Epidemics of 'Genital Shrinking' (Koro): Historical Review and Report of a Recent Outbreak in Southern China," *Curare* 9 (1986): 273.

6. W. S. Tseng et al., "A Sociocultural Study of Koro Epidemics in Guangdong, China," *American Journal of Psychiatry* 145, no. 12 (1988): 1540.

7. R. E. Bartholomew, "The Medicalization of Exotic Deviance: A Sociological Perspective on Epidemic Koro," *Transcultural Psychiatry* 35, no. 1 (1998): 5–38.

8. W. S. Tseng et al., "Koro Epidemics in Guangdong, China: A Questionnaire Survey," *Journal of Nervous and Mental Disease* 180, no. 2 (1992): 122.

9. Tseng et al., "Sociocultural Study," p. 1542; Tseng et al., "Koro Epidemics," p. 117.

10. S. Suwanlert and D. Coates, "Epidemic Koro in Thailand—Clinical and Social Aspects," abstract of the report by F. R. Fenton appearing in *Transcultural Psychiatric Research Review* 16 (1979): 65.

11. D. Andelman, "Thai Junta Re-Examines Relations with Neighbor Nations and U.S.," *New York Times*, October 18, 1976; D. Andelman, "Vietnam Accuses Thai Regime and Demands That It Free 800," *New York Times*, October 28, 1976, p. 30.

12. D. Andelman, "Campaign Grows against Vietnamese in Thailand Region," *New York Times*, December 12, 1976, p. 3.

13. W. G. Jilek and L. Jilek-Aall, "A Koro Epidemic in Thailand," *Transcultural Psychiatric Research Review* 14 (1977): 58.

14. Suwanlert and Coates, "Epidemic Koro," p. 65.

15. Jilek and Jilek, "A Koro Epidemic in Thailand," p. 58.

16. A. Chakraborty, S. Das, and A. Mukherji, "Koro Epidemic in India," *Transcultural Psychiatric Research Review* 20 (1983): 150–51.

17. P. S. Sachdev and A. Shukla, "Epidemic Koro Syndrome in India," *Lancet* 2 (1982): 1161.

18. Ibid.

19. S. T. C. Ilechukwu, "Letter from S. T. C. Ilechukwu, M.D. (Lagos, Nigeria) which Describes Interesting Koro-Like Syndromes in Nigeria," *Transcultural Psychiatric Research Review* 25 (1988): 310–14.

20. S. T. C. Ilechukwu, "Magical Penis Loss in Nigeria: Report of a Recent Epidemic of a Koro-Like Syndrome," *Transcultural Psychiatric Research Review* 29 (1992): 95.

21. Ibid., p. 95.

22. Ibid., p. 96.

23. Ilechukwu, "Letter from S. T. C. Ilechukwu," p. 313.

24. Ilechukwu, "Magical Penis Loss," pp. 96–97.

25. Ibid., pp. 101–102.

26. R. A. Emsley, "Koro in Non-Chinese Subject," *British Journal of Psychiatry* 146 (1985): 102.

27. G. S. Devan and O. S. Hong, "Koro and Schizophrenia in Singapore," *British Journal of Psychiatry* 150 (1987): 106–107; J. G. Edwards, "The Koro Pattern of Depersonalization in an American Schizophrenic Patient," *American Journal of Psychiatry* 126, no. 8 (1970): 1171–73; N. L. Gittelson and S. Levine, "Subjective Ideas of Sexual Change in Male Schizophrenics," *British Journal of Psychiatry* 112 (1966): 1171–73.

28. E. M. Kendall and P. L. Jenkins, "Koro in an American Man," *American Journal of Psychiatry* 144, no. 12 (1987): 1621.

29. A. Cremona, "Another Case of Koro in a Briton," *British Journal of Psychiatry* 138 (1981): 180.

30. G. E. Berrois and S. J. Morley, "Koro-Like Symptoms in a Non-Chinese Subject," *British Journal of Psychiatry* 145 (1984): 331–34.

31. Bartholomew, "Medicalization of Exotic Deviance"; R. E. Bartholomew, "The Social Psychology of 'Epidemic' Koro," *International Journal of Social Psychiatry* 40, no. 1 (1994): 46–60.

32. M. E. Thase, C. F. Reynolds, and J. R. Jennings, "Nocturnal Penile Tumescence Is Diminished in Depressed Men," *Biological Psychiatry* 24 (1988): 33–46; F. Oyebode, M. J. Jamieson, and K. Davison, "Koro—A Psychophysiological Dysfunction," *British Journal of Psychiatry* 148 (1986): 212–14.

33. D. F. Ross, J. D. Read, and M. P. Toglia, *Adult Eyewitness Testimony: Current Trends and Developments* (Cambridge: Cambridge University Press, 1994).

# PART 4

# THE
# HISTORICAL
# PICTURE

# 10

# THE DANCING MANIA OF THE MIDDLE AGES

While medieval dance frenzies have long been regarded as a classic example of stress-induced mental disorder affecting mostly women, there is much evidence to the contrary.

Pick up a textbook on abnormal psychology and in the first chapter you are likely to find a discussion of dance manias. The manias (also known as St. Vitus dance) swept across Europe between the eleventh and seventeenth centuries, as tens of thousands of people participated in frenzied public orgies and wild dances lasting for days and sometimes weeks. It is little wonder why psychiatrists and medical historians typify episodes as group mental disorder affecting those overwhelmed by the stresses of the period. During outbreaks many immodestly tore off their clothing and pranced naked through the streets. Some screamed and beckoned to be tossed into the air; others danced furiously in what observers described as strange, colorful attire. A few reportedly laughed or wept to the point of death. Some women howled and made obscene gestures while others squealed like animals. Some rolled themselves in the dirt or relished being struck on the soles of their feet. An Italian variant was known as tarantism, as victims were believed to have been bitten by the tarantula spider, for which the only cure was thought to be frenetic dancing to certain music which supposedly dissipated the "poison" from the victim's blood.[1]

The term "dancing mania" is derived from the Greek word *choros*, a dance, and *mania*, madness. The literal translation of *choros mania* is dancing madness. The name was adopted after a group of about 200 people danced so spiritedly on a bridge above the Maas River in Germany during 1278 that it collapsed, killing many participants. Survivors were treated in a nearby chapel dedicated to St. Vitus, and many were reportedly restored to full health. Prior to the twentieth century the condition was commonly referred to as epidemic chorea or choreomania. The word "chorea" was erroneously evoked to describe these behaviors as participants were often thought to be exhibiting symptoms of chorea, a central nervous system disorder characterized by brief irregular jerking movements which can resemble dancing.

The terms "tarantism" and "dancing mania" are often used interchangeably as they share overlapping features. Tarantism was mainly confined to southern Italy. Historian Harold Gloyne describes it as the "mass hysterical reaction" to perceived bites of the tarantula spider, as previously mentioned.[2] The first recorded episodes appeared during the thirteenth century and persisted on a widespread scale in southern Europe for 400 years, reaching its height in the seventeenth century, after which it virtually disappeared. Small annual episodes have persisted in southern Italy well into the twentieth century. Researcher Hans Schadewaldt investigated an outbreak in Wardo during 1957.[3] Italian religious history professor Ernesto de Martino identifies thirty-five cases of tarantism near Galatina in 1959.[4] De Martino conducted his survey between June 28 and 30, as June 29 is the festival day of St. Peter and St. Paul. On that day it is customary for the "victims" to travel from regional villages to the chapel of St. Paul to obtain a cure for various ailments.[5] More recently, tarantism has been observed near Sardinia, Italy.[6]

Medieval tarantism was reported almost exclusively during the height of the hot, dry summer months of July and August:

People, asleep or awake, would suddenly jump up, feeling an acute pain like the sting of a bee. Some saw the spider, others did not, but they knew that it must be the tarantula. They ran out of the house into the street, to the market place dancing in great excitement. Soon they were joined by others who like them had just been bitten, or by people who had been stung in previous years, for the disease was never quite cured. The poison remained in the body and was reactivated every year by the heat of summer. . . .

. . . Music and dancing were the only effective remedies, and people were known to have died within an hour or in a few days because music was not available.[7]

Symptoms included headache, giddiness, breathlessness, fainting, trembling, twitching, appetite loss, general soreness, and delusions. Sometimes it was claimed that a sore or swelling was caused by a tarantula bite, but such assertions were difficult to verify as the bite resembled those of other insects. The dance frenzy symptoms resemble typical modern episodes of epidemic hysteria, in addition to expected reactions from exhaustive physical activity and excessive alcohol consumption.

Psychiatrists classify tarantism as a form of epidemic hysteria due to its psychological character and claims that most of those affected were females.[8] Early medical observers theorized that a venomous species of tarantula found only near the Italian state of Apulia was capable of producing sporadic tarantism symptoms each summer, but tests on spiders of the region have failed to substantiate these suspicions.[9] *Latrodectus tarantula* is a nonaggressive, slow-moving spider common in Apulia that can produce psychoactive effects in people it bites, triggering hallucinations. In severe cases, it may temporarily mimic many tarantism symptoms, including twitching and shaking of limbs, weakness, nausea, and muscular pain.[10] Ironically, *Lycosa tarantula* was typically blamed for tarantism symptoms, as it is larger, more aggressive, ferocious in appearance and has a painful bite. Yet neither spider can account for the predominantly symbolic and psychogenic character of tarantism attacks. *Latrodectus tarantula* is also found in other countries where tarantism does not occur, including the United States.[11] There is no evidence that a venomous species of tarantula, native only to Apulia, may have existed during this period and later died out. As historian Henry Sigerist remarks:

"The same tarantula shipped to other parts of the country seemed to lose most of its venom, and what remained acted differently."[12] It is also doubtful that some other insect or agent was responsible for causing "attacks," as most participants did not even claim to have been bitten, and would only participate in tarantism at designated times.

Clearly most cases were unrelated to spider bites. Other psychological aspects include the only reliable cure: dancing to certain types of music. "Victims" would typically perform one of numerous versions of the tarantella, a rapid tempo score characterized by brief, repetitive phrases which mount in intensity. Such performances also allowed "victims" to exhibit social behavior that is prohibited during any other time. Dancing persisted intermittently for hours and days, and sometimes weeks. Participants would eventually proclaim themselves "cured" for the remainder of the summer, only to relapse in subsequent summers. Many "victims" never claimed to have been bitten, but were believed to have been infected from those who had, or from simply brushing against a spider. In those who had received bites, all that was needed to "reactivate" the venom was to hear the strains of certain music being played to cure those who had recently been bitten.

## DANCING MANIAS

A variation of tarantism spread throughout much of Europe between the thirteenth and seventeenth centuries, where it was known as the dancing mania or St. Vitus dance, on account that participants often ended their processions in the vicinity of chapels and shrines dedicated to this saint. Like its Italian counterpart, outbreaks seized groups of people who engaged in frenzied dancing which lasted intermittently for days or weeks. Social scientists typify "victims" as females who were maladjusted, deviant, irrational, or mentally disturbed. These activities were typically accompanied by symptoms similar to tarantism, including screaming, hallucinations, convulsive movements, chest pains, hyperventilation, crude sexual gestures, and outright intercourse. Instead of spider bites, participants usually claimed that they were possessed by demons who had induced an uncontrollable urge to dance. Like tarantism, however, music was typically played during episodes and was considered to be an effective remedy. Detailed accounts of many episodes appear in a classic book by German physician Justus Hecker, *Epidemics of the Middle Ages*, published in 1844. He considered the origin of these "epidemics" as due to "morbid sympathy" since they often coincided with periods of severe disease, such as widespread pessimism and despair that occurred after the Black Death.[13] This epic plague, which by some estimates killed half of the population of Europe, subsided about twenty years prior to 1374, the year that most scholars identify with the onset of the dance mania. Benjamin Gordon, in *Medieval and Renaissance Medicine* describes the onset of the dance mania this way:

> From Italy it spread to . . . Prussia, and one morning, without warning, the streets were filled. . . . They danced together, ceaselessly, for hours or days, and in wild delirium, the dancers collapsed and fell to the ground exhausted, groaning and sighing as if in the agonies of death. When recuperated, they swathed themselves tightly with cloth around their waists and resumed their convulsive movements. They contorted their bodies, writhing, screaming and jumping in a mad frenzy. One by one they fell from exhaustion. . . .
> . . . Many later claimed that they had seen the walls of heaven split open and that Jesus and the Virgin Mary had appeared before them.[14]

As with tarantism, dance manias are considered to have occurred spontaneously, with participants, largely confined to mentally disturbed females, unable to control their actions. Influential New York University psychiatrists Harold Kaplan and Benjamin Sadock state that the victims represent "collective mental disorder"; psychologist Robert Carson and associates view St. Vitus dance and tarantism as collective hysterical disorders; while abnormal psychologist Ronald Comer of Princeton University uses the term "mass madness."[15]

Let us examine these claims based on several dozen period chronicles translated by E. Louis Backman in his seminal study of religious dances.[16] Few if any textbooks on psychiatry and abnormal psychology of today cite these early chronicles. Instead they rely on a handful of often-cited influential medical historians of the early twentieth century, and use their assessments and well-worn quotations. Medical historians such as Henry Sigerist, George Mora, and George Rosen were giants in their field and astute enough to acknowledge Greek or Roman ritualistic elements in the dance manias, but each assumes that the participants used these rites to work themselves into frenzied states of physical and mental disturbance in order to experience cathartic reactions to intolerable social conditions. They also assume that most participants were hysterics.

George Mora writes that tarantism and dance manias used rituals as psychotherapeutic attempts to cope with either individual or societal mal-adjustments which fostered mental disturbances.[17] Sigerist held a similar view. An abnormal psychology text written by Robert Carson of Duke University and his colleagues cites Sigerist to support the view that Saint Vitus' dance and tarantism were similar to ancient Greek orgiastic rites which had been outlawed by Christian authorities but were secretly practiced anyway. The authors assume that these "secret gatherings . . . probably led to considerable guilt and conflict," which triggered collective hysterical disorders.[18] Dance frenzies appeared most often during periods of crop failures, famine, epidemics, and social upheaval, leading historian George Rosen to conclude that this stress triggered widespread hysteria.[19] Yet these same disasters prompted attempts at divine intervention through ritualized dancing, and often produced trance and possession states. Consistent with this latter view, many symptoms associated with tarantism and dancing mania are consistent with sleep deprivation, excessive alcohol consumption, emotional excitement, and vigorous, prolonged physical activity. A German chronicle reports that during a dance frenzy at Strasbourg in 1418, "many of them [the participants] went without food for days and nights."[20]

The European "dancing manias" and its Italian variant tarantism are portrayed within the psychiatric literature as spontaneous, stress-induced outbursts of psychological disturbance that primarily affected females. This depiction is based on the selective use of period quotations by medical historians such as George Rosen and Henry Sigerist, who were reflecting popular stereotypes of female susceptibility to mental disorders. However, based on a series of translations of medieval European chronicles describing these events, many firsthand, and by scrutinizing other historical sources which provide a degree of social, cultural, historical, and political perspective, it is evident that contemporary depictions of "dancing manias" have been misrepresented. Contrary to popular psychiatric portrayals, females were not over-represented among participants, episodes were not spontaneous but highly structured, and involved unfamiliar religious sects engaging in strange or unfamiliar customs that were redefined as a behavioral abnormality.[21] Let us examine the evidence.

# FALLACY #1:
# MOST "DANCERS" WERE CRAZY

Period chronicles reveal that most participants did not reside in the municipalities where the frenzies occurred, but hailed from other regions, traveling through communities as they sought out shrines and churchyards to perform in. As foreigners, they would naturally have had unfamiliar customs. The largest and best documented dance plague, that of 1374 involving throngs of "dancers" in Germany and Holland, were "pilgrims" who traveled, "according to Beka's chronicle, from Bohemia, but also from Hungary, Poland, Carinthia, Austria, and Germany. Great hosts from the Netherlands and France joined them."[22]

The behavior of these dancers was described as strange, because while exhibiting actions that were part of the Christian tradition, and paying homage to Jesus, Mary, and various saints at chapels and shrines, other elements were foreign. Radulphus de Rivo's chronicle *Decani Tongrensis* states that "in their songs they uttered the names of devils never before heard of . . . this strange sect." Petrus de Herenthal writes in *Vita Gregorii XI*: "There came to Aachen . . . a curious sect." The *Chronicon Belgicum Magnum* describes the participants as "a sect of dancers." The actions of dancers were often depicted as immoral as there was much uninhibited sexual intercourse. The chronicle of C. Browerus (*Abtiquitatum et Annalium Trevirensium*) states: "They indulged in disgraceful immodesty, for many women, during this shameless dance and mock-bridal singing, bared their bosoms, while others of their own accord offered their virtue." *A Chronicle of Early Roman Kings and Emperors* states that a number of participants engaged in "loose living with the women and young girls who shamelessly wandered about in remote places under the cover of night." If most of the participants were pilgrims of Bohemian and Czech origin as Backman asserts, the behavior was not uncharacteristic for them, as during this period Czechs and Bohemians were noted for a high incidence of perceived immorality, especially sexual, including prostitution and annual festivals involving the free partaking of sex.[23]

# FALLACY #2: THERE WAS A SPONTANEOUS, UNCONTROLLABLE URGE TO DANCE

Period chronicles reveal that dance manias mainly comprised pilgrims engaging in emotionally charged, highly structured displays of worship that occasionally attracted locals. This social patterning is evident in a firsthand account on September 11, 1374, by Jean d'Outremeuse in his chronicle *La Geste de Liege*, which states that "there came from the north to Liege . . . a company of persons who all danced continually. They were linked with clothes, and they jumped and leaped. . . . They called loudly on Saint John the Baptist and fiercely clapped their hands." Slichtenhorst, in describing the dance frenzy of 1375 and 1376 in France, Germany, and Gelderland (now southwestern Holland), notes that participants "went in couples, and with every couple was another single person . . . they danced, leaped and sang, and embraced each other in friendly fashion."[24]

A similar pattern is evident in tarantism. While *taranti* (as victims were known) are typically described as participating in uncontrollable behaviors in chaotic, frenzied throngs, like modern-day ecstatic religious sects, adherents worshipped in a set pattern. Australian medical historian and tarantism expert Jean Russell states that *taranti* would typically commence dancing at sunrise, stop during midday to sleep and sweat, then bathe before the resumption of dancing until evening, when they would again sleep and sweat, consume a light meal, then sleep until sunrise. This ritual was usually repeated over four or five days, and sometimes for weeks.[25]

Clearly tarantism episodes were not spontaneous, and the same is true of dance manias. German magistrates even contracted musicians to play for participants and serve as dancing companions. The latter was intended to reduce injuries and mischief during the procession to the Saint Vitus chapel.[26] Hecker states that the dancing mania was a "half-heathen, half-christian festival" which incorporated into the festival of Saint John's day as early as the fourth century "the kindling of the 'Nodfyr,' which was forbidden them by Saint Boniface."[27] This ritual involved the leaping through smoke or flames, which was believed to protect participants from various diseases over the ensuing year. A central feature of the dance frenzy was leaping or jumping continuously for up to several hours through what participants claimed were invisible fires, until exhaustion caused collapse.

Not only were episodes scripted, but dance processions were swollen by spectators, including children searching for parents who were among the dancers, and vice versa.[28] Some onlookers were threatened with harm for refusing to dance.[29] Many took part out of loneliness and carnal pleasures; others were curious or sought exhilaration.[30] Hecker remarks that "numerous beggars, stimulated by vice and misery, availed themselves of this new complaint to gain a temporary livelihood," while gangs of vagabonds imitated the dance, roving "from place to place seeking maintenance and adventures."[31] Similar observations have been noted of tarantism episodes.

## FALLACY #3: MOST "DANCERS" WERE HYSTERICAL FEMALES

A revisiting of the descriptions of dancing manias based on early chronicles of these events shows that both men and women were equally affected. Where the gender of the participants was noted, the following comments are representative: Petrus de Herenthal's chronicle *Vita Gregorii XI* remarks that "Persons of both sexes . . . danced"; Radulpho de Rivo's *Decani Tongrensis* states, "persons of both sexes, possessed by devils and half naked, set wreathes on their heads, and began their dances"; Johannes de Beka's *Canonicus Ultrajectinus et Heda, Wilhelmus, Praepositus Arnhemensis: De Episcopis Ultraiectinis, Recogniti*, states that in 1385, "there spread along the Rhine . . . a strange plague . . . whereby persons of both sexes, in great crowds . . . danced and sang, both inside and outside of churches, till they were so weary that they fell to the ground"; according to *Koelhoff's Chronicle* published in 1499, "Many people, men and women, old and young, had the disease [of dancing mania]"; Casper Hedion, in *Ein Ausserlessne Chronik von Anfang der Welt bis auff das iar nach Christi unsers Eynigen Heylands Gepurt M.D.*, writes that in 1374 "a terrible disease, called St. John's dance . . . attacked many women and girls, men and boys"; A. Slichtenhorst's *Gelsersee*

*Geschiedenissen* states that "men and women were smitten by the fantastic frenzy." This gender mixture is also reflected in more recent tarantism reports such as episodes in the vicinity of Sardinia, Italy, studied by Gallini which found that the vast majority of "victims" were male, while de Martino reported that most participants that he investigated near Apulia were female.[32]

## WHAT CAUSED THE DANCE MANIAS?

Ergot (pronounced "er-get") poisoning has been blamed for hallucinations and convulsions accompanying the dance mania. Nicknamed Saint Anthony's Fire, ergotism coincided with floods and wet growing seasons which foster the growth of the fungus *Claviceps purpura* which thrives in damp conditions and forms on cultivated grains, especially rye. While this could account for some symptoms, many outbreaks did not coincide with floods or wet growing or harvest periods. Convulsive ergotism could cause bizarre behavior and hallucinations, but chronic ergotism was more common and typically resulted in the loss of fingers and toes from gangrene, a feature that is distinctly not associated with dance manias.[33] As for tarantism, most episodes occurred only during July and August and were triggered by real or imaginary spider bites, hearing music, or seeing others dance, and involved structured annual rituals. Also, while rye was a key crop in central and northern Europe, it was uncommon in Italy. Surely a few participants were hysterics, epileptics, mentally disturbed, or even delusional from ergot, but the large percentage of the populations affected, and the circumstances and timing of outbreaks, suggests otherwise. Episodes were pandemic, meaning that they occurred across a wide area and affected a very high proportion of the population.[34]

So, what is the most likely explanation for dance manias? Based on an examination of a representative sample of medieval chronicles, it is evident that these episodes are best explained as deviant religious sects that gained adherents as they made pilgrimages through Europe during years of turmoil in order to receive divine favor. Their symptoms (visions, fainting, tremor) are predictable for any large population engaging in prolonged dancing, emotional worship, and fasting. Their actions have been "mistranslated" by contemporary scholars evaluating the participants' behaviors per se, removed from their regional context and meaning. Tarantism was a regional variant of dancing mania that developed into a local tradition that was primarily confined to southern Italy.

In reviewing the dance frenzies, it is important to consult original sources and realize that we are all, to some extent, products of our social, cultural, and historical milieu. When assessing the normality of a particular act, it is vital to not solely focus on the behaviors themselves, but the context of the participants and those making the evaluations. It is not that these prominent historians were trying to deceive, but their social and cultural milieu was different from our own. They had different assumptions and worldviews, and were writing at a time when it was taken for granted that women were innately susceptible to hysteria and were both physically and emotionally frail.[35] This situation affected their selective readings of medieval chronicles despite their scholarly backgrounds and evidence to the contrary in the very texts they translated.

That a person's milieu could affect her scholarship is not surprising. What is of concern is the persistence of several fallacies about dance manias into the last decade of the twentieth century, and the reliance on secondary sources by the authors of many textbooks on abnormal psychology and psychiatry. In their defense, unless they are specialists in medieval manuscripts, most of these authors would lack the time or resources to consult original, obscure texts. This underlines the importance of consulting original sources whenever possible, not relying solely on the interpretation of others.

Scientific progress and understanding is achieved by standing on the shoulders of giants. But occasionally those shoulders unwittingly face in the wrong direction. It is time to correct that mistake. One cannot help wondering how many more "facts" of today are based on the prejudices of yesterday, and will eventually be exposed, by revisiting original sources, as the fallacies of tomorrow.

The lesson of the dancing mania is the importance of examining "the" evidence, that is, consulting the original sources. It is vital to consider the context of historical behaviors. Until very recently, dancing mania participants were typified as hysterical females. This assessment has gone relatively unchallenged by scientists, but was not made through a rigorous consultation of period chronicles. Instead this view was espoused by later observers—many scholars—who assumed that females were innately prone to hysteria. This assessment of dance manias as rituals involving an equal proportion of both males and females would have occurred earlier if researchers had read through the original medieval chronicles. The evidence has always been there. No one bothered to recheck these sources, instead relying on translations from the 1800s and early 1900s by researchers with antiquated ideas about female inferiority and their propensity to become hysterical.

## REVIEW QUESTIONS

1. Briefly list the various explanations that have been offered to explain dance frenzies. Which view do you support as being the most likely?
2. Why is it important to examine original sources from medieval chronicles which describe dance manias? Which should we place more credibility in—old chronicles or modern textbooks?
3. Why is it unlikely to think that insect and spider bites were responsible for people acting strangely and engaging in the dance manias?
4. Compare modern-day dance raves and medieval dance manias. How are they similar? Different?
5. What degree of certainty can scientists have as to what really caused the dance manias?
6. What biases did people hold that led them to suggest that hysterical females were susceptible to dance frenzies when the facts do not bear this out?
7. What role may have ergot poisoning played in triggering some dance manias? Do you think ergot poisoning can explain most or every dance mania?

## NOTES

1. J. F. C. Hecker, *Epidemics of the Middle Ages*, trans. B. Babington (London: The Sydenham Society, 1844); G. Rosen, *Madness in Society* (London: Routledge and Kegan Paul, 1968); F. Sirois, "Perspectives on Epidemic Hys-

teria," in *Mass Psychogenic Illness: A Social Psychological Analysis*, ed. M. Colligan, J. Pennebaker, and L. Murphy (Hillsdale, N.J.: Lawrence Erlbaum, 1982), pp. 217–36.

2. H. F. Gloyne, "Tarantism: Mass Hysterical Reaction to Spider Bite in the Middle Ages," *American Imago* 7 (1950): 29.

3. H. Schadewaldt, "Musik und Medizin" (Music and Medicine), *Arztliche Praxis* 23 (1971): 1846–51, 1894–97.

4. E. de Martino, *La Terre du Remords* (The Land of Self-Affliction), trans. Claude Poncet (Paris: Gallimard, 1966).

5. "Tarantism, St. Paul and the Spider," *Times Literary Supplement* (London), April 27, 1967, pp. 345–47.

6. C. Gallini, *La Ballerina Variopinta: Une Festa Guarigione in Sardegna* (The Multi-colored Dancer: A Healing Festival in Sardinia) (Naples: Liguori, 1988).

7. H. E. Sigerist, *Civilization and Disease* (Ithaca, N.Y.: Cornell University Press, 1943), pp. 218–19.

8. Ibid., p. 218; Rosen, *Madness in Society*, p. 204.

9. Gloyne, "Tarantism," p. 35.

10. I. M. Lewis, "The Spider and the Pangolin," *Man* 12, no. 3 (1991): 514.

11. J. F. Russell, "Tarantism," *Medical History* 23 (1979): 416; Lewis, "The Spider and the Pangolin," p. 517.

12. Sigerist, *Civilization and Disease*, p. 221.

13. Hecker, *Epidemics of the Middle Ages*, p. 87.

14. B. L. Gordon, *Medieval and Renaissance Medicine* (New York: Philosophical Library, 1959), p. 562.

15. H. I. Kaplan and B. J. Sadock, eds., *Comprehensive Textbook of Psychiatry*, vol. 2 (Baltimore: Williams and Wilkins, 1985), p. 1227; R. C. Carson, J. N. Butcher, and S. Mineka, *Abnormal Psychology and Modern Life,* 10th ed. (New York: HarperCollins, 1998), p. 37; R. J. Comer, *Fundamentals of Abnormal Psychology* (New York: W. H. Freeman and Company, 1996), p. 9.

16. E. L. Backman, *Religious Dances in the Christian Church and in Popular Medicine*, trans. E. Classer (London: Allen and Unwin, 1952).

17. G. Mora, "A Historical and Socio-Psychiatric Appraisal of Tarantism," *Bulletin of the History of Medicine* 37 (1963): 436–38.

18. Carson et al., *Abnormal Psychology*, p. 37.

19. Rosen, *Madness in Society*.

20. F. Rust, *Dance in Society: An Analysis of the Relationship between the Social Dance and Society in England from the Middle Ages to the Present Day* (London: Routledge and Kegan Paul, 1969), p. 20.

21. R. E. Bartholomew, "Dancing with Myths: The Misogynist Construction of Dancing Mania," *Feminism & Psychology* 8, no. 2 (1998): 173–83.

22. Backman, *Religious Dances*, p. 331.

23. Ibid., p. 290.

24. Cited in ibid., p. 210.

25. Russell, "Tarantism," p. 413.

26. J. F. C. Hecker, *The Dancing Mania of the Middle Ages*, trans. B. Babington (New York: B. Franklin, 1970 [1837]), p. 4.

27. Ibid., p. 6.

28. Ibid., p. 4; H. W. Haggard, *The Doctor in History* (New Haven, Conn.: Yale University Press, 1934), p. 187.

29. Backman, *Religious Dances*, p. 147.

30. Rust, *Dance in Society*, p. 22.

31. Hecker, *Dancing Mania*, pp. 3–4.

32. de Martino, *La Terre du Remords*; Gallini, *La Ballerina Variopinta*.

33. L. J. Donaldson, J. Cavanagh, and J. Rankin, "The Dancing Plague: A Public Health Conundrum," *Public Health* 111 (1997): 203.

34. T. Lidz, "Hysteria," in *The Encyclopedia of Mental Health*, vol. 3, ed. A. Deutsch and H. Fishman (New York: Franklin Watts, 1963), p. 822; T. Millon and R. Millon, *Abnormal Behavior and Personality: A Biosocial Learning Approach* (Philadelphia: W. B. Saunders, 1974), p. 22.

35. B. Ehrenreich and D. English, *For Her Own Good: 150 Years of the Experts' Advice to Women* (Garden City, N.Y.: Anchor Press, 1978); C. Smith-Rosenberg, "The Hysterical Woman: Sex Roles and Role Conflict in Nineteenth-Century America," *Social Research* 39, no. 4 (1972): 652–78; M. S. Micale, *Approaching Hysteria: Disease and its Interpretations* (Princeton, N.J.: Princeton University Press, 1995).

# 11

A small group of people living near lumberjack camps on the northern fringes of New England and southern Quebec have exhibited what appeared to be a strange affliction. Did the "Jumpers" suffer from a bizarre medical problem or a conditioned habit picked up from playing "the horse kicking game?"

# THE JUMPING FRENCHMEN OF MAINE

*with Dr. Stephen R. Whalen*

*Custom is a second nature, and no less powerful.*

—Michel Montaigne[1]

Ask most New Englanders if they have heard of "the jumping Frenchmen of Maine," and they may think you're referring to a visiting gymnastics troupe. But ask a neurologist in the region—or the world for that matter—and most will recognize the phrase. For more than a century, "jumping" has been a mystery in the fields of neurology and cross-cultural psychiatry. It was (and may still be) located along the northern fringe of Maine and New Hampshire, and in the adjacent Canadian province of Quebec.[2] In these areas, small pockets of people, especially in isolated communities and lumberjack camps, exhibited dramatic responses when suddenly startled. These behaviors included a combination of jumping, screaming, swearing, flailing out and striking bystanders, and throwing objects that may be in their hands. The most remarkable display was "automatic obedience," briefly doing whatever they were told. Jumping was prominent among residents of French-Canadian heritage in Maine, hence the nickname.

"Jumping" has long been a part of the heritage and legend of northern New England. In 1902 Holman Day published a book of stories on Maine folklore, *Pine Tree Ballads*.[3] He included a poem, "The Jumper," describing a man who jumped at the slightest stimulus, and who unintentionally struck his wife in bed on numerous occasions after being startled by the whistle of a passing train.

The "Jumping Frenchmen" first gained public attention in 1878, when prominent New York neurologist Dr. George Beard told a group of doctors that he had heard stories of a group of lumberjacks in northern Maine who suffered from a strange nervous condition. When suddenly startled, these individuals struck out at nearby people or objects. In 1880 Dr. Beard boarded a train to the Moosehead Lake region of Maine to see if the accounts were true. He was not disappointed. One case involved a twenty-seven-year-old man who was sitting in a chair while holding a knife that he was about to use to cut tobacco. Suddenly he was struck hard on the shoulder and ordered to "throw it." The knife flew from his hand and struck a beam. He was again forcefully commanded to "throw it." Beard wrote, "He threw the tobacco and the pipe on the grass at least a rod away with the same cry and the same suddenness and explosiveness of movement."[4] Dr. Beard noted that the condition seemed to run in families. He noted that jumping began in childhood, lasted a lifetime, and was rare in women.

The publication of Beard's reports on the "Jumping Frenchmen" led to increased attention in scientific circles on the subject of exaggerated response to the startle reflex. Experts widely assumed that Beard's "jumpers" were a culture-specific variation of *latah*, believed at the time to be a strange mental disorder among the people of Malay and Indonesia in Southeast Asia (for a detailed description of *latah*, see chapter 7). Beard was the first to publicly make this connection.[5] Beard's observations of the "Jumping Frenchmen" raised issues regarding whether the behavior had a cultural origin, and to what degree race played a role in the symptoms. Was there any link between the Malay people who experience *latah* and the North Americans exhibiting "jumping"?

# JUMPING AND RACISM

To what extent were *latah* and jumping the same? Did these conditions indicate a racial or ethnic defect in the genes of those affected? Beard's reputation soon attracted attention to these questions.[6] Within a few years, scientists were cataloging various exotic behaviors as identical to jumping or *latah*. Yet, the few similar reports of so-called *latah* in widely separated geographical and cultural locations were not totally convincing. Most of the "evidence" was old, scattered, and incomplete.[7] With the various languages involved, misunderstandings and mistranslations were common. One article, mistranslated from English into Russian, identified the "Jumping Frenchmen of Maine" as a group of gymnasts![8] How could the translator have gotten it so wrong? Beard described a jumper throwing a "tumbler" (a type of drinking glass), but the translator apparently assumed that he meant an acrobat.[9]

While researchers often cite the "Jumping Frenchmen" as an example of *latah* in a culture unrelated to Malaysia or Indonesia, there were too many dissimilarities to label them as identical. Jumping almost always affected males and typically became prominent during childhood; *latah* rarely if ever involved jumping, was rare in children, and most of those affected were elderly women. Beard noticed these inconsistencies and assumed that jumping was an inherited condition that was triggered by habitual tickling. He never associated jumping with diminished capacity to think, and he suggested that everyone is a potential jumper.[10] Even though Beard's conclusions discounted a racial element in the jumping reflex, this ran counter to popular views of *latah*. During the 1880s, Western scientists used the prevalence of *latah* among Malays and Indonesians to paint a picture of the natives as inherently nervous, mentally unstable, and irrational. This stereotype of the Malays as ideal followers justified colonial domination.[11] In contrast, Beard described the jumpers as physically and mentally strong.[12] Beard speculated that jumping was caused by temporary degeneration from exposure to their rustic environment, but he made no conclusions about racial heredity or a diminished capacity for the ability to make rational judgments.

## MODERN INVESTIGATIONS OF "JUMPING"

Renewed interest in "jumping" arose in the 1960s and led to a debate as to whether it was a disorder or habit. In 1963, neurologist Dr. Harold Stevens examined a fifty-nine-year-old man of French-Canadian descent whose father was a lumberjack in northern Maine. Dr. Stevens noted that the man was easily startled, and when struck by a reflex hammer, "he jumped about ten inches off the bed."[13] Dr. Stevens said the man exhibited similar reactions to the sound of a telephone ring or an instrument dropping on the floor.

Dr. Reuben Rabinovitch, a Canadian neurologist, wrote in 1965 about his childhood experience with jumping. He said that while growing up in Quebec, Canada, the exaggerated reflex was common to all of the children in his village. Each spring, lumberjacks came out of the woods and set up camp nearby. They shared with the children their food, music, and entertainment. In this way, Rabinovitch was exposed to "the horse kicking game," in which children snuck up on their victim and suddenly poked them while making the neighing sound of a horse. The "victim" then jumped up in the air and flailed out while blurting out the horse cry. Horses were a vital part of logging camps and were used to haul logs to the riverbank, where they could then be floated to their destination. The horses were often temperamental and the lumberjacks could be badly hurt from being kicked when entering a stall. Dr. Rabinovitch wrote that typically one lumberjack would sneak into the stall next to his intended victim's horse and wait. When the victim arrived, the prankster would "reach over and suddenly and violently poke his victim and give vent to the loud neighing cry of an enraged horse. This would most often frighten the victim into jumping away from what he thought was his own horse about to kick him."[14] Rabinovich's anecdote suggests that social and cultural factors appear to be important in the development of jumping.

Dr. E. Charles Kunkle, a Maine neurologist, also emphasized the influence of learned roles in analyzing the game reported by Dr. Rabinovitch. Dr. Kunkle notes that this game involved subjects who, when startled, were "expected to produce a formalized response of jumping violently, flailing out, and shouting angrily, often imitating the cry of a kicking horse." Adults, especially those in isolated communities and lumberjack camps, sometimes practiced this "horse play." Kunkle felt that this represented a "socially conditioned reflex, reinforced by example and by repeated stimulation." Kunkle described jumping as a "part of regional folklore." As a physician he was able to talk to and examine fifteen jumpers. Dr. Kunkle said that jumping seemed to develop and flourish in "relatively closed and unsophisticated communities and in entirely masculine work groups."[15]

During the mid-1980s, three Canadian scientists studied eight jumpers in the region of Beauce, Quebec, where men traditionally worked as lumberjacks in Maine. In six of those examined, the symptoms began with their work as lumberjacks. One man, when startled "would run, swear, throw an object he was holding, strike at bystanders, or obey commands."[16] He said that one time he "jumped from a height of 10 feet after a sudden command." The researchers noted that all eight subjects would scream, most would throw an object in their hand or strike out, and half briefly obeyed commands shouted at them immediately after being startled, such as "jump," "run," or "dance."

Are the jumpers a local variant of a universal condition or disorder, or the result of environmental factors? Similar behaviors have been recorded in peoples in various parts of the world. Some scientists believe these symptoms occur in hyperstartlers, rare individuals suffering from a dysfunction of the human startle response. Others think it is much more common and akin to a regional habit and is not a disease or disorder. It appears that jumping resulted from a set of social conditions, but it is also related to other examples of hyperstartle. While there is probably a genetic predisposition to excessive startle in the general population, this does not explain the prevalence of jumping in isolated Maine communities.[17] While certain medical conditions can cause excessive startle (magnesium deficiency, tetanus, and degenerative brain disorders),[18] jumpers have no known medical condition. This suggests a possible social and cultural link. The "Jumping Frenchmen" in Maine is unique in the context of the environment of logging communities of the time period, and in the attention they received from the scientific community.

The most plausible explanation for jumping is that a local social interaction became institutionalized among a select group of people. If the inhabitants of a logging camp lived with the knowledge that they may be surprised by a sudden "poke," and that an exaggerated startle was the expected response, then this "reflex irritation" became a normal part of social intercourse. Kunkle suggested this when he wrote that "jumping may represent a special variety of socially conditioned reflex, reinforced by example and by repeated stimulation from attentive colleagues."

How then do we explain the "jumping"? Dr. Rabinovitch suggested that lumberjacks were confined to the northern woods from autumn to spring. Isolated and bored, they invented distractions involving the only protagonists available, men and horses. The jumping syndrome then grew out of the lumber camps and moved to surrounding towns and villages. Jumping appeared to die out with the passing of the traditional logging camp. As tractors replaced horses, and as lumberjacks became less isolated, the incidence of jumping declined. The experts have noted that even severe "jumpers" lost their exaggerated responses as they were removed from the continual stimuli.[19] This suggests that jumping may result from operant conditioning—learning based on the consequences of the response. In other words, responses are associated with their consequences. Acts that are reinforced tend to be repeated, while those that are not tend to diminish in frequency.[20]

## REVIEW QUESTIONS

1. Build a case supporting the likelihood that "jumping" is a result of nature and not nurture.
2. Build a case supporting the likelihood that "jumping" is a result of nurture not nature.
3. Why do you think early Western scientists labeled *latah* in Southeast Asia as a mental disorder among people who were not particularly intelligent or rational, while "jumping" was labeled as a less serious condition that was triggered by habitual tickling?

# NOTES

1. Quoted in R. T. Tripp, comp., *The International Thesaurus of Quotations* (New York: Thomas Y. Crowell, 1970), p. 210.

2. Because the last scientific study of jumping dates to 1986, (see M. H. Saint-Hilaire, J. M. Saint-Hilaire, and Luc Granger, "Jumping Frenchmen of Maine," *Neurology* 36 [September 1986]: 1269–71), and this study examined subjects aged fifty-five to seventy-seven, it is questionable as to whether the syndrome still exists. For ease of reading and because this is an historical account, we have described jumping in the past tense.

3. H. F. Day, *Pine Tree Ballads* (Boston: Small, Maynard & Company, 1902).

4. George M. Beard, "Experiments with the 'Jumpers' or 'Jumping Frenchmen' of Maine," *Journal of Nervous and Mental Disease* 7 (1880): 487–90.

5. Ibid., p. 490.

6. R. Porter, *A Social History of Medicine: Stories of the Insane* (London: Weidenfeld and Nicolson, 1987), p. 9; and A. Kleinman, *Rethinking Psychiatry: From Cultural Category to Personal Experience* (New York: The Free Press, 1988), pp. 12–14.

7. H. B. M. Murphy, "History and Evolution of the Syndromes: The Striking Case of Latah and Amok," in *Psychopathology: Contributions from Social, Behavioral, and Biological Sciences*, ed. M. Hammer, K. Salzinger, and S. Sutton (New York: Wiley, 1973), pp. 33–55.

8. H. Stevens, "'Jumping Frenchmen of Maine': Myriachit," *Archives of Neurology* 12 (1965): 312.

9. Beard, "Experiments," p. 489.

10. Ibid., p. 488.

11. R. E. Bartholomew, *Exotic Deviance: Medicalizing Cultural Idioms— From Strangeness to Illness* (Boulder: University Press of Colorado, 2000).

12. Beard, "Experiments," p. 489.

13. Stevens, "'Jumping Frenchmen of Maine': Myriachit," p. 313.

14. R. Rabinovitch, "An Exaggerated Startle Reflex Resembling a Kicking Horse," *Canadian Medical Association Journal* 93 (1965): 130.

15. E. Charles Kunkle, "The 'Jumpers' of Maine: A Reappraisal," *Archives of Internal Medicine* 119 (1967): 355–57.

16. Saint-Hilaire et al., "Jumping Frenchmen of Maine," pp. 1269–71.

17. Ibid., p. 1270. The Saint-Hilaires and Granger cited a study that identified American military recruits with at least 1 in 2,000 with an excessive startle

response. See F. C. Thorne, "Startle Neurosis," *American Journal of Psychiatry* 101 (1944): 105–109.

18. Kunkle, "The 'Jumpers' of Maine: A Reappraisal," p. 358.

19. Saint-Hilaire et al., "Jumping Frenchmen of Maine," p. 1271.

20. D. Coon, *Introduction to Psychology: Exploration and Application* (Pacific Grove, Calif.: Brooks/Cole Publishing, 1998), pp. 278, 284.

# 12

# THE BIRTHPLACE OF THE FLYING SAUCER

The "flying saucer" myth can be traced to a single press dispatch sent by a reporter at a newspaper office in Pendleton, Oregon. The rest is history.

Historical examination is a powerful tool in understanding contemporary events, providing distance from popular assumptions and folk beliefs and often yielding unique insights into the context and meaning of situations and circumstances, allowing us to view them in a new light. This is no more evident than in the history of unidentified flying objects (UFOs), where the state of Oregon has a unique place in history.[1] This is because a wire service dispatch was sent from Pendleton, Oregon, in 1947, which created worldwide public awareness of flying saucers.

The flying saucer era began in 1947 during a Western moral panic over the rapid, global spread of communism which ushered in the Cold War. It is within this "Red Scare" context that waves of claims and public discourse about the existence of flying saucers should be understood. The genesis of the first wave of sightings of mysterious aerial saucer-shaped objects can be traced to the western United States during the summer of that year.

On Tuesday, June 24, 1947, Boise, Idaho, businessman Kenneth Arnold (1915–1984), owner of Great Western Fire Control Supply of Boise, installed his equipment at the Central Air Service complex in Chehalis, Washington. There he talked with another pilot about the possible crash site of a missing C-46 Marine transport plane, believed to have been lost in the vicinity of Mount Rainier, Washington. Relatives of those on board were offering a $5,000 reward to anyone who could locate the crash site. Though his next planned flight was to Yakima, Washington, Arnold decided to re-route over the search area in hopes of spotting the wreckage. Shortly before 3 P.M. on June 24, Arnold was flying his private plane near the Cascade Mountains when he saw what appeared to be nine glittering objects flying in an echelon formation from north to south near Mount Rainier. He kept the rapidly moving objects in sight for about three minutes before they traveled south over Mount Adams and were lost to view.[2]

Worried that he may have observed remote-controlled Soviet guided missiles, Arnold eventually flew to Pendleton, Oregon, where he tried reporting what he saw to the Federal Bureau of Investigation (FBI) office there, but finding it closed, he went to the offices of Pendleton's lone newspaper, the *East Oregonian*. Two reporters at the paper, Nolan Skiff and Bill Bequette, listened to Arnold's story for only about five minutes because their deadline was fast approaching. Skiff took notes and wrote a brief story which Bequette managed to fit onto the front page of the June 25 edition of the *East Oregonian*, under the headline, "Impossible! Maybe, but Seein' Is Believin', Says Flier."[3]

According to the article,

Kenneth Arnold, with the fire control at Boise and who was flying in southern Washington yesterday afternoon in search of a missing marine plane, stopped here en route to Boise today with an unusual story—which he doesn't expect people to believe but which he declared is true.

He said he sighted nine saucer-like air craft flying in formation at 3 P.M. yesterday, extremely bright—as if they were nickel plated—and flying at an immense rate of speed. He estimated they were at an altitude between 9,500 and 10,000 feet and clocked them from Mt. Rainier to Mt. Adams, arriving at the amazing speed of about 1200 miles an hour. "It seemed impossible," he said, "but there it is—I must believe my eyes."

He landed at Yakima somewhat later and inquired there, but learned nothing. Talking about it to a man from Ukiah in Pendleton this morning whose name he did not get, he was amazed to learn that the man had sighted the same aerial objects yesterday afternoon from the mountains in the Ukiah section!

He said that in flight they appeared to weave in an [sic] out in formation.

Bequette recalls that he then hurriedly keyed in a second similar report to the Associated Press (AP). "We were only minutes from 'putting the paper to bed' so we didn't have much time to give him [referring to Arnold]."[4] It is notable that both stories were misleading, as Arnold had described the objects as crescent-shaped, referring only to their movement as "like a saucer would if you skipped it across the water."[5] However, Bequette's Associated Press account describing Arnold's "saucers" appeared in scores of newspapers across the country.

Bequette was obligated to file an AP story, as member papers were required to provide the AP with local teletype transmission reports that editors deemed to be of wider regional or national interest. Bequette later recalled that at the time, Oregon papers belonging to the AP cooperative were linked by the "C wire." Bequette said that "Other papers were free to use stories from the C wire and the AP bureau took whatever stories the Portland editors thought had . . . [broader] interest and transmitted them on the AP's main, or trunk, wire." Bequette filed his story onto the C wire, but he said it was picked up on the main wire, and by the following morning, "almost every newspaper in the country published the story on page 1."[6] Bequette's story appeared on teletype machines as follows:

PENDLETON, Ore., June 25 (AP)—Nine bright saucer-like objects flying at "incredible speed" at 10,000 feet altitude were reported here today by Kenneth Arnold, Boise, Idaho, pilot who said he could not hazard a guess as to what they were.

Arnold, a United States Forest Service employee engaged in

searching for a missing plane, said he sighted the mysterious objects yesterday at three P.M. They were flying between Mount Rainier and Mount Adams, in Washington State, he said, and appeared to weave in and out of formation. Arnold said that he clocked and estimated their speed at 1200 miles an hour.

Enquires at Yakima last night brought only blank stares, he said, but he added he talked today with an unidentified man from Utah, south of here, who said he had seen similar objects over the mountains near Ukiah yesterday.

"It seems impossible," Arnold said, "but there it is."[7]

This report was not technically responsible for the first use of the term "flying saucer." After an examination of press clippings surveyed between June 25 and 26, 1947, Herbert Strentz of the Journalism Department at Northwestern University found that the use of the words "flying saucer" is the collective product of American headline writers, and cannot be traced to any one person.[8] However, the AP report filed by Bequette was the proto-article from which the term "flying saucer" was created. Of key importance was his use of the term "saucer-like" in describing Arnold's sighting. The term "flying saucer" allowed the placement of "seemingly inexplicable observations in a new category."[9] Bequette's use of the word "saucer" provided a motif for the worldwide wave of flying saucer sightings during the summer of 1947, and other waves since.[10] It also encouraged others who had observed mysterious aerial phenomena to report their sightings and heightened fears of a Soviet attack.[11] Hence, the massive global 1947 flying saucer wave is a social construction of reality unique to the twentieth century,[12] with popular opinion as to what perceptions constitute a "saucer" being a manufactured concept created and propagated by the mass media.[13]

In the June 26 edition of the *East Oregonian*, Bequette described Arnold as having seen "nine mysterious objects" that were "somewhat bat-shaped," and it was not until near the end of this account that he added that Arnold had "also described the objects as 'saucer-like.'" Many years later, Bequette remarked that he could not recall "whether or not Arnold used the words 'saucer-shaped craft,' but I am inclined to credit his version (that he only spoke of objects moving like a saucer if you skipped it across the water)."[14] This recollection of events is consistent with a description furnished by Arnold on June 26, 1947, when he appeared as a live guest on Pendleton, Oregon, radio station KWRC where he was interviewed by announcer Ted Smith. During the interview, Arnold never referred to the objects that he reported seeing two days earlier, as "saucer-like" or "flying saucers," but stated that they looked "like a pie plate that was cut in half with a sort of convex triangle in the rear."[15] The other notable feature of this interview is the atmosphere of excitement and Cold War urgency evident throughout. For instance, Ted Smith, in his closing remarks, states:

> I know that the press associations . . . [have] been right after you every minute. . . . It has been on every newscast over the air and in every newspaper I know of. . . . I understand United Press is checking on it out of New York now, with the Army and also with the Navy, and we hope to have some concrete answer before nightfall. . . . And we urge our listeners to keep tuned to this station because any time this afternoon or this evening, that we get something . . . we'll have it on the air.[16]

The *Oregon Journal* of June 27 referred to Arnold as having seen "nine shiny crescent-shaped planes" and quoted him as saying they "were half-moon shaped, oval in front and convex in the rear." But many other newspapers, including the *East Oregonian*, continued to use a variety of descriptions that reinforced the "flying saucer" motif. For example, the *Portland Daily Journal* of June 26, used such terms as "flying disk," "mysterious objects," and "shiny, 'piepan' shaped objects." The front page of the *Boise Idaho Statesman* of June 27 used the term "flying saucers." Meanwhile, Arnold was growing weary of the remarkable public reaction to his sighting.

Of the hundreds of UFO reports that followed Kenneth Arnold's sighting, one prominent incident occurred in Portland, Oregon. On July 4, 1947, at 1:05 P.M., a Portland City Police Department patrolman, Kenneth A. McDowell, reported seeing five "disc-shaped" objects moving at great speed. McDowell was on duty and feeding pigeons in a parking lot behind Precinct #1 when he noticed the birds become excited and fly off. In looking for the source of the disturbance, he spotted "five large discs in the air east of Portland: two discs flying south and three discs in an easterly direction." He said "they were dipping in an up and down oscillating motion."[17]

UFO researcher Jerome Clark, who has access to a vast amount of UFO-related data in his capacity as an associate with the J. Allen Hynek Center for UFO Studies in Chicago, states that "There were at least twenty other sightings on the twenty-fourth [of June 1947], all but two in the Pacific Northwest."[18] However, none of these reports appeared prior to Arnold's. While I have not examined these other reports, it is a classic characteristic feature of UFO sighting waves that an initial spectacular sighting which triggers a subsequent wave of reports typically prompts others who may have perceived ambiguous aerial stimuli prior to or at about the time of the initial sighting, to redefine it as related to the initial prominent sighting. In other words, people who might have seen something "odd" around the time of Arnold's sighting may have redefined or reinterpreted their own sighting to more closely match Arnold's. My guess is that most of these reports from June 24 would fit into this category. One such report that was made public retrospectively involved an Oregon man. On August 20, 1947, Lt. Col. Donald L. Springer, an intelligence officer with the Headquarters of the Fourth Air Force at Hamilton Field in California, received a letter from prospector Fred M. Johnson of "106 No. West 1st Ave" in Portland, Oregon. Johnson claimed that he was prospecting in the vicinity of Mount Adams on June 24 when he observed several UFOs. He said that he "saw the same flying objects [as Arnold] at about the same time." Johnson continued: "Having a telescope with me at the time I can asure [sic] you they are real and noting [sic] like them I ever saw before [and] they did not pass very high over where I was standing." Johnson said they were noiseless, moved at tremendous speed, flew about 1,000 feet high, and he could discern "an object in the tail and looked like a big hand of a clock shifting from side to side like a big magnet."[19]

# THE CONTEXT: DOMESTIC OR FOREIGN SECRET WEAPONS

Why would Bill Bequette have believed Arnold's story and decided to write his now-famous wire report? Firstly, by all accounts, Arnold was an articulate man, and in 1962 he even stood as a candidate (albeit unsuccessful) for the position of Idaho lieutenant governor. Another important factor was the recent memory of World War II, which had ended just two years before. Between 1944 and 1945, 93,000 Japanese Fugo balloon-carrying incendiary bombs were launched into the "jet stream" and sent in the direction of the Pacific Northwest in hopes of setting fire to forests and farmland. Only 297 were known to have reached the United States and Canada, causing relatively minor damage, although psychologically the threat struck widespread fear into coastal residents.[20] Memories of these secret Japanese weapons were still vivid in 1947, prompting speculations as to whether the flying saucers were "an indication of a similar activity on the part of the Soviet Union."[21]

In the year immediately prior to the saucer wave, there were mass sightings of mysterious aerial objects, especially in Scandinavia and occasionally in Europe, and observers almost exclusively described them as resembling guided missiles or German V-rockets, with the most common descriptive term being "ghost rocket." This motif is an obvious reflection of the immediate post–World War II political landscape and widely held view in Northern Europe at the time that remote-controlled German V-rockets confiscated by the Soviets at the close of World War II were being test-fired as a form of political intimidation. Russian forces had occupied Peenemunde, a German village on the island of Usedom, the former center of German rocket science, and controlled much of northern Europe during this period, and it was unclear as to how much Scandinavian territory they might claim in the political uncertainty following the war.[22] The 1947 saucer wave reflects a transition stage with "ghost rocket" sightings of the previous year which received considerable U.S. and domestic press coverage.

From the time of Arnold's sighting until 1950, many observations of missile-like aerial objects were recorded, reflecting the popular notion that the mysterious sightings represented a domestic or foreign secret weapon. However, from the very beginning of the 1947 wave, most sightings were saucer-shaped, and by 1950, the missile motif had virtually disappeared, leaving most people to report disk or saucer-like objects. For instance, Bloecher's *Report on the UFO Wave of 1947* catalogues a minimum of 800 sightings during this wave alone. Of these, approximately two-thirds were saucer-shaped.[23]

Interestingly, virtually no one during the 1947 "saucer" wave believed the mysterious objects were of an extraterrestrial origin. The American obsession with the Cold War and possible atomic conflict was reflected in the sighting explanations. Less than two months after Arnold's sighting, on August 15, 1947, a Gallup Poll revealed that 90 percent of Americans surveyed were aware of flying saucers, and many (16 percent) believed they were U.S. or Russian secret weapons.[24] "Nothing [in the poll] was said about 'alien visitors,' not even a measurable 1 percent toyed with the concept."[25] For several weeks after Arnold reported his sighting, the FBI was seriously concerned that many reports were disinformation spread by Soviet agents who were attempting to promote fear and panic, and as of late July, local Bureau offices conducted background checks on saucer witnesses.[26] These concerns reflect American preoccupation with the spread of communism during this period. Two typical incidents reflect the social paranoia over the communist threat. After someone soaked a twenty-eight-inch "saucer" with turpentine and set it alight on top of a Seattle, Washington, house on July 15, 1947, a witness erroneously thought he could see a hammer and sickle on the disc, causing FBI and military bomb experts to rush to the site.[27] Eight days later, the Salmon River Bridge in Oregon was destroyed by a fire of undetermined origin. The FBI investigated the possibility of communist sabotage to the 400-foot long wooden structure. The ambiguous nature of the fire, and its appearance near the peak of a UFO wave, led to speculation that flying saucers were responsible.[28] During this period, the U.S. Air Force was concerned that the stimulus for some sightings may have been unconventional Soviet aircraft intended to "negate U.S. confidence in the atom bomb as the most advanced and decisive weapon in warfare"; "perform photographic reconnaissance missions"; "test air defenses"; or "conduct familiarization flights over U.S. territory."[29]

# THE WEST COAST, 1896, BIRTHPLACE OF THE AIRSHIP MANIA

Half a century before Kenneth Arnold's sighting, the press also played an instrumental role in affecting the outcome of a UFO wave—but this time the actions of various Oregon newspaper editors and journalists served to extinguish a flurry of UFO sightings that was spreading rapidly across the Pacific Northwest. Let us briefly examine the context and circumstances surrounding "the Great Airship Wave" of 1896–1897.

During the last decade of the nineteenth century, an extraordinary social delusion spread across the United States. Amid rumors that an American inventor had perfected the world's first heavier-than-air flying machine, citizens from various parts of the country and numbering in the tens of thousands reported seeing an imaginary airship. It was typically described as oval or cigar-shaped with an attached undercarriage, having a powerful headlight and giant fans or wings protruding from both sides. Some observers even claimed that the wings slowly flopped up and down like a bird. The airship was almost exclusively seen at night, and far exceeded the period technology, as the Wright brothers' crude attempt at piloted powered flight would not occur until 1903, during which the longest period of sustained flight was just fifty-nine seconds. We can also rule out the possibility that citizens were misperceiving a free-flying spherical balloon as night flight was treacherous, and a sudden wind gust could have disastrous consequences. Further, the airship was often seen simultaneously in different states, prompting some observers to comment that there must have been a fleet of vessels.

The airship sightings have been described as a classic case of mass hysteria, occurring between mid-November 1896 and May 1897, at which time it was seen in most American states.[30] The episode transpired during a period of rapid technological change which fostered a widespread feeling that almost any invention was possible. The second half of the nineteenth century was marked by a series of revolutionary inventions that would permanently alter lifestyles. These included the telephone (1876), gramophone (1877), filament lamp (1879), motor car (1884), steam turbine (1884), diesel engine (1893), X-rays (1895), and radio (1896). In the twenty years preceding the airship mania, the American public became preoccupied with the popular literature on science and inventions.[31] Of particular interest was the age-old dream of heavier-than-air flight, as during this period "magazines devoted to science and engineering vied with Jules Verne's *Robur the Conquerer* and other fictional publications to describe the flier which would soon succeed."[32] The voluminous literature on aviation "fed the public a steady diet of aeronautical speculation and news to prime people for the day when the riddle of aerial navigation finally would receive a solution."[33] It was within this setting—characterized by a collective mood that almost any invention was possible—that the airship mania transpired.

# AIRSHIPS AND YELLOW JOURNALISM

On Tuesday, November 17, 1896, the first recorded sightings of the air-ship episode occurred in Sacramento, California, as hundreds of residents reported seeing an illuminated airship fly low over the city between 6 and 7 P.M.[34] Some even claimed to hear voices and music coming from the craft.[35] Rail car operator R. L. Lowry described the craft "as an oblong mass, propelled by fanlike wheels operated by four men, who worked as if on bicycles."[36] Many newspapers reflected popular sentiments that a local man had invented the world's first practical heavier-than-air flying machine and was testing it under the cover of darkness, describing the sighting as plausible or as fact.[37]

Mass sightings across California began on November 19, as a myste-rious light was seen near Eureka.[38] The next afternoon the airship was spotted near Tulare.[39] That evening numerous Sacramento residents again observed what appeared to be a light "attached to some aircraft," while in Oakland, witnesses claimed to discern huge fan-like propellers, while others said they saw giant wings attached to each side of an airship.[40] On November 22 between 5 and 6 P.M., hundreds of Sacramento residents watched what they thought was an airship with a brilliant arc lamp pass to the southwest.[41]

During the last week of November and first week of December, air-ship sightings were reported in such California communities as Red Bluff, Riverside, Antioch, Chico, Visalia, Hanford, Ferndale, Box Springs, Salinas, Maxwell, Tulare, Merced, Fresno, and Pennington.[42] There were scattered sightings during the episode in the adjacent states of Oregon, Washington, Nevada, and Arizona which received minor press coverage.[43] The wave was primarily confined to California, where widespread sight-ings continued until dramatically declining by mid-December, with the exception of a few intermittent cases from around the state.

An interesting feature of the California episode were several reports of close encounters with terrestrial airship pilots or crew who typically offered to give the witness a ride in the vessel, although one involved an encounter with what appeared to have been Martians.[44]

Speculative stories about the possible existence of an airship and inventors, and reports of other sightings, appeared in almost every state, starting with a trickle of reports in mid-January 1897 and climaxing during April before petering out in May. The West Coast states where the episode began in November 1896 were virtually spared.

Press sensationalism played a major role in creating and perpetuating the sightings, first in California, and later across the United States. Amid intense public interest in airship development, newspaper editors published a barrage of articles speculating as to whether someone had invented the world's first practical airship. Publisher William Randolph Hearst remarked in the *San Francisco Examiner* that he could not recall a clearer example of "Fake journalism . . . than the persistent attempt to make the public believe that the air in this vicinity is populated with airships. It has been manifest for weeks that the whole airship story is pure myth."[45] Hearst was notorious for exaggerating or fabricating news stories in order to sell his papers, and his position on the existence of the airship was characteristically hypocritical in order to exploit the situation and increase sales. During November and December 1896, his *San Francisco Examiner* adhered to a strict editorial policy of deriding the airship's existence. Meanwhile, Hearst's flagship newspaper in the eastern United States, the *New York Journal*, was publishing sensational accounts proclaiming the California airship's reality. A bitter rival of Hearst at the time, the *San Francisco Call*, took great relish in pointing out this conspicuous discrepancy which it said proved the "Jekyll and Hyde features of 'Little Willie's' journalistic character."[46] The *Examiner*'s skeptical position on the California airship was almost certainly in response to claims made at the very beginning of the wave in the *Call*, suggesting the airship's reality.

This "yellow journalism" typified the period prior to and encompassing the sightings, and refers to the reporting of sensational, exaggerated, and often falsified stories in order to boost circulation. This strategy was common among many American newspapers between 1880 and 1900.[47] Other editors attacked the sensationalism of the airship rumors and sightings by portions of the California press.[48] However, while yellow journalism in California was instrumental in propagating the episode, many witnesses were usually seeing objects in the sky, typically stars and planets.

# OREGON AND THE UFO WAVE
# THAT DIDN'T HAPPEN

The California airship wave had been building up for about a week and dominated the California press amid sensational, near saturation-level press coverage, when sightings spread to nearby states, and eventually across the country. One of the first sightings in the Pacific Northwest was at McMinnville, Oregon, on the night of November 24, 1896, when a report in that city's *Telephone-Register* newspaper, referred to the incident with a brief two-sentence story: "Tuesday night several of the boys about town saw the Sacramento air ship sail over this city, at least they saw lights in the heavens. This they swear to."[49] A deluge of airship sightings ensued across the Pacific Northwest, except in Oregon. This prompted the *Portland Evening Telegram* to remark that "It is news to say that the ship has not been seen in Portland" and had nearly missed the state altogether.[50]

The answer for the apparent immunity in Oregon from what some people labeled as "airshipitis," appears to have resulted from a combination of cloudy weather, responsible journalism, and an almost universal resentment by the Oregon press of the widely perceived California avant-garde lifestyle. As soon as the sightings began in Oregon on November 24, stormy weather set in over most of the state that lasted for several days. Simultaneously, state newspaper editors attributed the sightings within the region to sensational California journalism designed to sell newspapers, and labeled the affair a hoax. These included the *Dalles Times Mountaineer* which used the headlines, "California's Fake," and the *Roseburg Plaindealer* which echoed these sentiments, calling them "Aladdin's Lamp stories" that were akin to sea serpent tales.[51] Meanwhile, the *Albany* (Oregon) *Weekly Herald-Disseminator* described the reports as "an entirely sensational piece of fiction."[52] In a lengthy article that was both humorous and acerbic, the editor of the *Portland Oregonian* savaged the California press, noting that "California has proved the richest American soil for propagation of the 'fake'—a noxious weed introduced into the country within the present generation by what is called modern journalism." In defining this term, it was observed that "The fake at its best is a lie well told; that is, a piece of pure fiction dressed with an air of probability and presented as truth."[53] When on the evening of December 1 a display of aerial lights caused by trolley cars lit up the Portland sky, one press account emphatically proclaimed that it was not airship-related:

**AN AURORA BOREALIS LAST NIGHT**
**SMALL EDITION OF ONE FURNISHED**
**BY "SPARKING" TROLLEYS**

Pretty Electrical Display in the East Side Suburbs—
Wasn't an Airship Searchlight

The big black bank of clouds which was hovering over the Columbia river in the northeast and eastern sky last night portended a storm, and not a few persons were probably deceived into believing that an electrical storm was approaching. At least, some East Siders thought much was the case, until they made an investigation and found that the brilliant flickerings in the sky were caused by the trolley cars in the suburbs. One man came into a store on East Burnside street, with wide-distended eyes, and vowed he had seen the searchlight of the famous California airship turned on the town.[54]

The Marshfield *Coos Bay News* said that "If it was a genuine flying machine, there would be no need for it to meander around in the heavens under cover of night."[55] The *Eugene Register* stated the flying machine stories "reminds one of the old saying that California has the largest trees, smallest matches and d–nest liars of any place on earth."[56] Following several reports of sightings near Alturas, the *Lake County Examiner* noted: "Alturas has several well-developed cases of 'airship.' Wonder what kind of whisky they have down in that section."[57] When a mysterious light was reported hovering above Knox's Butte, someone at the *Albany State Rights Democrat* quipped: "It is in order for the *San Francisco Call* to come up here and make a night flying machine out of it."[58]

# UNIDENTIFIED FLYING METEORS?

What, from the available evidence, is the most likely trigger for the 1896–1897 airship wave, and Kenneth Arnold's famous 1947 "saucer" sightings? A compelling explanation is offered by *San Francisco Chronicle* science writer Keay Davidson, who observes that November 17, 1896, is the peak date of the Leonid meteor shower, and descriptions of the object sighted that evening in Sacramento "sounds . . . very much like a meteoric fireball."[59]

During the early 1990s, Davidson, working on a suggestion by aviation writer Philip Klass, began researching the possibility that on June 24, 1947, Kenneth Arnold saw a disintegrating meteor. Davidson says that Arnold's observation resembled previous fireballs. While Arnold said the objects were in view for up to three minutes, Davidson notes that time estimates under stress are commonly overestimated, such as a 1989 California earthquake that many San Francisco Bay–area residents estimated to have lasted over a minute. In reality, it was fifteen seconds.[60] There have been historical reports of individual meteors lasting up to fifty seconds (times that were also likely overestimated). Internal evidence from Arnold's account suggests that he further overestimated the duration of the sighting by confusing the meteor fragments with the resulting contrail, which could have persisted for a number of minutes. Some large meteors break into smaller pieces as they burn. Davidson points out that Arnold described the objects as glowing tadpoles that pulsated and fluttered. "That sounds like chunks of a disintegrating meteor that glow, then dim as they cool," said Davidson.[61] Later, private UFO researcher Brad Sparks of Irvine, California, found indirect evidence for the meteor hypothesis. At almost exactly the same time as Arnold's sighting, Idaho Lt. Gov. Donald Whitehead and Boise justice J. M. Lampert described "an object that bears a strong resemblance to a meteor contrail."[62] Whitehead said the object resembled a comet, was in view for about twenty minutes, and "had a brilliant head and a filmy smoke for a tail."[63] Finally, why wasn't the meteor widely observed? Davidson reviewed weather maps and found that on June 24, 1947, "a huge system of bad weather covered much of Canada and the United States east of the Cascades."[64]

## OREGON AND PRESS RESPONSIBILITY: A TALE OF TWO ERAS

An examination of the events and circumstances surrounding the United States airship mania of 1896–1897, and flying saucer waves beginning in 1947, provides valuable insights into the origin and nature of modern-day

UFO reports. The parallels between the two episodes are remarkable, and highlight the potential impact of the mass media in creating popular delusions. Social psychology also plays an important role. Human perception is unreliable, and is greatly influenced by one's mental set or perceptual outlook at the time of the observation.[65] Stars and planets can appear to move, change colors, and flicker, and misidentifications of stars and planets (especially Venus) are the most common explanation for contemporary UFO reports.[66] Many airship reports were triggered by illuminated kites or fire balloons set aloft by pranksters, and similar devices are not uncommon today. Popular during the time of the airship mania, fire balloons (also called tissue balloons) were commonly sold at shops selling pyrotechnics. They consisted of paper balloons with candles attached near the mouth. Heat from the candle made the balloon buoyant. However, misperceptions of Venus, prominent at the time, were clearly responsible for the majority of airship sightings, and are the most common stimulus for flying saucer reports.[67]

The airship delusion occurred over a hundred years ago as humanity stood at the dawn of the twentieth century, amid great enthusiasm for rapid technological progress and trepidation over the potential for misuse of these new machines. The airship episode of 1896–1897 is perhaps best described as a mass wish fulfillment. As we begin the twenty-first century, enthusiasm for an impending technological revolution led by computers characterizes our time, along with concerns over how such a revolution will affect social life (and even possibly extinguish it, in the case of nuclear weapons). At this critical historical juncture, one cannot help but wonder if people will again look to the heavens and create new symbols that will reflect the prevailing social conditions on Earth. These new symbols are likely to tell us little about extraterrestrial life, but much about the creative capacity of the human mind and its search for meaning.

Humanity seems to be growing more reliant on technology to provide basic information that is necessary to the successful function of everyday life. What role will the media play in creating or extinguishing as yet unhatched social delusions? In this regard, it is important to learn from the lessons of the past, such as the airship mania. Even more pertinent is an understanding of the most persistent, widespread social delusion of the twentieth century—the flying saucer—born in an obscure newspaper office in Pendleton, Oregon.[68]

Could knowledge of critical thinking have prevented the 1947 flying saucer wave? Perhaps. Reporters covering Arnold's description of the crescent- or boomerang-shaped objects inadvertently misrepresented his description as "saucer-shaped," which appears to have structured subsequent UFO descriptions during that summer and since 1947 as "flying discs" and "saucers." They should have asked for a more detailed description or a rough sketch of the objects. This should have extinguished the legend of the flying saucer before it even began. In terms of tolerating uncertainty, what Arnold reported remains the subject of vigorous debate. We may never know exactly what he saw, though the meteor explanation seems the most plausible. Arnold's report also highlights the notoriously unreliable nature of human perception, and the role of the mass media in influencing public opinion. Since 1947, there has been considerable speculation in popular books that flying saucer sightings involve observations of extraterrestrial spaceships in the complete absence of rigorous evidence to support such claims. Why, since 1947, have there been numerous best-selling books whose writers claimed proof of the existence of alien visitors? The existence of aliens seems to have touched an emotional chord. In an increasingly secular world, aliens may be viewed as saviors from the sky. If they were to make contact and be friendly (as most UFO abduction books claim), a sharing of their technological capabilities could offer medical breakthroughs that could extend the human life span and perhaps even lead to immortality.

## REVIEW QUESTIONS

1. How did a single wire service dispatch sent from Pendleton, Oregon, trigger mass sightings of saucer-shaped objects in the summer of 1947?
2. When "flying saucers" were created in 1947, the popular public explanation of them had little to do with alien spacecraft. What did most Americans think they were?
3. How did "yellow journalism," especially the actions of William Randolph Hearst, contribute to the American airship wave of 1896–1897?
4. Why was Oregon relatively immune from seeing imaginary air-

ships whereas California experienced a massive sighting wave at about the same time?

5. Compare the airship sightings with modern UFO waves. What are the similarities between the two?

6. What did Kenneth Arnold most likely see on June 24, 1947? Why had there been so few similar sightings of what Arnold reported?

## NOTES

1. This study avoids the issue of whether otherworldly life forms exist or have visited Earth. Instead, it focuses on certain social aspects of the UFO phenomenon. Most UFO sightings and encounters have prosaic explanations. The long-standing dispute between "believers" and "skeptics" is over the origin and nature of the small percentage of reports which defy conventional explanations. Irrespective as to the reality of alien visitors, social studies of UFOs can contribute to our understanding of human consciousness and myth-making, which at the very least comprise a significant part of the UFO phenomenon. For instance, the contemporary belief that some UFOs represent extraterrestrials is maintained and propagated through a complex interaction of psychological, sociological, and folkloric processes. UFO-related examples of experiences in each of the aforementioned categories appear in Robert Emerson Bartholomew and George S. Howard, *UFOs & Alien Contact: Two Centuries of Mystery* (Amherst, N.Y.: Prometheus Books, 1998); and Robert Emerson Bartholomew, *UFOlore: A Social Psychological Study of a Modern Myth in the Making* (Stone Mountain, Ga.: Arcturus Books, 1989).

While there is no unambiguous, incontrovertible evidence at present for the existence of otherworldly beings in the universe outside of Earth, this possibility cannot be discounted. As for my personal opinion on UFOs, I believe that 99 percent of cases result from prosaic factors, and the remaining 1 percent are not likely to be of otherworldly origin, but these may provide important discoveries for science.

2. Pierre Lagrange, "'It Seems Impossible, but There It Is,'" in *Phenomenon: Forty Years of Flying Saucers*, ed. John Spencer and Hilary Evans (New York: Avon, 1989), pp. 26–45; Kenneth Arnold, *The Flying Saucer as I Saw It* (Boise, Idaho: The author, 1950); Kenneth Arnold and Ray A. Palmer, *The Coming of the Saucers: A Documentary Report on Sky Objects That Have Mystified the World* (Amherst, Wisc.: The authors, 1952); "Idaho 'Flying Saucer' Sighter Dies," *Boise Idaho Statesman*, January 22, 1984; Jerome Clark, *The*

*UFO Encyclopedia: The Phenomenon from the Beginning, Volume One: A–K*, 2d ed. (Detroit: Omnigraphics, Incorporated, 1998), pp. 139–43; Martin Gardner, *The New Age: Notes of a Fringe Watcher* (Amherst, N.Y.: Prometheus Books, 1988); personal communication from Brad Sparks dated February 1, 2000. Sparks notes that Arnold's total time estimate kept varying from under two minutes to as many as four minutes.

3. "An Interview with Bill Bequette." Comprised of undated personal correspondence between French sociologist Pierre Lagrange and Bill Bequette, made available to the public in Lagrange, "It Seems Impossible," p. 1. A small portion of Bequette's replies were in the form of face-to-face conversations in July 1988 with Lagrange and Bequette, the latter of whom was living at the time in Tri-Cities, Washington, where the conversations took place.

4. Ibid., p. 1.

5. Martin Gardner, *Fads and Fallacies in the Name of Science* (New York: Dover, 1957), p. 56; Ronald Dean Story, *The Encyclopedia of UFOs* (New York: Doubleday, 1980), p. 25; Margaret Sachs, *The UFO Encyclopedia* (New York: Perigee, 1980), pp. 207–208.

6. "An Interview with Bill Bequette," p. 1.

7. This initial description of Arnold as "a United States Forest Service employee," is incorrect. See "Boise Flier Maintains He Saw 'Em," *East Oregonian*, June 26, 1947, p. 1.

8. Herbert J. Strentz, *A Survey of Press Coverage of Unidentified Flying Objects, 1947–1966.* Ph.D. diss. Northwestern University, department of journalism. Brad Sparks (personal communication), is skeptical of this statement by Strentz, as he provides no supporting details. These suspicions may be well founded. After searching hundreds of newspapers for UFO reports during the time of Arnold's sighting, to date Jan Aldrich has located but a single press report dated June 26, 1947, using the term "flying saucer."

9. David Michael Jacobs, *The UFO Controversy in America* (Bloomington: Indiana University Press, 1975), p. 37; Joseph A. Blake, "UFOlogy: The Intellectual Development and Social Context of the Study of Unidentified Flying Objects," in *On the Margins of Science: The Social Construction of Rejected Knowledge*, ed. R. Wallis (Keele, England: University of Keele, 1979), pp. 315–37. Sociological Review Monographs 27.

10. DeWayne B. Johnson, *Flying Saucers—Fact or Fiction?* Master's thesis, University of California at Los Angeles journalism department, 1950; Thomas Edward Bullard, *Mysteries in the Eye of the Beholder: UFOs and Their Correlates as a Folkloric Theme Past and Present.* Ph.D. diss., Indiana University folklore department, 1982.

11. Ted Bloecher, *Report on the UFO Wave of 1947* (Washington, D.C.: The author, 1967).

12. There are a few scattered historical references to disc-shaped objects, but no consistent pattern emerges until 1947. There were only a handful of occasions prior to 1947 that a witness actually used the word "saucer" to describe mysterious aerial objects. The first known instance occurred on January 22, 1878, when John Martin observed an orange object "about the size of a large saucer" near Denison, Texas (*Denison Daily News*, January 25, 1878). In this instance, Martin refers to the size, and not the shape, as saucer-like.

13. Herbert Hackett, "The Flying Saucer: A Manufactured Concept," *Sociology and Social Research* 32 (1948): 869–73. As for what Arnold had actually observed on June 24, 1947, no one can be certain. However, various naturalistic explanations have been offered by astronomer Donald Menzel. See Menzel, *Flying Saucers* (Cambridge, Mass.: Harvard University Press, 1953); Donald Howard Menzel and Lyle G. Boyd, *The World of Flying Saucers: A Scientific Examination of a Major Myth of the Space Age* (Garden City, N.Y.: Doubleday & Company, 1963).

14. "An Interview with Bill Bequette," p. 1.

15. "Transcript of KWRC Radio's Interview with Kenneth Arnold at Pendleton, Oregon, on June 26, 1947 at 12:00 P.M.," p. 2. Located, transcribed, and made available to the public by French sociologist Pierre Lagrange, who found the tape while examining the papers of Ray Palmer, who co-authored *The Coming of the Saucers* (Amherst, Wisc., and Boise, Idaho: The authors) with Ken Arnold in 1952. In a 2000 personal communication, Brad Sparks notes that Arnold himself added to the confusion surrounding the term "flying saucer" as on several occasions he used "saucer" shapes in his retellings.

16. "Transcript of KWRC Radio's Interview," p. 2.

17. A previously classified and confidential United States Air Force investigation report of the episode (referred to as Incident #5), and made public by Jan Aldrich, with assistance from Barry Greenwood and Ed Stewart. Aldrich states that the Air Force concluded that the stimulus for this incident was "chaff" or "windows"— aluminum strips designed to confound radar.

18. Clark, *UFO Encyclopedia*, p. 141.

19. A letter dated August 20, 1947, from Fred M. Johnson to Donald L. Springer, the latter serving as an assistant chief of staff, A-2, at the headquarters of the Fourth Air Force at Hamilton Field, California. In a confidential letter dated August 25, 1947, Springer told the Special FBI Agent in Charge at the U.S. Justice Department in room 422 of the Federal Office Building in San Francisco, that "A possibility exists that Mr. Johnson might have read some of this in the

newspapers when Arnold was published re this matter." Credit Jan Aldrich for making both letters available to the public at his Project 1947 Web site: www.project1947.com.

20. Henry Stevenson, "Balloon Bombs: Japan to North America," *British Columbia Historical News* 28, no. 3 (1995): 22–23. Stevenson also recounts the only recorded deaths from a Fugo balloon, which occurred in a tragic incident in Oregon on May 5, 1945, when the Rev. Archie Mitchell of the Christian and Missionary Alliance Church in Bly went for a picnic on Gearhart Mountain with his wife, Elyse, and five Sunday school students. Elyse and the children suffered horrific injuries and died shortly after approaching an object buried in the snow. The Reverend Mitchell was the only survivor (p. 23).

21. Donald Howard Menzel and Ernest Henry Taves, *The UFO Enigma: The Definitive Explanation of the UFO Phenomenon* (Garden City, N.Y.: Doubleday & Company, 1977), p. 7.

22. B. Sundelius, ed., *Foreign Policies of Northern Europe* (Boulder, Colo.: Westview, 1982). It is within this context of long-held Russian invasion fears and postwar political ambiguity involving possible Russian claims on Swedish territory that plausible rumors began circulating as to potentially hostile Russian intentions. See "Russians Cry 'Slander' to Rocket-Firing Charge," *New York Times*, September 4, 1946, p. 10; "The Russians Talk about Lies and Panic," *Svenska Dagbladet*, September 4, 1946, p. 3; "Sic transit," *Ny Dag*, August 6, 1946; "Sweden Used as a Shooting Range," *Halsingborgs Dagblad*, July 26, 1946; "Rocket, Meteor or Phantom?" *Aftonbladet*, August 7, 1946; *Smalands Folkblad*, July 27, 1946; "The Ghost Bomb a Serious Threat. 'Monster in Miniature for the Next War,'" *Svenska Dagbladet*, August 7, 1946, p. 7; Robert Emerson Bartholomew, "Redefining Epidemic Hysteria: An Example from Sweden," *Acta Psychiatrica Scandinavia* 88 (1993): 178–82; Anders Liljegren and Clas Svahn, "Ghost Rockets and Phantom Aircraft," in *Phenomenon: Forty Years of Flying Saucers*, ed. John Spencer and Hilary Evans (New York: Avon, 1989), pp. 53–60.

23. Bullard, *Mysteries*, p. 259.

24. George Gallup, "Nine out of Ten Heard of Flying Saucers," *Public Opinion News Service*, August 15, 1947.

25. Loren Eugene Gross, *UFOs: A History*, vol. 1, *July 1947–December 1948* (Scotia, N.Y.: Arcturus Books, 1982), p. 30.

26. Bruce Sargent Maccabee, "UFO Related Information from FBI File: Part 1," *The UFO Investigator*, official publication of the now defunct National Investigations Committee on Aerial Phenomena (November 1977), p. 3; Gross, *UFOs*, p. 16.

27. Gross, *UFOs*, p. 37.

28. Arnold and Palmer, *Coming of the Saucers*, pp. 188–89; Gross, *UFOs*, p. 29.

29. Declassified formerly top secret U.S. Air Force Air Intelligence Report produced for the Directorate of Intelligence in Washington, D.C., on April 28, 1949, entitled, "Analysis of Flying Object Incidents in the U.S., Summary and Conclusions," NO. 100-203-79, CY. NO. 102 OF 103, p. 2. This document was made available to the public by Jan Aldrich on his Project 1947 Web site: www.project1947.com.

30. For a detailed discussion of this event as a case of mass hysteria, refer to Robert Emerson Bartholomew, "The Airship Hysteria of 1896–97," *Skeptical Inquirer* 14, no. 2 (1990): 171–81; Robert Emerson Bartholomew and George S. Howard, *UFOs & Alien Contact: Two Centuries of Mystery* (Amherst, N.Y.: Prometheus Books, 1998).

31. Ivan Frederick Clarke, "American Anticipations: The First of the Futurists," *Futures* 18, no. 4 (1986): 584–96.

32. Bullard, *Mysteries*.

33. Ibid.

34. "Voices in the Sky . . . People Declare They Heard Them and Saw a Light," *Sacramento Evening Bee*, November 18, 1896, p. 1.

35. Ibid., p. 1.

36. "A Lawyer's Word for That Airship," *San Francisco Chronicle*, November 22, 1896, p. 16.

37. "That Peculiar Night Visitant," *The (San Francisco) Call*, November 20, 1896, p. 1; "Floating in the Air . . . All the Stories Coincide," *Oakland Tribune*, November 23, 1896, p. 1; "Body Like a Bird," *The (San Francisco) Call*, November 24, 1896, p. 1; "Mission of the Aerial Ship," *The (San Francisco) Call*, November 25, 1896, p. 1; "New Converts," *The (San Francisco) Call*, November 26, 1896, p. 1; "Saw the Airship," *San Jose Daily Mercury*, November 26, 1896, p. 5.

38. "Singular Phenomenon," *Western Watchman* (Eureka, Calif.), November 21, 1896, p. 3; "That Mysterious March," *Western Watchman*, November 28, 1896, p. 3.

39. "Sailed High Overhead," *The (San Francisco) Call*, November 22, 1896, p. 13.

40. "That Airship Again," *The (San Francisco) Call*, November 21, 1896, p. 3; "Saw the Mystic Flying Light," *The (San Francisco) Call*, November 22, 1896, p. 13.

41. "Have We Got 'Em Again," *Sacramento Evening Bee*, November 23, 1896, p. 1.

42. "A Singular Phenomenon. Was It an Airship . . . ," *Red Bluff Daily People's Cause*, November 24, 1896; "The Airship Again," *Riverside Daily Press*, December 10, 1896, p. 5; "A Strange Phantom," *Weekly Antioch Ledger*, November 28, 1896, p. 3; "Seen Again. Many People of Chico Gaze at the Supposed Airship," *Morning Chronicle-Record* (Chico, Calif.), November 25, 1896, p. 3; "The Air Ship," *Weekly Visalia Delta*, November 26, 1896, p. 2; "Seen at Hanford," *Weekly Visalia Delta*, November 26, 1896, p. 2; "The Air Ship. The Vessel Seen Again . . . ," *Weekly Visalia Delta*, December 3, 1896, p. 1; "Was It an Air-Ship?" *Ferndale Semi-Weekly Enterprise*, December 1, 1896, p. 5; "The Air Ship," *Riverside Daily Press*, December 2, 1896, p. 5; "Observations," *Daily Colusa*, December 1, 1896, p. 2; "County News," *Daily Colusa*, December 3, 1896, p. 3; "Our Neighbors," *Weekly Visalia Delta*, December 3, 1896, p. 3; "The Air Ship at Tulare," *Tulare County Times* (Visalia, Calif.), December 3, 1896, p. 4; *Merced Express*, December 4, 1896, p. 3; *Fresno County Enterprise* (Selma, Calif.), November 27, 1896, p. 4; "Pennington Points," *Sutter County Farmer* (Yuba City, Calif.), December 4, 1896, p. 6.

43. *McMinnville (Oregon) Telephone-Register*, November 26, 1896, p. 3; "The Tourist of the Air" [editorial], *Tacoma (Washington) News*, November 28, 1896, p. 4; "Beats the Airship," *Tacoma (Washingon) News*, November 30, 1896, p. 2; "The Airship of Winnemucca," *Carson City (Nevada) Morning Appeal*, November 26, 1896, p. 3; "The Airship," *Reno Evening Gazette*, December 3, 1896, p. 1; "The Airship Again," *Reno Evening Gazette*, December 5, 1896, p. 3; "That Airship," *Carson City (Nevada) Morning Appeal*, December 6, 1896, p. 2; "Airship Burned," *Carson City (Nevada) Morning Appeal*, December 9, 1896, p. 3; "Airship Yarns," *Territorial Enterprise* (Virginia, Nev.), December 12, 1896, p. 2; "What Could It Have Been?" *Central Nevadan*, December 10, 1896, p. 3; "The Air Ship. It Reached Carson Saturday Night," *Carson Weekly*, December 7, 1896, p. 6; "Local Briefs," *Arizona Gazette* (Phoenix, Ariz.), December 4, 1896, p. 8.

44. "Others Who Saw It," *The (San Francisco) Call*, November 23, 1896; "Piercing the Void, or on to Honolulu," *San Francisco Examiner*, December 2, 1896; "How about This? A San Josean Declares That He Traveled on the Ship," *Oakland Tribune*, December 1, 1896, p. 1; "We Are in It," *San Luis Obispo (California) Tribune*, December 11, 1896, p. 1; *San Jose Daily Mercury*, December 1, 1896, p. 8; *Marysville (California) Daily Appeal*, December 2, 1896, p. 3; "The Airship Described by Fishermen," *The (San Francisco) Call*, December 3, 1896, p. 1; ". . . Strange and Circumstantial Story of a Sailor Passenger," *The (San Francisco) Call*, December 5, 1896, p. 2; "Three Strange Visitors. Who Possibly Came from the Planet Mars," *Evening Mail* (Stockton, Calif.), November 27, 1896, p. 1.

45. "The Airship Nuisance," *San Francisco Examiner*, December 5, 1896, p. 6.

46. "Hearst and His Two Faces," *The (San Francisco) Call*, December 5, 1896, pp. 1–2.

47. Ray Eldon Hiebert, Thomas W. Bohn, and Donald F. Ungurait, *Mass Media: An Introduction to Modern Communication Media* (New York: David McKay Company, 1974), pp. 209–10; John Tebbel, *The Life and Good Times of William Randolph Hearst* (New York: E. P. Dutton, 1952).

48. "A Necessity," *San Luis Obispo Tribune*, December 18, 1896, p. 3; "A Journalistic Failure," *San Francisco Examiner*, December 6, 1896, p. 6; "Coincidents," *Merced Express* (Merced, Calif.), December 4, 1896, p. 3; "Credit Where It Is Due," *San Francisco Chronicle*, December 5, 1896, p. 6.

49. *McMinnville (Oregon) Telephone-Register*, November 26, 1896, p. 3. McMinnville would become the scene of one of the most famous UFO cases of the modern UFO era. On May 11, 1950, Evelyn Trent reported seeing a saucer-shaped object of metallic appearance move slowly from the north or northeast at about 7:30 P.M. After she summoned her husband Paul, he eventually took two photos. The sighting occurred on the Trents' farm about nine miles from McMinnville. On June 8, the pictures were published in the *McMinnville Telephone-Register* with an accompanying story by local reporter William Powell, entitled "At Long Last—Authentic Photographs of Flying Saucer?" Within two days the story made headlines around the world. The photos were even featured in *Life* magazine on June 26, 1950, under the title "Farmer Trent's Flying Saucer." The case later became a focal point for flying saucer proponents after publication of the so-called Condon Report in 1969, which concluded on page 407: "This is one of the few UFO reports in which all factors investigated, geometric, psychological, and physical appear to be consistent with the assertion with an extraordinary flying object, silvery, metallic, disk-shaped, tens of meters in diameter, and evidently artificial, flew within sight of two witnesses." However, an editor for the influential publication *Aviation Week & Space Technology*, Philip Klass, and a former computer systems programmer at NASA's Goddard Space Flight Center, Robert Sheaffer, have suggested that the case was hoaxed after showing discrepancies in witness accounts, and concluding that the photo had been taken in the morning and not in the early evening as the Trents had claimed. This view is supported by former Harvard University astronomer Donald Howard Menzel. However, American physicist and photographic expert Bruce Maccabee disputes this claim, as does respected UFO researcher Jerome Clark, who hold the credibility of Evelyn and Paul Trent in high regard. See Edward Uhler Condon, *Scientific Study of Unidentified Flying Objects* (New York: Bantam, 1969), pp. 396–407;

Robert Merrill Sheaffer, *The UFO Verdict: Examining the Evidence* (Amherst, N.Y.: Prometheus Books, 1981); Philip Julian Klass, *UFOs Explained* (New York: Random House, 1974); "Farmer Trent's Flying Saucer," *Life*, June 26, 1950, p. 40; Menzel and Taves, *UFO Enigma*, pp. 109–10; Bruce Sargent Maccabee, "The McMinnville Photos," in *The Spectrum of UFO Research: The Proceedings of the Second CUFOS Conference, Held September 25–27, 1981, in Chicago, Illinois*, ed. Mimi Hynek (Chicago: J. Allen Hynek Center for UFO Studies, 1988), pp. 13–57; Jerome Clark, *The UFO Encyclopedia: The Phenomenon from the Beginning*, vol. 2, *L–Z*, 2d ed. (Detroit: Omnigraphics, Incorporated, 1998), pp. 600–602.

50. "That California Airship . . . It Slid over Portland in the Fog," *Evening Telegram* (Portland, Ore.), December 1, 1896, p. 3.

51. "California's Fake," *Dalles (Oregon) Times Mountaineer*, November 28, 1896, p. 2; "Coincidents," *Roseburg Plaindealer*, November 30, 1896, p. 1.

52. *Weekly Herald-Disseminator* (Albany, Ore.), November 26, 1896, p. 4.

53. "The Liar or the Faker," *Portland Oregonian*, November 29, 1896, p. 4.

54. *Portland Evening Telegram*, December 2, 1896, p. 2.

55. *Coos Bay News* (Marshfield, Ore.), December 2, 1896, p. 3.

56. *Eugene (Oregon) Register*, December 11, 1896, p. 1.

57. *Lake County Examiner* (Lakeview, Ore.), December 3, 1896, p. 2.

58. *Albany (Oregon) State Rights Democrat*, December 11, 1896, p. 4.

59. Keay Davidson, *Carl Sagan: A Life* (New York: John Wiley & Sons, 1999), p. 440.

60. Keay Davidson, "Flying Saucer Saga," *San Francisco Examiner Magazine*, June 1, 1997, pp. 12–13.

61. Ibid., p. 13.

62. Letter from Keay Davidson to Robert Bartholomew dated January 24, 2000.

63. "Whitehead, Lampert Join 'Disc List,'" *Idaho Daily Statesman*, July 3, 1947, p. 1.

64. Davidson, "Flying Saucer Saga," p. 13.

65. Regarding the unreliability of human perception, see Elizabeth F. Loftus, "Reconstructing Memory: The Incredible Eyewitness," *Psychology Today* 8 (1974): 116–19; Elizabeth F. Loftus, *Eyewitness Testimony* (Cambridge, Mass.: Harvard University Press, 1979); David Ross, J. Donald Read, and Michael P. Toglia, *Adult Eyewitness Testimony: Current Trends and Developments* (Cambridge, Mass.: Cambridge University Press, 1994). For information on how mindset influences perceptions, see Robert Buckhout, "Eyewitness Testimony," *Scientific American* 231 (1974): 23–33; James E. Alcock, *Parapsy-*

*chology: Science or Magic?* (New York: Pergamon Press, 1981), pp. 73–74; Gary L. Wells and J. W. Turtle, "Eyewitness Identification: The Importance of Lineup Models," *Psychological Bulletin* 99 (1968): 320–29.

66. Edward Uhler Condon, *Scientific Study of Unidentified Flying Objects* (New York: Bantam, 1969).

67. Fred L. Whipple, "Introduction," in Menzel and Taves, *UFO Enigma*, pp. xiii–xiv.

68. I am indebted to Dr. Thomas Bullard, Clas Svahn, and Anders Liljegren Sweden, who provided many press accounts used in this article. I am also grateful to Robert Girard for access to a wealth of UFO-related material, and Jan Aldrich for making available to the public several 1947 UFO press reports and declassified United States government documents related to 1947 UFO sighting claims. I also thank Pierre Lagrange, Keay Davidson, and Brad Sparks for sharing advice and information. Finally, I am thankful to Hal McCune, News Editor of the *East Oregonian*, for granting permission to reprint press clippings.

# 13

For forty years, mysterious black helicopters have been spotted roaming the English countryside. Speculation as to their origin ranges from IRA terrorists to illegal aliens, space aliens, and secret government missions. Or do they symbolize popular fears?

# ENGLAND'S BLACK HELICOPTERS

*with David Clarke*

*Helicopters fly the night sky, what do they carry —terrorists who will blow up our cities, foreigners who will take away "our way of life," Russian agents who stir up trouble, or Satanists who will drink the blood of our cattle? Whatever, it bodes no good . . .*

—Peter Rogerson[1]

During the winter of 1973–1974, a wave of nighttime black helicopter sightings was reported in northwest England.

Two popular explanations arose: illegal immigrants and Irish terrorists. Linking helicopters with the smuggling of immigrants seemed logical, as before the helicopter craze citizens were concerned over illegal immigrants. In May 1972, an aircraft was tracked by radar at Royal Air Force (RAF) at Coningsby. Within minutes the blip disappeared below radar cover and was assumed to have landed along the coast. Numerous police cars searched without success for the mystery plane thought to be carrying illegal aliens.[2] This isolated example illustrates the background context against which the helicopter scare of 1973–1974 occurred.

The fear of terrorists soon replaced that of illegal aliens. Throughout the 1970s the Irish Republican Army (IRA) mounted a bombing campaign in Britain. Police feared that helicopters and aircraft might form part of an IRA network to bypass sea terminals to smuggle arms and explosives to the mainland. A helicopter could also be used in raids on vulnerable explosive stores. Shortly before the sightings began, the IRA had used a hijacked helicopter to spring an IRA sympathizer from a prison in Northern Ireland, and on another occasion a police station was attacked from the air.[3] A regular ferry service between Northern Ireland and Liverpool also placed northwest England, particularly Manchester and the industrial Mersey valley, on a list of potential terrorist targets.

Given these circumstances, it is no surprise that the Metropolitan Police Special Branch began investigating the reports of unidentified night-flying helicopters in November 1973 after sightings were made regularly from the Derbyshire Peak District, a rustic 542-square-mile national park in the English Midlands. Fears were heightened when several sightings were made near quarries, where high explosives were stored for use in mining operations.

The involvement of Special Branch detectives was reported by regional and national newspapers during a flurry of sightings, many of them made by police patrols early in January 1974.[4] Both the Home Office and Ministry of Defence were concerned that the sightings were a by-product of terrorist activities. Detectives from the Special Branch became involved shortly after the first sightings in September 1973 and a memo from a chief superintendent to Operations, noted that after six months of investigations senior officers remained skeptical that a "real" helicopter had ever been involved. The superintendent wrote: "the helicopter is an extremely noisy machine and is dangerous at night in all but the most excellent hands. Had one not been recently used successfully in Ireland, I would have discounted the value of the information absolutely."[5]

The Special Branch file mentions twelve sightings reported to police in Derbyshire over two weeks in September 1973. The sighting that appears to have triggered the "scare" occurred on September 18 at the complex of quarries and Mine Research laboratories near Buxton in Derbyshire. At 1 A.M. a resident of Harpur Hill who lived opposite the large Hillhead limestone quarry observed what she believed was a helicopter rising directly out of the complex and called Peak Security. Security guard Simon Crowe said after receiving her report he went back to check the quarry magazine (where the explosives were stored) with three other men. At that point he saw the helicopter approaching the quarry again and ordered all the lights to be switched off. He said, "I think the helicopter must have seen them as it veered off. I assume that it was a helicopter as it seemed to climb and not bank as an aircraft would."[6]

Peak Security reported the sighting to Derbyshire Police who immediately issued a statement to the local media appealing for information "from anyone who saw an unidentified aircraft or helicopter in the Buxton area." On the night of October 26, police in Yorkshire, Derbyshire, and Cheshire were said to have been overwhelmed with reports from people who saw what they described as a "flying saucer" streaking across the Pennines, a high mountain range that runs through northern England.[7] One report from Scarborough on the east coast described an object heading out to sea, while an observer in Sheffield described it as cigar-shaped and added "I would not have said it was a helicopter."[8] The air traffic control center for northern England at Preston, which received reports describing a "flying saucer," said that no unusual flights had been recorded for that night. The ATC's radar coverage was, however, unlikely to detect the movements of a "hedge-hopping" helicopter on the edge of its area of coverage.[9]

Nevertheless, the police in Buxton, Derbyshire, issued a statement which said a piston-engined helicopter had flown low over the town, and had been sighted in the same area earlier the same week! "A hedge-hopping helicopter was definitely seen last night," said a spokesman. "It was on an unscheduled flight and we are calling for information."[10]

According to a report drawn up for the Metropolitan Police Special Branch on November 22, a number of witnesses along with two officers

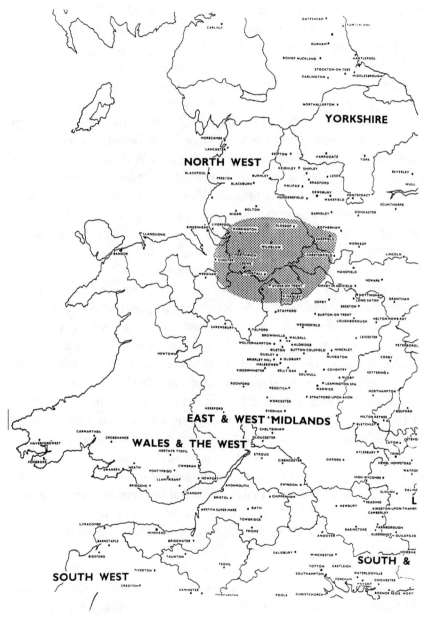

The main area where phantom helicopters have been seen is hilighted. Courtesy David Clarke.

from Derbyshire Police had made "a positive identification of an Augusta Bell 206A Jet Ranger helicopter" flying by night over the area. The report continued:

> The machine was observed on a number of occasions over a period of two weeks to be apparently practising landings in the vicinity of the sites of quarries and explosives stores in the Derbyshire countryside. . . . [Special Branch constable] has made numerous enquiries to discover the ownership and reasons for the flights from various sources but has yet to establish any positive facts. He has contacted an experienced Royal Air Force helicopter pilot with night flying experience who explained that night flying in the Derbyshire area would be extremely dangerous due to the nature of the terrain and to the number of overhead pylons in the area.[11]

The report concluded there was "a strong possibility" of the flights being "of an illegal nature." A list of current owners of Bell Augusta helicopters was quickly drawn up and forwarded to Derby County and Borough Police for further enquiries to be made with private pilots who were clearly under suspicion. Newspaper reports suggested there were three types of civilian helicopters at this time that carried between three to fifteen passengers. The Bell Augusta aircraft mentioned in the Special Branch file was a medium-sized five-seater with a range of about 250 miles.[12]

At this stage the mystery had received little coverage outside the local media and police inquiries were based upon information provided by witnesses who had spotted the machine flying in the Buxton area. Newspaper reports in January 1974 suggested that the security guard, Simon Crowe, had reported seeing the helicopter on five separate occasions while he was on duty in the Buxton area late at night.[13] Peak Security had, it emerged, already received "a warning" from police sources to be vigilant as it was known that IRA units were operating on the British mainland. One of their targets was believed to be depots where high explosives were stored. Subsequently, Crowe reported that he had been visited by two plainclothes policemen from Liverpool, who he assumed were members of the Criminal Investigation Department (CID) or Special Branch. They questioned him about the sightings and advised him not to talk to the press about the matter.[14]

No further sightings of the helicopter were made until January 1974, when a series of reports by police in northwest England suddenly placed the subject again into the media spotlight. On January 15 the regional and national press carried reports of phantom helicopter sightings made after midnight on the previous morning over the moorland border between Cheshire and Derbyshire counties. Police patrols spotted a helicopter flying in the Cat and Fiddle area of Cheshire and immediately contacted colleagues in the neighboring force by radio. They gave chase and said the pilot appeared to veer off toward Sheffield to avoid identification.[15] The same night police in the Macclesfield area of Cheshire mounted a fruitless search of fields near the giant Jodrell Bank radio telescope after reports were made that the machine had landed in a field nearby. A spokesman said, "Our officers spotted the helicopter and then lost it. They managed to spot it again and it gave the impression that it had landed, but the helicopter took off before the officers could get to it."[16] On this occasion it appears that radars at the air traffic control center in Preston did track an unidentified flying object following a route from Manchester to Stockport and then toward Buxton. This evidence was presented at a secret meeting organized by the Home Office, Ministry of Defence, and Special Branch, but it is not known if the radar tapes corroborated the visual sightings made by police. According to a newspaper source, the radar incident occurred shortly before midnight on Sunday January 13, 1974.[17]

Officially, air traffic control staff at Preston and Manchester were said to be unsurprised that the helicopter had largely managed to evade their coverage, because the aircraft appeared to be hiding beneath their radar height. Staff at the airport were said to be skeptical of the reports, but one pilot told a journalist that cattle had been stolen in the High Peak of Derbyshire and "a helicopter would be an ideal getaway vehicle" for conducting this sort of nocturnal crime.[18] The media coverage of these events marked the beginning of a period of rumor spread. Police statements added to the aura of mystery by failing to provide clear dates, times, and details of sightings. Reports in newspapers, radio, and TV news suggested the copter had been seen in rural parts of south Derbyshire and Staffordshire and the desolate High Peak area for six months. Rumors suggested that nocturnal visits had been made to Liverpool, Matlock, and Wirksworth.[19] One report boldly claimed that the machine had been seen four times and always disappeared in the direction of Sheffield.[20]

Collage of press reports on the phantom helicopter over Great Britain. The press was influential in perpetrating and maintaining the scare.

According to the police, the helicopter usually flew after midnight at altitudes of one hundred feet or less, without lights and seemingly with civil aviation markings blacked out. On other occasions it appeared the pilot was using a searchlight to guide its way through the darkness.

On Tuesday, January 15, the same day the press exposure to the mystery occurred, a series of new sightings was made. The first occurred at Buxton in the late afternoon and others followed in Staffordshire at Audley, near Stoke-on-Trent and Mow Cop, where a policeman saw a helicopter flying from Manchester toward Sandbach. Later that evening it was reported again in the Cheshire area. A police spokesman told the press these were "definite sightings . . . the people who got in touch with us were rational, sensible people who were not imagining things."[21]

Two more sightings were made by police officers. In the early hours of January 16 a detective driving a Crewe Division CID car spotted a helicopter apparently landing near a crossroads on the road from Sandbach to Congleton in Cheshire. As he sped toward the machine, it flew off.[22] A similar incident occurred when two policemen on duty near a disused airfield at Meir, near Stoke-on-Trent, heard the rotor blades of a helicopter and saw lights as if it had touched down. Once again it "veered away" before their patrol car was able to reach the landing area. Asked what they believed lay behind the nocturnal flights, a Staffordshire police spokesman said, "We do not know what is involved but we are determined to find out."[23]

A senior officer from Derbyshire said they had "pretty well ruled out that it is anything to do with illegal immigrants" but admitted the reason for the flights were "a complete mystery."[24] The absence of hard facts was replaced by speculation and rumors spread that the helicopter was linked with drug smugglers or cattle rustling. One intriguing idea was that an accomplice on the ground made a flare path for the pilot to follow and that he helped to refuel the machine. The London *Daily Telegraph* reported two newer rumors, that "it might be a 'home-made' helicopter which the owner, unable to obtain an air-worthiness certificate, is flying—and dangerously so—at night or, it is suggested it might be a modern—and wealthy—lover who finds it the most convenient way to reach his mistress or girlfriend."[25]

Undeterred by newspaper speculations, police inquiries continued to be centered on the possibility of terrorists. One newspaper said police were following a number of lines of inquiry, including the idea that "it could be used for drug or gun-running, for the UDA [terrorists] who are alleged to be operating in Bolton, or for trial runs for a major jail-break."[26]

As the rumors mushroomed, the national press adopted the mysterious pilot as a celebrity in his own right. The *Daily Mirror* called him "a devil-may-care pilot" and said the scare had "all the drama of a James Bond spy spectacular."[27] The *Mirror* sent a reporter, Edward Macauley, to the northwest to take a jaunt over the phantom's stomping ground as a passenger in a Jet Ranger helicopter. The pilot, Alex Parker, was an experienced ex-Army flyer. The pair flew in daylight on January 17 at an altitude of 500 feet. In comparison, the phantom flew at night between 50 and 100 feet from the ground. This led Alex to observe that, "to try to get through these hills at such a low level makes this guy a madman—or a great pilot. Whichever he is, I still feel he has been lucky to get away without having an accident."[28] His views were echoed by Lt. Col. Bob Smith, another former Army helicopter pilot, who said:

It's quite likely this man received his training in the services. To fly safely the way he does he would need at least £30,000 worth of extra equipment including radios, blind flying instruments, a very wide range of navigational aids, homing devices and a moving map display. It is possible to fly without all these aids but he could never find his way from A to B. This man must be an extremely competent pilot, because flying at night in the sort of country he is in you can meet all sorts of hazards. There's always the possibility you will fly into a high-tension cable or the side of a mountain. I would like to meet him![29]

Three hundred private helicopter pilots registered with the Civil Aviation Authority had their movements checked and were ruled out as suspects during the course of the police investigation. Strong night glasses and dogs were reportedly brought in to help patrols track down the landing ground used by the mystery helicopter. RAF and army units were also said to be on stand-by to give chase if the helicopter showed up again, but the armed forces were reluctant to be drawn into the hunt. They said it would be "far too hazardous" to use a second machine to give chase. A spokesman for RAF Valley in Anglesey, North Wales, said they "would not want to know . . . only owls and fools fly by night under those circumstances. It would be foolhardy, to put it mildly, to try and tail someone at night who is flying so low."[30]

Derbyshire and Cheshire police said they had built up "a full sightings file on him [the pilot] for the last six months" and more reports coming in. "He seems to be up and about after midnight most of the time and mainly at about three o'clock in the morning. We've alerted special patrols, officers with strong night glasses, to look for him. As soon as they see him, we want to get as many men into the area as possible before he clears off." Police had visited places where it was believed the helicopter had touched down, without finding any traces. "We only know it's medium sized, with a single rotor on top and a tail rotor. We feel it is coming from not too far away, and it uses so much fuel when it veers off straight flight and starts hovering and changing direction, that it's [sic] range becomes limited."[31]

Between January 16 and 17, the police in Cheshire and Staffordshire received twenty reports of the phantom's activities, most of them directly from members of the public as a result of newspaper appeals. All were checked without success and a spokesman said he was "surprised if anyone was flying the strong winds last night."[32] Nevertheless, two further "touchdowns" were reported, both near the Jodrell Bank telescope at Goostrey, where a police observation point had been set up. In one case, the machine appeared to remain on the ground for over an hour as police searched for it, only to see red and green tail lights flashing as it circled before leaving the area.[33] At 1:30 A.M. on the morning of January 18 the helicopter was even reported to have hovered above a house in Macclesfield for a couple of minutes "making a terrific noise."[34]

## DOUBTS BEGIN TO MULTIPLY

At this point, doubts about the credibility of the reports began to surface in the media. Throughout the world an oil crisis was causing concern and fuel shortages, yet the phantom flier seemed to be untroubled by this problem. A Shell Oil company spokesman said helicopters used large amounts of aviation fuel that was available only at airfields and airports. "Someone can't just go and buy it in cans and store it in the garden. Whoever it is must have access to supplies from some legitimate source."[35] Even if supplies were available, it was pointed out that it would cost roughly £100 to keep a helicopter in the air for one hour.

Following a week of unproductive police appeals the *Daily Mail* put forward the theory that the phantom helicopter "may prove to be an illusion." The newspaper said that senior officers remained skeptical because of a lack of clear evidence. Psychology professor John Cohen of Manchester University said the first reports of the phantom may have triggered off a series of spurious sightings. He said, "It is contagious . . . plant an idea and you get a kind of visual epidemic."[36]

In this instance it was the police who had planted the idea as a result of genuine concerns that the initial sightings may have been the result of terrorist activities. It was the police who had subsequently made the most extensive sightings and had even identified a specific model of helicopter. Their press statements had created a media sensation and encouraged others to report "sightings," both of helicopters and more ambiguous "lights in the sky." This policy appeared to have backfired when, late in January 1974, the police triggered a "visual epidemic" of poor quality reports, many of which appeared to relate to bona fide aircraft flying to and from Manchester's international airport. All these factors were considered when the Home Office and Ministry of Defence decided to hold a meeting to discuss the authenticity of the sightings that had been reported up to the end of March 1974. The meeting was held at Horseferry House in central London on March 21 and was attended by senior officers from the Derbyshire and Cheshire constabularies, Special Branch, the Home Office, and two Ministry of Defence representatives.[37]

In advance of the meeting, a summary report was prepared by the Special Branch squad responsible for the investigation for the attention of their chief superintendent. His feelings were that if a real helicopter was involved it should have been easily identified as there were so few specialist aircraft and pilots capable of operating in the Peak District. "Rumours of clandestine activities by light aircraft, including helicopters are common-place. They usually originate from laymen and only in the rarest cases prove to be accurate in detail; even less frequently do these reports lead to a serious police interest," he wrote. "It would be naive to think that there are no illegal activities taking place by the medium of light aircraft. However, the sightings [detailed in the report] seem to me to be only loosely connected and may in fact simply be a random amalgam of the frequent sighting reports which are made to one authority or another on a daily basis."[38] This senior officer seems to have recognized that the border between the helicopter sightings and UFO reports received by the police and Ministry of Defence on a daily basis was thin. "Helicopter flights at night are a highly specialized undertaking, requiring a fully equipped aircraft and an expert pilot. Blind landings at night are a risky undertaking and this point is well taken by the MoD who are reluctant to place even one of their fully equipped aircraft in such a night-flying situation."[39]

The meeting considered the reports prepared by Special Branch along with "some allegedly corroborative reports available through the Civil Aviation Authority, from the Air Traffic Control Centre at Preston and

Manchester Air Traffic Control." A report by chief superintendent of "B" Squad, Special Branch, summarized the conclusions reached: "In the event there were found to be only three 'hard' sightings and no useful pattern of timing or positioning was discernible; in addition, no crimes were reported at the times of the alleged flights. I was able to report that the Metropolitan Police Special Branch had no hard information to place potential subversive activities in the area."[40] The meeting ended with an agreement that the Ministry of Defence would prepare a paper on the services they could provide if further reports were received. No further sightings were reported during 1974 and, according to the Home Office, "the helicopter and pilot were never identified."[41]

A background of unsolved mystery continued to surround the events of 1973–1974 for a number of years. In subsequent winters, when further reports of unidentified, low-flying aircraft were made in the same area of Pennine hills, newspapers continued to label them as "the phantom copter." In January 1975 the drama of the previous year was repeated further north, in the foothills above Oldham in Greater Manchester, where strange flashing lights were pursued by police patrols in the early hours of three successive mornings. On January 17 at 3:10 A.M. two officers chased flashing white lights first by car and then by foot as the lights glided over barren moorland above the town.[42] This category of sighting soon became part of popular folklore in the Pennine foothills with rumors linking the activities of the "phantom copter" to terrorists and illegal immigrants. Both were potent "folk devils" that could easily be exchanged for the more culturally ingrained UFO when the circumstances were correct.

## GOVERNMENT CONSPIRACY?

During the 1970s sightings of phantom helicopters were linked with "cattle mutilations" in the United States. In recent years, copter sightings have been re-interpreted again within a new framework by UFO researchers—one of whom goes so far to speculate that alien spaceships camouflage themselves as helicopters in order to pursue some unknown agenda.[43] This tradition of paranoia has been kept alive most recently in the writings of Nick Redfern, which broadly follow the "Government conspiracy" motif.[44] Redfern links together many disparate rumors and *memorates* to provide a new niche for the phantom helicopters reported in northern England, albeit within a traditional "conspiracy" context. The term "memorates" was coined by Swedish folklorist Carl von Sydow in 1848 and refers to personal folk stories as opposed to more communal "fabulates." In this scenario the helicopter scare is directly connected with rumors that claim a UFO crashed into a Welsh mountain on January 23, 1974. The "crash" coincided with a major earth tremor centered upon the Bala Mountains and reports of lights in the sky that appear to have been fireball meteors. In the folklore version, anonymous informants describe how the disabled craft was subsequently recovered by government agencies and the bodies of the dead occupants removed to the secret Ministry of Defence Chemical and Biological Defence station at Porton Down, Wiltshire. A further "coincidence" were rumors of a sudden influx of American CIA agents into the United Kingdom, reported by the national press during the same month. Redfern feels this collection of coincidence, rumor, and modern legend was sufficient evidence to pose the following question: "Were the helicopters seen over Cheshire, Staffordshire and Derbyshire attached to a secret UFO crash-retrieval team?"[45]

The most likely explanation views mystery copter sightings as a rumor-generated visual illusion. This conclusion appears to have been reached independently by the police Special Branch investigation at the time. The police concluded that of the many hundreds of "reports" received, just three were deemed to be "authentic." The others were misperceptions of everyday objects—aircraft and "genuine" helicopters—reinterpreted within a sinister context as a result of the publicity hunt for the phantom received in the media.

The interpretation of the "trigger" event is important in fostering the episode. If the source emanates from someone respected, and is given immediate publicity as the helicopter reports were from January 1974, an ambiguous event can induce others to report experiences and trigger a visual epidemic. The involvement of the police led newspapers to place the story on their daily agenda and as a consequence the public began to treat the subject as important. Following the police appeals, people began to report lights in the sky as "phantom helicopters" they might otherwise have ignored.

The process whereby people conclude that an ambiguous aerial menace is a helicopter or a UFO is similar to the transmission of rumor. A rumor is a recurrent story or message "through which people caught together in an ambiguous situation attempt to construct a meaningful interpretation of it by pooling their intellectual resources."[46] Phillis Fox lists three social conditions needed to transmit rumor.[47] First is the perception of a stimuli that is both ambiguous and important followed by an effective means of spreading the reports, a role played by the media. Statements by "experts" or persons of status in the community, for example the police or government, are vital in terms of the how the population as a whole will respond to this information. When the second condition—the lack of any convincing official interpretations—is met, rumors find a fertile breeding ground.

Fox's third condition for rumor transmission is supportive social interaction. "In the absence of official explanations people tend to improvise their own, attempting through their conversations with each other to place an unusual event in its proper context." It is this process that produces the conclusion that phantom helicopters are sent by Irish terrorists and that UFOs are flying saucers from another world. Human beings, she adds, do not observe events in the way that a camera captures images on celluloid. "To a considerable extent, people see what they expect to see; and what they expect to see is not simply a result of their personalities but also of their social and cultural milieu."[48]

In different social contexts a UFO/helicopter "scare" can be triggered by the sheer quantity of numbers of sightings (for example in the case of a satellite re-entry), by the quality of report by a "credible" witness (for example, a police officer or airline pilot), or the activities of a promoter who brings a mystery into the public eye. This last role is often played by journalists, as in the case of the UFO "window" at Warminster, Wiltshire, that was largely inspired by the writings of Arthur Shuttlewood, a reporter with the town's weekly newspaper during the 1960s.[49]

England's black helicopter scare of 1973–74, and subsequent similar scares, flourished in an atmosphere of anxiety and fear and is reminiscent of the "mad gasser" of Mattoon. As with Mattoon, the press played a significant role in fostering the belief that black copters, up to no good, were roaming the skies. Reporters must be instant experts on the topics they cover, and most are not experts on the dynamics of folklore, rumor, myth, and the fallibility of eyewitness perception. It was widely assumed that illegal immigrants or IRA terrorists were responsible for the reports, as the journalistic accounts mirrored popular sentiment and the press reporting was tainted by such assumptions. Speculation gave rise to more sightings of nocturnal lights, which in turn engendered further speculation, and so it went. The same can be said for police who initially issued appeals for witnesses. In the end, the mystery unraveled as it became apparent that there was no solid evidence as to their reality. This assessment was reached not on emotion or speculation, but in the absence of hard evidence.

## REVIEW QUESTIONS

1. How has the social context influenced the various theories on popular opinion as to what England's phantom helicopters were widely believed to be?
2. Discuss the parallels between present-day UFO sightings and the mystery helicopter scare.
3. What responsibility did the media play in fostering and maintaining the helicopter sightings?
4. How might British authorities have unwittingly contributed to the scare?
5. How does the helicopter scare fit with the evidence of rumor transmission?

## NOTES

1. Peter Rogerson, "A Panorama of UFOlogical Visions," *Merseyside UFO Bulletin* (New Series) 3 (summer 1976): 12.

2. "Search for Mystery Aircraft in North Lincolnshire," *Scunthorpe Evening Telegraph* (Lincolnshire), May 2, 1972.

3. "Terrorists Launch First Air Attack," *Liverpool Echo*, January 24, 1974.

4. "Police Hunt Phantom Helicopter," *Daily Mirror* (London), January 15, 1974.

5. Memo to Commander (Ops) from Chief Superintendent, Special Branch, March 20, 1974, file 371/74/94.

6. "Riddle of Midnight Helicopter," *Buxton (Derbyshire) Advertiser*, September 21, 1973.

7. "Search for Mystery Helicopter," *Manchester Evening News*, October 27, 1973.

8. "Hedge-Hopper Starts Flying Saucer Scare," *Daily Mirror* (London), October 27, 1973.

9. "Copter Puzzle at Buxton," *Derby Evening Telegraph*, October 30, 1973.

10. "Mystery of Low Level Helicopter," *Morning Telegraph* (Sheffield, Yorkshire), October 29, 1973.

11. Special Report, "Unidentified Helicopter Sighted in Derbyshire," November 22, 1973, Special Branch file 371/74/94.

12. Edward Macauley, "The Great Helicopter Mystery," *Daily Mirror* (London), January 17, 1974.

13. "That Mysterious Man in His Flying Machine Keeps the Police Guessing," *Macclesfield (Cheshire) Express*, January 24, 1974.

14. Personal communication with Simon Crowe, January 1989.

15. "Police Puzzled by Helicopter's Mystery Flights," *Derbyshire Times* (Chesterfield, Derbyshire), January 18, 1974.

16. "Police Appeal over Mystery Helicopter," *Staffordshire Evening Sentinel* (Stoke-on-Trent), January 15, 1974.

17. "Phantom Flier May Have Landed in Field," *Daily Telegraph* (London), January 16, 1974.

18. *Manchester Evening News*, January 15, 1974.

19. *Derbyshire Times*, January 18, 1974.

20. *Manchester Evening News*, January 15, 1974.

21. "Ghost Whirlybird in a New Riddle," *Daily Mirror* (London), January 16, 1974.

22. "Phantom 'Copter Mystery Has Police Baffled," *Staffordshire Evening Sentinel* (Stoke-on-Trent), January 16, 1974.

23. "Hunt Is on for Phantom Flier," *Birmingham Mail*, January 16, 1974.

24. "Mystery 'Copter Search Goes On," *Liverpool Echo*, January 22, 1974.

25. *Daily Telegraph*, January 16, 1974.

26. "Youth Spotted Mystery Copter," *Stockport Express* (Stockport, Greater Manchester), January 17, 1974.

27. *Daily Mirror* (London), January 17, 1974.

28. "On the Trail of the Phantom Flier," *Daily Mirror* (London), January 18, 1974.

29. "The Phantom Flier Is a Real Expert," *Manchester Evening News*, January 17, 1974.

30. "Sky-High Hunt for 'Copter Is Out," *Liverpool Echo*, January 17, 1974.

31. *Daily Mirror* (London), January 17, 1974.

32. *Staffordshire Evening Sentinel*, January 17, 1974.

33. "Police Seek the Flying Phantom," *Liverpool Echo*, January 16, 1974.

34. "Mystery Copter over House 2 Minutes," *Manchester Evening News*, January 18, 1974.

35. *Manchester Evening News*, January 18, 1974.

36. "That Copter May Be Just an Illusion," *Daily Mail* (London), January 21, 1974.

37. Personal correspondence from Andrew Brown, Metropolitan Police, March 8, 2001.

38. Memo from Chief Superintendent to Commander (Ops), Special Branch, March 20, 1974.

39. Ibid.

40. Memo, Chief Superintendent "B" Squad, Special Branch, March 22, 1974.

41. Personal correspondence from Andrew Brown, Metropolitan Police, March 8, 2001.

42. Jenny Randles, *The Pennine UFO Mystery* (London: Granada, 1983), pp. 29–32.

43. David Rees, "Mystery Helicopters," *Awareness* 7, no. 1 (spring 1978): 3–5; "Phantom Helicopters: A UK Selection," *Awareness* 8, no. 3, (autumn 1979): 17–21; "UEOs—Unidentified Everyday Objects," *Earthlink* 1, no. 3 (winter 1978–79): 5–7.

44. Nick Redfern, *A Covert Agenda: The British Government's UFO Top Secrets Exposed* (London: Simon & Schuster, 1997).

45. Nick Redfern, *Cosmic Crashes* (London: Simon & Schuster, 1999), pp. 124–44.

46. Phillis Fox, "Social and Cultural Factors Influencing Beliefs about UFOs," in *UFOs and the Behavioral Scientist*, ed. Richard F. Haines (Metuchen, N.J.: Scarecrow Press, 1978), p. 37.

47. Ibid.

48. Ibid.

49. Arthur Shuttlewood, *The Warminster Mystery* (London: Neville Spearman, 1967). Thanks to Nigel Watson, Granville Oldroyd, Simon Crowe, Jim Austin, Nick Redfern, Peter Warrington, Dennis Stillings, and Andrew Brown of the Metropolitan Police for assistance in my hunt for the lair of the phantom copter.

# 14

# INDIA'S MONKEY MAN MANIA

Recently reports of a monkey man on the loose in the streets of New Delhi, India, prompted not a few chuckles from Westerners. Yet, is it possible that our delusions are no less bizarre or ridiculous?

*To see ourselves as others see us can be eye-opening. . . . But it is from the far more difficult achievement of seeing ourselves amongst others, as a local example of the forms human life has locally taken, a case among cases, a world among worlds, that the largeness of mind . . . comes.*

—Clifford Geertz[1]

During the first three weeks of May 2001, residents in the vicinity of New Delhi, India, were alarmed by waves of claims and media reports about sightings and attacks by a mysterious creature dubbed "the monkey man." Encounters were reported almost exclusively at night by persons sleeping on rooftops of their suburban homes to avoid the extreme heat in the wake of power blackouts.[2] Descriptions varied widely of a half-human, half-monkey-like creature often said to have razor-sharp fingernails, superhuman strength, and an incredible leaping ability. Some reports claimed that it had steel claws and could press a button on a belt around its waist, rendering itself invisible. Most descriptions of the creature said it ranged from between three and six feet tall, although some said it was the size of a cat. In mid-May, at the height of the scare, vigilante groups roamed the city brandishing sticks. Two people were confirmed dead after frantic attempts to escape the clutches of the monkey man. Both had awakened to cries that the creature was in the vicinity. One man leapt off the roof of a one-story building in the southeastern suburb of Noida. The other, a pregnant woman, tumbled down a staircase.[3] The evening of May 16 was typical as police logged over forty telephone calls of creature attacks or sightings in disparate parts of the city, often simultaneously. After further investigation, each of the calls was determined to have been bogus. In one instance, the "victim" had clearly been bitten by a rat, while another caller was said to be testing police response time.[4] One man was arrested for wearing a monkey mask while breaking into a house.[5] By the end of the third week, reports to police rapidly dwindled to zero.

Although the episode is commonly described in the Indian and Western press as a case of "mass hysteria," most witnesses were clearly not hysterical in the clinical sense. "Hysteria" refers to the rapid spread of illness signs and symptoms for which there is no identifiable organic cause. The monkey man episode is not a delusion in the the way that psychiatrists use that word to describe people with mental illness or disturbance. Most witnesses did not appear to be suffering from psychotic delusions. The episode is best described as a social delusion—a term commonly used by sociologists and social psychologists to describe the rapid spread of false or exaggerated beliefs. The recipe for these exaggerated fears involve rumors, that is, stories of perceived importance set in ambiguous circumstances. Add a dash of media sensationalism and a pinch of human imagination, and anything is possible. During such episodes people typically begin over-scrutinizing their environment for any evidence of their fear. Not surprisingly, they often find it, redefining various objects, events, and circumstances as monkey man–related. Many Americans may dismiss the Indian monkey business as the product a backward or uneducated society, but mass delusions are limited only by plausibility, that is, if the stories are considered believable.

If reports of a monkey man in New Delhi bounding from building to building and pressing an invisibility button when cornered seem incredible, consider descriptions of a three- to four-foot-tall creature with a head resembling a horse and sporting bat-like wings. This is what was reported by over 100 people in more than two dozen communities who claimed to see the "Jersey Devil." This episode did not occur in some exotic far off land to some group of uneducated natives whose tribal name we could not pronounce. It happened in the United States of America during the twentieth century. The New Jersey Devils ice hockey team is named after the "Jersey Devil" delusion. Since the 1730s, stories of a bizarre creature have circulated among residents living in the desolate Pine Barrens region of central and southern New Jersey. Occasional sightings of the "devil" were recorded until January 1909, at which point the region was overwhelmed with reported sightings of the creature or its footprints. The episode is documented in *The Jersey Devil*, by folklorists James McCloy and Ray Miller, who state that during the brief scare, most residents stayed inside behind locked doors, the factories and schools closed, and posses searched for the creature.[6] Ironically, Western countries are haunted by their own unique social delusions, from accounts of the "Jersey Devil" and Martian invaders in America to fairy sighting waves in England and Tasmanian "tiger" encounters in mainland Australia—beliefs that the average Indian would likely find ridiculous.[7]

Many scientists dismiss social delusions as silly and irrational because they are imaginary. Yet, they contain powerful symbolic messages about prevailing beliefs, attitudes, and stereotypes that should be carefully heeded. We should neither treat them as real nor irrational, but as part of the ethnographic record of humankind. We should accept them as part of ourselves and strive to understand them. In doing so we will better understand ourselves, for they are our own creations. In this regard, the

Indian monkey man episode will not be solved by searching for clues on the streets of New Delhi and its environs, but by looking to the human mind and what psychological fears are being reflected. Monkeys often run wild in New Delhi, especially on the city outskirts, occasionally attacking bystanders or entering homes. During the heat wave, residents who were forced to sleep on their housetops may have felt vulnerable to such attacks, generating anxiety, rumors, and misperceptions of mundane occurrences. For social delusions do not occur in a vacuum but have a context that requires decoding. Far from being random or arbitrary, they are social barometers mirroring the state of any given society at a specific time and place. Every society is haunted by its bogey men and women who occasionally emerge from the shadows to terrorize its inhabitants. In reality, they are demons of our own making—living folklore whose meaning deserves to be studied and decoded. Imaginary—yes—but they need to be taken seriously, as beliefs have consequences that can turn out to be real, as any student of history can attest.

The monkey man episode illustrates the blinding nature of one's culture and environment, and the importance of considering interpretations other than the one that may seem obvious at the time. A strict analysis of the evidence by police soon revealed an absence of concrete physical proof of the creature's existence. Virtually all of the evidence was in the form of eyewitness testimony, which is highly unreliable. The incident offers a poignant lesson for those living in more "civilized," "educated," and "developed" societies—while the monkey man reports may seem obviously ridiculous to someone outside of India, each culture has its own unique fears and hopes, which become embedded in rumor and myth. Critical thinking helps us to reveal such myths and rumors for what they are by posing critical questions, sticking with the known facts, and not getting carried away by our emotions.

## REVIEW QUESTIONS

1. List some of the factors that may have triggered "monkey man" sightings in India.
2. Provide examples of equally strange social delusions in Western countries that rival those of the "monkey man."

3. Why do you think the "monkey man" stories and sightings appeared when and where they did?

4. While "monkey man" reports were imaginary, why should scholars take such tales seriously?

## NOTES

1. C. Geertz, *Local Knowledge: Further Essays in Interpretive Anthropology* (New York: Basic Books, 1983), p. 16.

2. Lalit Kumar, "DIG Says 'Shoot at Monkeyman' as Panic Spreads," *Times of India*, May 14, 2001.

3. "'Monkey' Gives Delhi Claws for Alarm," *The Australian*, May 17, 2001.

4. Prashant Pandey, "Cops Step Up Hunt as Panic Spreads," *The Hindu*, May 17, 2001.

5. James Palmer, "Prowling 'Monkey-Man' Causes Panic in Delhi," *The Independent*, May 16, 2001.

6. J. F. McCloy and R. Miller, *The Jersey Devil* (Wallingford, Penn.: Middle Atlantic Press, 1976).

7. Hadley Cantril, *The Invasion from Mars: A Study in the Psychology of Panic* (Princeton, N.J.: Princeton University Press, 1940 [1947]); letter to Robert Bartholomew from Leslie Shepard, former president of the now defunct Fairy Investigation Society, based in the United Kingdom, June 5, 1984; Hilary Evans, *Visions, Apparitions, Alien Visitors* (Wellingborough, U.K.: Aquarian, 1984); A. Park, "Tasmanian Tiger: Extinct or Merely Elusive?" *Australian Geographic* 1 (1986): 66–83.

## 15

# HOW TO RECOGNIZE MASS DELUSIONS

Collective delusions are an important topic to address, as they have the potential to influence millions of people.

The word "delusion" is used by psychiatrists to describe a persistent pathological belief associated with serious mental disturbance, usually psychosis. Sociologists and social psychologists use the term "mass or collective delusion" in a different sense, to describe the spontaneous, temporary spread of false beliefs within a given population. Excluded from this definition are mistaken beliefs that occur in an organized or ritualistic manner. The two terms are also a common source of confusion since the term is often used as a "catch-all" category to describe a variety of different behaviors under one convenient heading. There are four common types of mass delusions. Being familiar with the processes involved in each, and recognizing their features, is the first line of defense to counteract their influence. Mass delusions differ from prominent religious myths and popular folk beliefs in that the delusions occur in an unorganized, spontaneous fashion, although they may become institutionalized. Examples include church groups incorporating claims of widespread satanic cult sacrifices into their teachings, or the formation of organizations intended to confirm the existence of alien visitors or Bigfoot.

History is replete with examples of group delusions, many of which may seem humorous to those outside of the historical or cultural setting. For instance, in 1806 near Leeds, England, residents became terror-stricken believing that the end of the world was imminent after a hen began laying eggs with the inscription "Christ is Coming." Masses thronged to glimpse the miraculous bird—until discovering that the eggs had been inscribed with a corrosive ink and then forced back into the animal's body. This is one of many examples from Charles Mackay's classic, *Memoirs of Extraordinary Popular Delusions and the Madness of Crowds*.[1] Unfortunately, the outcomes are often more sinister: Nazism, mass suicide, moral witch-hunts, the hunt for real witches, communist infiltration scares, the Crusades, and unfounded fears about the casual transmission of AIDS, to name but a few.

While historical episodes of collective folly are legendary, modern occurrences are remarkably similar. The four broad categories to be surveyed all involve a rapid spread of false but plausible exaggerated beliefs that gain credibility within a particular social and cultural context. They can be positive and take the form of wish-fulfillment, but usually they are negative and spread by fear. Rumors are an essential ingredient common to each category of delusion. As persons try to confirm or dismiss the accuracy of these unsubstantiated stories of perceived importance, everyday objects, events, and circumstances that would ordinarily receive scant attention become the subject of extraordinary scrutiny. They are soon redefined according to the emerging definition of the situation, creating a self-fulfilling prophecy. Many factors contribute to the spread of episodes: the mass media, low education levels, the fallibility of human perception, cultural superstitions and stereotypes, group conformity, and reinforcing actions by authority figures such as politicians or institutions of social control such as military agencies.

# IMMEDIATE COMMUNITY THREATS

Community threats involve exaggerated feelings of danger within communities at-large, where members of the affected population are concerned over what is believed to be an immediate personal threat. Episodes usually persist from a few weeks to several months, and often recur periodically. Participants may express excitement and concern, but do not panic and take flight. The fallibility of human perception and the tendency for persons sharing similar beliefs in group settings to accept the opinion of the majority is the process underlying fantasy creation and its spread.

Examples of *immediate community threats* include the mass sightings of imaginary rockets flying across Sweden during 1946. In conjunction with rare cometary debris entering the atmosphere, rumors circulated that remote-controlled German V-rockets, confiscated by the Soviets at the close of World War II, were being test-fired as a form of political intimidation or a prelude to an invasion. The historical and political context were key factors in making the rumors believable, as the episode occurred amid a long history of Soviet mistrust, including invasion fears, border disputes, and spy scandals which have preoccupied Swedes for centuries. Public statements reinforcing the existence of the rockets were made by top Swedish military officials, politicians, scientists, police, and journalists. Convinced of their existence, many citizens began reinterpreting cometary spray that sporadically streaked across the sky as enemy rockets. Some even claimed to distinguish tail fins or a fuselage. Of 997 reports investigated by the Swedish military, including nearly 100 "crashes" in remote areas, not a single shred of evidence confirming the rockets' existence was found, despite the extreme measure the military took of draining some lakes.[2]

Occasionally the feared agent is a mysterious attacker believed to be terrorizing a community. During a two-week period in 1956, nearly two dozen residents in Taipei, Taiwan, claimed to have been slashed by a man wielding a razor-blade-type object. Police later determined the episode to have been entirely psychological. In the wake of rumors, lacerations from such mundane sources as incidental paper cuts or bumping into an umbrella on a crowded bus were redefined.[3] Sometimes the imaginary threat is from an agent that is believed to cause illness, such as the series of phantom attacks involving a "mad gasser" in Mattoon, Illinois, during two weeks in 1944[4] (discussed in chapter 4). In Auckland, New Zealand, in 1973, fifty drums of the chemical compound merphos were being unloaded at a wharf when it was noticed that several barrels were leaking, and a chemical smell permeated the air. After immediate requests for information on the toxicity of merphos, authorities were wrongly informed that it was extremely toxic, after which at least 400 dock workers and nearby residents received treatment for a variety of psycho-somatic complaints: headache, breathing difficulty, and eye irritation.[5] In fact, the substance is relatively harmless.

In non-Western settings, immediate community threats are closely associated with cultural traditions, as in the case of headhunting rumor-panics that have occurred for centuries in remote parts of Malaysia and Indonesia.[6] These episodes represent fears by "primitive" peoples of losing political control to a distant, central government. Headhunting scares are characterized by sightings of headhunters and finding their alleged paraphernalia. Just as the vast, ambiguous nighttime sky is an excellent catalyst for spawning UFO sightings, and lakes are conducive to sea serpent reports, the thickly vegetated southeast Asian jungle is ideal for misperceiving headhunters lurking in the foliage. Villages are often paralyzed with fear, travel severely restricted, sentries are posted, and schools commonly closed for months. Most headhunting scares coincide with the nearby construction of a government bridge or building, during which it is widely believed that one or more human heads are required to produce a strong, enduring foundation. Such rumors are a projection of the state of tribal–government relations reflecting "ideological warfare between the administrators and the administrated."[7]

## COMMUNITY FLIGHT PANICS

A second type of mass delusion involves *community flight panics* where residents attempt to flee an imaginary threat. Most episodes last from a few hours to several days or weeks, subsiding when it is realized that the harmful agent did not materialize. Perhaps the best known example is the minor panic that ensued in the United States on Halloween eve in 1938 following the realistic radio reenactment of H. G. Wells's book *War of the*

*Worlds* by the CBS Mercury Theater.[8] Researcher Hadley Cantril noted that, in general, those panicking failed to exercise critical thinking, such as telephoning the police or checking other media sources. There remains a great potential for similar hoaxes to be successful when they are presented with plausibility and a degree of realism for the participants.

Spontaneous mass flights from the city of London have occurred over the centuries in response to prophecies of its destruction by a great flood in 1524, the Day of Judgment in 1736, and an earthquake in 1761. One of many contemporary examples involving apocalyptic prophecies and mass panic occurred in Adelaide, Australia, in the weeks leading up to January 19, 1976. Many people fled the city and some even sold their homes after "psychic" John Nash predicted that an earthquake and tidal wave would strike at midday on that date. In examining the circumstances of the event, many of those who sold their homes or just headed to the hills for the day were first-generation Greeks and Italians. Both countries have a long history of devastating earthquakes, and the belief in clairvoyants in those nations is generally taken very seriously.[9]

# SYMBOLIC COMMUNITY SCARES

*Symbolic community scares* typically endure in a waxing and waning fashion for years, encompassing entire countries and geographical regions. There is less of an immediate concern for safety and welfare, and more of a general long-term threat. They are primarily symbolic and rumor-driven, consisting of fear over the exaggerated erosion of traditional values. These moral panics are characterized by self-fulfilling stereotypes of ethnic minorities and deviants who are wrongfully indicted for evil deeds, having much in common with the infamous continental European witch persecutions that took place from 1400 to 1650. In *Collective Behavior*, sociologist Erich Goode aptly summarizes these events, noting that they originated from the disintegration of the Roman Catholic Church during the later Middle Ages and early Renaissance.[10] The feudal hierarchy was unraveling and peasants were migrating to cities. Scientific rationalism with its secular philosophy conflicted with Church doctrine, and new religious denominations were being formed beyond the Church's control. In an unconscious attempt to counteract secularism and re-establish traditional authority, the Church-sponsored persecution of witches attempted to redefine moral boundaries, and Church inquisitors focused on eradicating various deviants who were viewed as a threat.

Two prominent moral panics have persisted for the past decade: satanic ritual abuse and child sex abuse. Scores of Western communities with predominantly Judeo-Christian traditions have experienced ongoing concern in conjunction with rumors about the existence of a network of Satanic cults kidnapping and sacrificing children. These rumors coincide with the widespread perception of declining Western morality and traditional values. Under similar historical circumstances, subversion myths have appeared in which a particular alien group is believed to threaten the moral fabric of society. Common scapegoats include minority ethnic groups, Jews, Africans, communists, heretics, deviants, and the poor. Such myths flourish in areas experiencing economic hardship and social unrest, and are characterized by dramatic, plausible rumors containing meaningful, timely morals or messages reflecting popular fears. When the stories are told, local details are included and then supplanted, and a credible source is identified. The function of such stories is primarily metaphorical. Sociologist Jeffery Victor notes that the contemporary Satanic cult scare coincides with the disintegration of traditional family structures, intensifying fears, and the desire "to blame someone."[11] Unlike scares involving imminent danger, subversion myths present a more generalized threat to not only people, but a way of life, as rumors and urban legends of local Satanic cults function as cautionary cultural metaphors about the inability of the weakened family to protect children.[12] A similar symbolic process drives the child sex abuse panics which have appeared periodically in certain regions for decades.[13] They, too, seem to be metaphors for the disintegrating traditional family and our uneasy reliance on day care and neighbors ("strangers") to watch our children.

## COLLECTIVE WISH-FULFILLMENT

Mass wish-fulfillment involves similar processes that cause community threats and moral panics, except that the object of interest is esteemed and satisfies psychological needs. Cases typically persist for a few weeks to a few months, and recur periodically in clusters. Episodes involve a subconscious wish that is related to human mortality in conjunction with a plausible belief, fostering a collective quest for transcendence. Examples include Virgin Mary "appearances," "moving" religious statues in Ireland, waves of claims and public discourse surrounding widespread reports of fairies in England before the twentieth century, and flying saucers worldwide since 1947.[14] These myths are supported by a spiritual void left by the ascendancy of rationalism and secular humanism. Within this context, and fostered by sensationalized documentaries, news stories, movies, and books, contemporary populations have been conditioned to scan the heavens for UFOs representing what Carl Jung termed "technological angels."[15] These sightings serve as a projected Rorschach ink blot test of the collective psyche, underscoring the promise of rapid technological advancement during a period of spiritual decline.

Accounts of UFO occupants and fairies depict god-like beings capable of transcending natural laws and, thus, potentially elevating humans to their immortal realm. They reflect similar themes found in religion, mythology, and folklore throughout the world, camouflaged for contemporary acceptance.[16] Transcendence and magical or supernatural powers are an underlying theme in most wish fulfillments. Education builds resistance, but does not provide immunity to what philosopher Paul Kurtz terms "the transcendental temptation."[17] Even observations of imaginary or extinct creatures such as Bigfoot and the Tasmanian Tiger, respectively, once considered the sole domains of zoology, have undergone recent transformations with the emergence of a new motif among paranormal researchers which links extraterrestrial or paranormal themes with phantom animals.[18] The existence of such animals can be viewed as antiscientific symbols undermining secularism. Like claims of contact with UFOs or the Virgin Mary, evidence for the existence of Bigfoot and Tasmanian Tigers ultimately rests with eyewitness testimony, which is notoriously unreliable.[19]

# A NOTE ON NON-WESTERN DELUSIONS

Human gullibility is limited only by plausibility. This is especially apparent in non-Western countries where superstitions are often rampant. For example, in some cultures it is widely believed that eating certain foods or having contact with ghosts can cause one's sex organs to rapidly shrivel. It is a remarkable example of the power of self-delusion that men in parts of Asia continue to experience *koro* epidemics—convinced that they are the victims of a contagious disease that causes their penises to shrink (see chapter 9).

While *koro* may seem to represent extreme irrationality to outsiders, outbreaks differ from mass delusions in Western countries in only one significant respect—the rumor-related object. The external sex organs regularly change size, shape, and firmness under a variety of conditions. For the mass delusion to occur, the object of scrutiny must be of perceived importance, and the rumor credible. Hence, in theory, the only factor preventing similar epidemics in the West is the absence of *koro* cultural traditions.

## THE SEDUCTIVE ALLURE OF MASS DELUSIONS

Collective delusions possess a powerful seductive lure that continuously changes in a chameleon-like fashion to enable us to confirm our deepest fears or realize our greatest desires. Most Westerners can easily distinguish *koro* and headhunting scares as the products of myth and superstition. Yet many of these same people are likely to believe in the reality of flying saucers, ghosts, or psychic phenomena. We must always be prepared to evaluate incredible claims based on the available facts and avoid making emotional judgments. The underlying themes of collective delusions remain constant. Circumstances surrounding the Adelaide earthquake panic of 1976 are virtually identical to the London earthquake panic of 1761. Modern-day child molestation and satanic cult fears resemble the persecution of various deviants and ethnic groups during the infamous medieval European witch-hunts. Contemporary wish-fulfillments parallel transcendent elements that have been prominent fixtures in religious movements for millennia. Only the form changes to reflect the social and cultural context.

# REVIEW QUESTIONS

1. How is the word "delusion" defined differently by sociologists as opposed to psychiatrists?
2. List the four common types of mass delusions and their characteristic features.
3. All episodes of mass hysteria are collective delusions, but not all collective delusions involve mass hysteria. Explain.
4. Most episodes of mass wish-fulfillment appear to provide psychological comfort to those involved. What parallels exist between mass wish-fulfillments and religious beliefs?
5. According to sociologist Jeffery Victor, the contemporary satanic cult scare in the United States is related to the breakdown of traditional family life. What does he mean by this?
6. Most mass delusions last only a few weeks or months, at which time they collapse due to a conspicuous absence of evidence. What strategies can people undertake to shorten the duration of episodes?

# NOTES

1. C. Mackay, *Memoirs of Extraordinary Popular Delusions and the Madness of Crowds*, vol. 2 (London: Office of the National Illustrated Library, 1852).

2. R. Bartholomew, "Redefining Epidemic Hysteria: An Example from Sweden," *Acta Psychiatrica Scandinavica* 88 (1993): 178–82.

3. N. Jacobs, "The Phantom Slasher of Taipei: Mass Hysteria in a Non-Western Society," *Social Problems* 12 (1965): 318–28.

4. D. Johnson, "The 'Phantom Anesthetist' of Matoon: A Field Study of Mass Hysteria," *Journal of Abnormal Psychology* 40 (1945): 175–86.

5. W. R. McLeod, "Merphos Poisoning or Mass Panic?" *Australian and New Zealand Journal of Psychiatry* 9 (1975): 225–29.

6. G. Forth, "Construction Sacrifice and Head-Hunting Rumours in Central Flores (Eastern Indonesia): A Comparative Note," *Oceania* 61 (1991): 257–66; R. H. Barnes, "Construction Sacrifice, Kidnapping and Head Hunting Rumours on Flores and Elsewhere in Indonesia," *Oceania* 64 (1991): 146–58.

7. R. A. Drake, "Construction Sacrifice and Kidnapping: Rumor Panics in Borneo," *Oceania* 59 (1989): 275.

8. H. Cantril, *The Invasion from Mars: A Study in the Psychology of Panic* (Princeton, N.J.: Princeton University Press, 1940).

9. R. Bartholomew, "A Brief History of Mass Hysteria in Australia," *The Skeptic* (Australia) 12 (1992): 23–26.

10. E. Goode, *Collective Behavior* (New York: Harcourt Brace, Jovanovich, 1992).

11. J. Victor, "The Spread of Satanic Cult Rumors," *Skeptical Inquirer* 14 (1990): 287–91.

12. R. D. Hicks, "Police Pursuit of Satanic Crime Part II: The Satanic Conspiracy and Urban Legends," *Skeptical Inquirer* 14 (1990): 378–89; J. Victor, "A Rumor-Panic about a Dangerous Satanic Cult in Western New York," *New York Folklore* 15 (1989): 23–49.

13. A. Cockburn, "Abused Imaginings," *New Statesman and Society* 85 (1990): 19–20.

14. R. Yassa, "A Sociopsychiatric Study of an Egyptian Phenomenon," *American Journal of Psychotherapy* 34 (1980): 246–51; M. Persinger and J. Derr, "Geophysical Variables and Behavior: LIV. Zeitoun (Egypt) Apparitions of the Virgin Mary as Tectonic Strain-Induced Luminosities," *Perceptual and Motor Skills* 68 (1989): 123–28; C. Toibin, *Moving Statues in Ireland: Seeing Is Believing* (County Laois, Ireland: Pilgrim Press, 1985); R. Kirk, *The Secret Commonwealth of Elves, Fauns and Fairies* (London: Longman, 1812); W. Y. Evans-Wentz, *The Fairy Faith in Celtic Countries* (Rennes, France: Oberthur, 1909); R. Sheaffer, *The UFO Verdict* (Amherst, N.Y.: Prometheus Books, 1981).

15. C. Jung, *Flying Saucers: A Modern Myth of Things Seen in the Sky* (New York: Harcourt Brace and World, 1959).

16. T. E. Bullard, "UFO Abduction Reports: The Supernatural Kidnap Narrative Returns in Technological Guise," *Journal of American Folklore* 102 (1989): 147–70.

17. P. Kurtz, *The Transcendental Temptation: A Critique of Religion and the Paranormal* (Amherst, N.Y.: Prometheus Books, 1991).

18. A. Park, "Tasmanian Tiger: Extinct or Merely Elusive?" *Australian Geographic* 1 (1986): 66–83; J. Clark and L. Coleman, *Creatures of the Outer Edge* (New York: Warner, 1978); T. Healy and P. Cropper, *Out of the Shadows: Mystery Animals of Australia* (Ironbark, New South Wales: Chippendale, 1994).

19. E. Loftus, *Eyewitness Testimony* (Cambridge, Mass.: Harvard University Press, 1979); R. Buckhout, "Nearly 2000 Witnesses Can Be Wrong," *Bulletin of the Psychonomic Society* 16 (1980): 307–10; D. Ross, J. Read, and M. Toglia, *Adult Eyewitness Testimony: Current Trends and Developments* (Cambridge: Cambridge University Press, 1994).

# ABOUT THE AUTHORS AND CONTRIBUTORS

**ROBERT E. BARTHOLOMEW, PH.D.**, has taught sociology in Australia at Flinders University of South Australia and James Cook University in Queensland. A former broadcast journalist and contributor to news organizations such as the Associated Press and United Press International, he has conducted ethnographic field-work in Southeast Asia on so-called culture-specific psychiatric disorders. He has published dozens of articles in scientific journals on various topics.

**DAVID CLARKE** holds a Ph.D. in English Cultural Tradition and Folklore from the National Centre for English Cultural Tradition at the University of Sheffield, where he teaches and serves as an honorary research fellow.

**ROBERT LADENDORF** is a freelance writer, newspaper columnist, and cofounder of the Rational Examination Association of Lincoln

Land (REALL), an Illinois-based pro-science, anti-superstition organization. A public affairs staff writer and editor for the Illinois Department of Transportation, he resides in Springfield, Illinois.

JULIAN O'DEA received a Ph.D. in biology and serves as a research fellow in the Division of Archeology and Natural History at the Australian National University in Canberra.

BENJAMIN RADFORD is a freelance writer and the managing editor of the *Skeptical Inquirer*, an internationally refereed journal addressing issues in science and fringe science. He has been active in promoting critical thinking with a special interest in urban legends, Bigfoot, and mass hysterias. He has a Bachelor of Arts in Psychology from the University of New Mexico (1993).

STEVEN WHALEN has a master's in history from St. Michael's College in Vermont, and a doctorate in history from the University of Maine. He teaches in the Department of History at Castleton State College in Castleton, Vermont.

# INDEX